# GETTING STARTED

## Welcome

Congratulations, you have just gained access to the highest quality practice tests for the AWS Certified Cloud Practitioner Certification Exam. While we can't update the title of this book, all 390 practice questions have been fully updated to cover the latest version of the exam. These ultimate practice tests will prepare you thoroughly for the real exam so that you get to pass first time with confidence.

There are 6 practice exams with 65 questions each, and each set of practice exams includes questions from the five domains of the latest CLF-C01 exam. All 390 practice questions were designed to reflect the difficulty of the real AWS exam. With these Practice Tests, you'll know when you are ready to pass your AWS Cloud Practitioner exam first time! We recommend re-taking these practice tests until you consistently score 80% or higher - that's when you're ready to sit the exam and achieve a great score!

If you want easy to pass questions, then these Practice Tests are not for you! Our students love these high-quality practice tests because they simulate the actual certification exam and help them understand the AWS concepts. Students who have recently passed the AWS exam confirm that our AWS practice questions closely match the exam pattern and difficulty.

I hope you get great value from this resource and feel confident that you'll ace your AWS Certified Cloud Practitioner exam through diligent study of these questions.

Wishing you all the best with your AWS Certification exam.

Neal Davis

**AWS Solution Architect & Founder of Digital Cloud Training**

# How to best use this resource

We have organized the practice questions into 6 sets and each set is repeated once without answers and explanations and once with answers and explanations. This allows you to choose from two methods of preparation.

### 1. Exam simulation

To simulate the exam experience, use the "PRACTICE QUESTIONS ONLY" sets. Grab a pen and paper to record your answers for all 65 questions. After completing each set, check your answers using the "PRACTICE QUESTIONS, ANSWERS & EXPLANATIONS" section.

To calculate your total score, sum up the number of correct answers and multiply them by 1.54 (weighting out of 100%) to get your percentage score out of 100%. For example, if you got 50 questions right, the calculation would be 50 x 1.54 = 77%. The pass mark of the official AWS exam is 72%.

### 2. Training mode

To use the practice questions as a learning tool, use the "PRACTICE QUESTIONS, ANSWERS & EXPLANATIONS" sets to view the answers, read the explanations and look up the reference links as you move through the questions.

# Key Training Advice

**AIM FOR A MINIMUM SCORE OF 80%:** Although the actual AWS exam has a pass mark of 72%, we recommend that you repeatedly retake our AWS practice exams until you consistently score 80% or higher. We encourage you to put in the work and study the explanations in detail! Once you achieve the recommended score in the practice tests - you are ready to sit the exam and achieve a great score!

**CONFORM WITH EXAM BLUEPRINT:** Using our AWS Certified Cloud Practitioner practice exams helps you gain experience with the test question format and how the questions in the real AWS exam are structured. With our practice tests, you will be adequately prepared for the real AWS exam.

**DEEPEN YOUR KNOWLEDGE:** Please note that though we match the AWS exam pattern, our AWS practice exams are NOT brain dumps. Please don't expect to pass the real AWS certification exam by simply memorizing answers. Instead, we encourage you to use our AWS Cloud Practitioner practice tests to deepen your knowledge. This is your best chance to successfully pass your exam no matter what questions you are presented with in your real exam.

# Your Pathway to Success

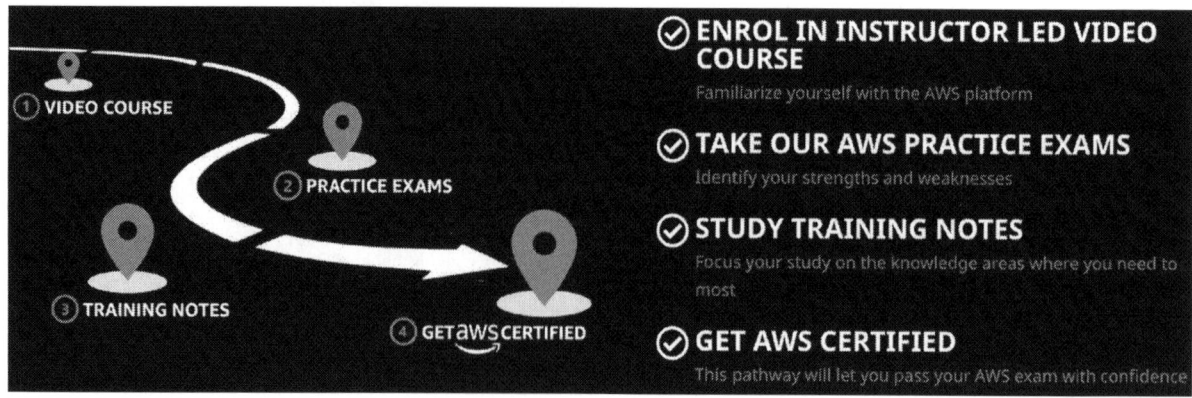

**Instructor-led Video Course**

If you're new to AWS, we'd suggest first enrolling in the online instructor-led AWS Certified Cloud Practitioner Video Course from Digital Cloud Training to familiarize yourself with the AWS platform before assessing your exam readiness with these practice exams.

**Online practice exam simulator**

If you are looking for more practice questions online, use the online exam simulator on the Digital Cloud Training website. With over 500 practice questions, you get to evaluate your progress and identify your strengths and weaknesses. Simply the best way to assess your exam readiness! We offer multiple learning modes and a pool of over 500 questions that are regularly updated.

**Training Notes**

As a final step, use the Training Notes for the AWS Certified Cloud Practitioner from Digital Cloud to get a more detailed understanding of the AWS services and focus your study on the knowledge areas where you need to most. Deep dive into the CLF-C01 exam objectives with 200 pages of detailed facts, tables and diagrams to shortcut your time to success.

## Limited Time Bonus Offer

As a special bonus, we are now offering **FREE Access to the Exam Simulator** on the Digital Cloud Training website. The exam simulator randomly selects 65 questions from our pool of over 500 unique questions - mimicking the real AWS exam environment. The practice exam has the same format, style, time limit, and passing score as the real AWS exam.

Navigate to the BONUS OFFER section at end of this book for instructions on how to claim your bonus.

## Contact, Support & Sharing

We want you to get great value from these training resources. If for any reason you are not 100% satisfied, please message us at feedback@digitalcloud.training. We promise to address all questions and concerns, typically within 24hrs. We really want you to have a 5-star learning experience!

For technical support, contact us at:
support@digitalcloud.training.

If you enjoy reading reviews, please consider paying it forward. Reviews really matter - they guide students and help us continuously improve our courses. We celebrate every honest review and truly appreciate it. We'd be thrilled if you could leave a rating at amazon.com/ryp or your local amazon store (e.g. amazon.co.uk/ryp).

The AWS platform is evolving quickly, and the exam tracks these changes with a typical lag of around 6 months. We are therefore reliant on student feedback to keep track of what is appearing in the exam. Our private Facebook group is a great place to ask questions and share knowledge and exam tips with the AWS community. Join the discussion and share your exam feedback to our Facebook group:

https://www.facebook.com/groups/awscertificationqa

© 2020 Digital Cloud Training

# TABLE OF CONTENTS

**Getting Started** .................................................................................................... 1
    Welcome ........................................................................................................... 1
    How to best use this resource ......................................................................... 2
    Key Training Advice ......................................................................................... 2
    Your Pathway to Success ................................................................................ 2
    Limited Time Bonus Offer ............................................................................... 3
    Contact, Support & Sharing ............................................................................. 3

**Table of Contents** .................................................................................................. 5

**Set 1: Practice Questions only** ............................................................................... 6

**Set 1: Practice Questions, Answers & Explanations** ............................................. 19

**Set 2: Practice Questions only** ............................................................................. 52

**Set 2: Practice Questions, Answers & Explanations** ............................................. 65

**Set 3: Practice Questions only** ............................................................................. 96

**Set 3: Practice Questions, Answers & Explanations** ........................................... 109

**Set 4: Practice Questions only** ........................................................................... 143

**Set 4: Practice Questions, Answers & Explanations** ........................................... 156

**Set 5: Practice Questions only** ........................................................................... 188

**Set 5: Practice Questions, Answers & Explanations** ........................................... 201

**Set 6: Practice Questions only** ........................................................................... 232

**Set 6: Practice Questions, Answers & Explanations** ........................................... 245

**Conclusion** ......................................................................................................... 276
    Reach out with any question .......................................................................... 276
    Limited Time Bonus Offer ............................................................................... 276

**OTHER BOOKS & COURSES BY NEAL DAVIS** ....................................................... 277
    AWS Certified Cloud Practitioner Video Course ............................................ 277
    AWS Certified Cloud Practitioner (online) Practice Tests .............................. 278
    AWS Certified Cloud Practitioner Training Notes .......................................... 279
    AWS Certified Solutions Architect Associate Video Course .......................... 280
    AWS Certified Solutions Architect Associate (online) Practice Tests ........... 281
    AWS Certified Solutions Architect Associate (offline) Practice Tests ........... 282

**ABOUT THE AUTHOR** ........................................................................................ 284

# SET 1: PRACTICE QUESTIONS ONLY

### 1. Question

**Which service records API activity on your account and delivers log files to an Amazon S3 bucket?**

1. Amazon CloudWatch
2. Amazon S3 Event Notifications
3. Amazon CloudTrail
4. Amazon CloudWatch Logs

### 2. Question

**What can you use to quickly connect your office securely to your Amazon VPC?**

1. AWS managed VPN
2. Route Table
3. Direct Connect
4. Internet Gateway

### 3. Question

**What advantages do you get from using the AWS cloud? (choose 2)**

1. Comply with all local security compliance programs
2. Increased capital expenditure
3. Stop guessing about capacity
4. Trade capital expense for variable expense
5. Gain greater control of the infrastructure layer

### 4. Question

**What is the scope of a VPC within a region?**

1. Spans all Availability Zones globally
2. Spans all Availability Zones within the region
3. At least 2 subnets per region
4. At least 2 data centers per region

### 5. Question

**Which types of pricing policies does AWS offer? (choose 2)**

1. Pay-as-you-go
2. Global usage discounts
3. Save when you reserve
4. Enterprise license agreement (ELA)
5. Non-peak hour discounts

## 6. Question

Which items can be configured from within the VPC management console? (choose 2)

1. Subnets
2. Regions
3. Security Groups
4. Auto Scaling
5. Load Balancing

## 7. Question

Which AWS service is primarily used for software version control?

1. AWS Cloud9
2. AWS CodeCommit
3. AWS CodeStar
4. AWS CodeDeploy

## 8. Question

Which services can be used for asynchronous integration between application components? (choose 2)

1. Amazon SQS
2. AWS CloudFormation
3. Amazon Step Functions
4. Amazon EC2 Auto Scaling
5. AWS Route 53

## 9. Question

What advantages does deploying Amazon CloudFront provide? (choose 2)

1. Automated deployment of resources
2. Improved performance for end users
3. Reduced latency
4. Provides serverless compute services
5. A private network link to the AWS cloud

## 10. Question

Under the AWS shared responsibility model what is the customer responsible for? (choose 2)

1. Physical security of the data center
2. Replacement and disposal of disk drives
3. Configuration of security groups
4. Patch management of infrastructure
5. Encryption of customer data

## 11. Question

**Which tool enables you to visualize your usage patterns over time and to identify your underlying cost drivers?**

1. AWS Budgets
2. AWS Cost Explorer
3. Total Cost of Ownership (TCO) Calculator
4. AWS Simple Monthly Calculator

## 12. Question

**Which of the statements below is accurate regarding Amazon S3 buckets? (choose 2)**

1. Bucket names must be unique regionally
2. Buckets are region-specific
3. Buckets are replicated globally
4. Bucket names must be unique globally
5. Buckets can contain other buckets

## 13. Question

**Which AWS services are used for analytics? (choose 2)**

1. Amazon S3
2. Amazon Athena
3. Amazon RDS
4. Amazon EMR
5. Amazon ElastiCache

## 14. Question

**Which service can be used for building and integrating loosely-coupled, distributed applications?**

1. Amazon EBS
2. Amazon SNS
3. Amazon EFS
4. Amazon RDS

## 15. Question

**What is the term for describing the action of automatically running scripts on Amazon EC2 instances when launched to install software?**

1. Bootstrapping
2. Containerization
3. Golden Images
4. Workflow automation

## 16. Question

**Identify the services that have a global (rather than regional) scope? (choose 2)**

1. Amazon Route 53
2. AWS Lambda
3. Amazon S3
4. Amazon EC2
5. Amazon CloudFront

## 17. Question

**How does AWS assist organizations with their capacity requirements?**

1. With AWS you don't pay for data centers
2. You don't own the infrastructure
3. You don't need to guess your capacity needs
4. With AWS you only pay for what you use

## 18. Question

**What strategy can assist with allocating metadata to AWS resources for cost tracking and visibility?**

1. Labelling
2. Tagging
3. Access Control
4. Categorizing

## 19. Question

**Which AWS storage technology can be considered a "virtual hard disk in the cloud"?**

1. Amazon Elastic File Storage (EFS) filesystem
2. Amazon Elastic Block Storage (EBS) volume
3. Amazon Glacier archive
4. Amazon S3 object

## 20. Question

**A company plans to create a hybrid cloud architecture. What technology will allow them to create a hybrid cloud?**

1. Direct Connect
2. VPC Peering
3. Elastic Network Interface
4. Internet Gateway

## 21. Question

**Which feature of Amazon Rekognition can assist with saving time?**

1. Identification of the language of text in a document
2. Identification of objects in images and videos
3. Adds automatic speech recognitions (ASR) to applications
4. Provides on-demand access to compliance-related information

## 22. Question

**Which AWS service can you use to install a third-party database?**

1. Amazon EMR
2. Amazon RDS
3. Amazon DynamoDB
4. Amazon EC2

## 23. Question

**Which AWS service can be used to convert video and audio files from their source format into versions that will playback on devices like smartphones, tablets and PC?**

1. Elastic Transcoder
2. Elastic Beanstalk
3. Auto Scaling
4. Elastic Load Balancer

## 24. Question

**Which type of Amazon Elastic Load Balancer operates at layer 7 of the OSI model?**

1. F5 Load Balancer
2. Application Load Balancer
3. Classic Load Balancer
4. Network Load Balancer

## 25. Question

**Which AWS service allows you to use block-based volumes on-premise that are then asynchronously backed up to Amazon S3?**

1. AWS Storage Gateway Volume Gateway
2. Amazon S3 Transfer Acceleration
3. AWS Storage Gateway File Gateway
4. Amazon S3 Multi-Part upload

## 26. Question

**Which AWS service allows you to connect to storage from on-premise servers using standard file protocols?**

1. Amazon EBS
2. Amazon S3
3. Amazon EFS
4. Amazon Glacier

## 27. Question

**Which statement below is incorrect in relation to Network ACLs?**

1. Process rules in order

2. Support allow and deny rules
3. Operate at the Availability Zone level
4. Stateless

## 28. Question

Which service can be used to help you to migrate databases to AWS quickly and securely?

1. AWS Migration Hub
2. AWS DMS
3. AWS SMS
4. AWS KMS

## 29. Question

Which of the following statements is correct in relation to consolidated billing? (choose 2)

1. One bill is provided per AWS organization
2. Only available to Enterprise customers
3. Volume pricing discounts cannot be applied to resources
4. Used to consolidate billing across organizations
5. Paying accounts are independent and cannot access resources of other accounts

## 30. Question

Which AWS support plan should you use if you need a response time of < 15 minutes for a business-critical system failure?

1. Basic
2. Developer
3. Business
4. Enterprise

## 31. Question

Which feature of AWS allows you to deploy a new application for which the requirements may change over time?

1. High availability
2. Disposable resources
3. Fault tolerance
4. Elasticity

## 32. Question

What is an availability zone composed of?

1. A collection of VPCs
2. A collection of edge locations
3. One or more DCs in a location
4. One or more regions

## 33. Question

**Which database service is a NoSQL type of database that is fully managed?**

1. Amazon RDS
2. Amazon DynamoDB
3. Amazon ElastiCache
4. Amazon RedShift

## 34. Question

**Which service can you use to provision a preconfigured server with little to no AWS experience?**

1. Amazon Elastic Beanstalk
2. AWS Lambda
3. Amazon EC2
4. Amazon Lightsail

## 35. Question

**For which services does Amazon not charge customers? (choose 2)**

1. Amazon VPC
2. Amazon EBS
3. Amazon CloudFormation
4. Amazon S3
5. Amazon SNS

## 36. Question

**What is the most cost-effective EC2 pricing option to use for a non-critical overnight workload?**

1. On-Demand
2. Spot
3. Reserved Instance
4. Dedicated Host

## 37. Question

**What benefits does Amazon EC2 provide over-using non-cloud servers? (choose 2)**

1. Fault tolerance
2. Inexpensive
3. High-availability with an SLA of 99.999%
4. Elastic web-scale computing
5. Complete control of the hypervisor layer

## 38. Question

**Which AWS service can an organization use to automate operational tasks on EC2 instances using existing Chef cookbooks?**

1. AWS CodeDeploy

2. AWS Config
3. AWS Service Catalog
4. AWS OpsWorks

## 39. Question

**Which AWS service can be used to process a large amount of data using the Hadoop framework?**

1. Amazon EMR
2. Amazon Kinesis
3. AWS Glue
4. Amazon Athena

## 40. Question

**Which statement below is incorrect in relation to Security Groups?**

1. Stateless
2. Evaluate all rules
3. Support allow rules only
4. Operate at the instance level

## 41. Question

**How can an organization compare the cost of running applications in an on-premise or colocation environment against the AWS cloud?**

1. AWS Budgets
2. AWS Simple Monthly Calculator
3. TCO Calculator
4. AWS Cost Explorer

## 42. Question

**Under the shared responsibility model, what are examples of shared controls? (choose 2)**

1. Patch management
2. Storage system patching
3. Service and Communications Protection
4. Physical and environmental
5. Configuration management

## 43. Question

**Which service can be used to track the CPU usage of an EC2 instance?**

1. Amazon CloudTrail
2. Amazon CloudFront
3. Amazon CloudFormation
4. Amazon CloudWatch

## 44. Question

**Which service allows you to automatically expand and shrink your application in response to demand?**

1. AWS Auto Scaling
2. Amazon Elastic Load Balancing
3. Amazon DynamoDB
4. AWS ElastiCache

## 45. Question

**Which of the following is a method of backup available in the AWS cloud?**

1. Route 53 Alias Record
2. EBS Snapshots
3. EFS File Systems
4. Availability Zones

## 46. Question

**Which type of cloud deployment enables customers to leverage the benefits of the public cloud and co-existing with on-premises infrastructure?**

1. Public Cloud
2. Private Cloud
3. Hybrid Cloud
4. Legacy IT Infrastructure

## 47. Question

**Which storage service allows you to connect multiple EC2 instances concurrently using file-level protocols?**

1. Amazon Glacier
2. Amazon S3
3. Amazon EBS
4. Amazon EFS

## 48. Question

**The AWS global infrastructure is composed of? (choose 2)**

1. Availability Zones
2. Fault Zones
3. Clusters
4. Regions
5. IP subnets

## 49. Question

**Which of the following are features of Amazon CloudWatch? (choose 2)**

1. Records account activity and service events from most AWS services

2. Used to gain system-wide visibility into resource utilization
  3. Can be accessed via API, command-line interface, AWS SDKs, and the AWS Management Console
  4. Provides visibility into user activity by recording actions taken on your account
  5. Used for auditing of API calls

## 50. Question

**What considerations are there when choosing which region to use? (choose 2)**

  1. Data sovereignty
  2. Available compute capacity
  3. Latency
  4. Pricing in local currency
  5. Available storage capacity

## 51. Question

**Which pricing model should you use for EC2 instances that will be used in a lab environment for several hours on a weekend and must run uninterrupted?**

  1. On-Demand
  2. Reserved
  3. Spot
  4. Dedicated Instance

## 52. Question

**What benefits are provided by Amazon CloudFront? (choose 2)**

  1. Used to enable private subnet instances to access the Internet
  2. Content is cached at Edge Locations for fast distribution to customers
  3. Built-in Distributed Denial of Service (DDoS) attack protection
  4. Provides a worldwide distributed DNS service
  5. Allows you to register domain names

## 53. Question

**What method can you use to take a backup of an Amazon EC2 instance using AWS tools?**

  1. Take full and incremental file-level backups using the backup console
  2. Take application-consistent backups using the EC2 API
  3. Take a snapshot to capture the point-in-time state of the instance
  4. Use Cross Region Replication (CRR) to copy the instance to another region

## 54. Question

**Which service allows you to run code as functions without needing to provision or manage servers?**

  1. AWS Lambda
  2. Amazon EKS
  3. Amazon EC2
  4. Amazon CodeDeploy

### 55. Question

**What are two ways that moving to an AWS cloud can benefit an organization? (choose 2)**

1. Gain greater control of data center security
2. Depreciate assets over a longer timeframe
3. Stop guessing about capacity
4. Increase speed and agility
5. Switch to a CAPEX model

### 56. Question

**A company would like to maximize their potential volume and RI discounts across multiple accounts and also apply service control policies on member accounts. Which service or tool can they use to gain these benefits?**

1. AWS Budgets
2. AWS Cost Explorer
3. AWS IAM
4. AWS Organizations

### 57. Question

**Which AWS service is used to enable multi-factor authentication?**

1. Amazon STS
2. AWS KMS
3. AWS IAM
4. Amazon EC2

### 58. Question

**Which AWS database service supports complex queries and joins and is suitable for a transactional database deployment?**

1. Amazon RDS
2. Amazon DynamoDB
3. Amazon EMR
4. Amazon RedShift

### 59. Question

**When instantiating compute resources, what are two techniques for using automated, repeatable processes that are fast and avoid human error? (choose 2)**

1. Performance monitoring
2. Infrastructure as code
3. Bootstrapping
4. Fault tolerance
5. Snapshotting

## 60. Question

Which service supports the resolution of public domain names to IP addresses or AWS resources?

1. Amazon Route 53
2. Amazon CloudFront
3. Amazon SNS
4. Hosted Zones


## 61. Question

Which feature can you use to grant read/write access to an Amazon S3 bucket?

1. IAM Role
2. IAM User
3. IAM Policy
4. IAM Group


## 62. Question

Which services are integrated with KMS encryption? (choose 2)

1. Amazon RDS
2. Amazon EC2
3. AWS CloudFormation
4. Amazon EBS
5. Amazon SWF


## 63. Question

What architectural best practice aims to reduce the interdependencies between services?

1. Services, Not Servers
2. Removing Single Points of Failure
3. Automation
4. Loose Coupling


## 64. Question

What is the most cost-effective support plan that should be selected to provide at least a 1-hour response time for a production system failure?

1. Enterprise
2. Business
3. Developer
4. Basic


## 65. Question

The IAM service can be used to manage which objects? (choose 2)

1. Security groups
2. Key pairs

3. Roles
4. Access policies
5. Network ACLs

# SET 1: PRACTICE QUESTIONS, ANSWERS & EXPLANATIONS

### 1. Question

Which service records API activity on your account and delivers log files to an Amazon S3 bucket?

1. Amazon CloudWatch
2. Amazon S3 Event Notifications
3. Amazon CloudTrail
4. Amazon CloudWatch Logs

**Answer: 3**

**Explanation:**

- AWS CloudTrail is a web service that records activity made on your account and delivers log files to an Amazon S3 bucket
- CloudTrail is for auditing (CloudWatch is for performance monitoring)
- S3 Event Notifications is a feature that notifies you when certain events happen in your S3 buckets, it does not record API activity at the account level
- Amazon CloudWatch Logs lets you monitor and troubleshoot your systems and applications using your existing system, application and custom log files

**References:**

https://digitalcloud.training/certification-training/aws-certified-cloud-practitioner/monitoring-and-logging-services/

### 2. Question

What can you use to quickly connect your office securely to your Amazon VPC?

1. AWS managed VPN
2. Route Table
3. Direct Connect
4. Internet Gateway

**Answer: 1**

**Explanation:**

An AWS managed VPN can be used to quickly connect from an office to an Amazon VPC

Direct Connect provides high-bandwidth, low-latency connectivity but takes weeks to months to setup (and is much more expensive)

An Internet Gateway is used to connect a public subnet to the Internet (egress)

A Route Table is part of a VPC and is used to control how traffic is routed within the VPC

**References:**

https://digitalcloud.training/certification-training/aws-certified-cloud-practitioner/aws-networking/

### 3. Question

**What advantages do you get from using the AWS cloud? (choose 2)**

1. Comply with all local security compliance programs
2. Increased capital expenditure
3. Stop guessing about capacity
4. Trade capital expense for variable expense
5. Gain greater control of the infrastructure layer

**Answer: 3,4**

**Explanation:**

The 6 advantages of cloud are:

- 1 Trade capital expense for variable expense
- 2 Benefit from massive economies of scale
- 3 Stop guessing about capacity
- 4 Increase speed and agility
- 5 Stop spending money running and maintaining data centers
- 6 Go global in minutes

You do not gain greater control of the infrastructure layer as AWS largely control this, and though AWS is compliant with lots of security compliance programs, not all programs in all local countries will be included

**References:**

https://digitalcloud.training/certification-training/aws-certified-cloud-practitioner/cloud-computing-concepts/

### 4. Question

**What is the scope of a VPC within a region?**

1. Spans all Availability Zones globally
2. Spans all Availability Zones within the region
3. At least 2 subnets per region
4. At least 2 data centers per region

**Answer: 2**

**Explanation:**

- A VPC spans all availability zones within a region
- VPCs do not span regions, you create VPCs in each region
- VPCs are not limited by subnets, subnets are created within AZs and you can have many subnets in an AZ
- An AZ uses one or more data centers. AWS does not publicize the details

**References:**

https://digitalcloud.training/certification-training/aws-certified-cloud-practitioner/aws-networking/

## 5. Question

**Which types of pricing policies does AWS offer? (choose 2)**

1. Pay-as-you-go
2. Global usage discounts
3. Save when you reserve
4. Enterprise license agreement (ELA)
5. Non-peak hour discounts

**Answer: 1,3**

**Explanation:**

- Amazon pricing includes options for pay-as-you-go, save when you reserve and pay less by using more
- Amazon does not offer ELAs, non-peak hour discounts, or global usage discounts

**References:**

https://digitalcloud.training/certification-training/aws-certified-cloud-practitioner/aws-billing-and-pricing/

https://aws.amazon.com/pricing/

## 6. Question

**Which items can be configured from within the VPC management console? (choose 2)**

1. Subnets
2. Regions
3. Security Groups
4. Auto Scaling
5. Load Balancing

**Answer: 1,3**

**Explanation:**

- Subnets and Security groups can be configured from within the VPC console
- Regions are not configured, resources within regions are configured
- Load balancing and auto scaling is configured from the EC2 console

**References:**

https://digitalcloud.training/certification-training/aws-certified-cloud-practitioner/aws-networking/

## 7. Question

**Which AWS service is primarily used for software version control?**

1. AWS Cloud9
2. AWS CodeCommit
3. AWS CodeStar
4. AWS CodeDeploy

**Answer: 2**

**Explanation:**

- AWS CodeCommit is a fully-managed source control service that hosts secure Git-based repositories. It makes it easy for teams to collaborate on code in a secure and highly scalable ecosystem
- AWS CodeStar enables you to quickly develop, build, and deploy applications on AWS. AWS CodeStar provides a unified user interface, enabling you to easily manage your software development activities in one place
- AWS Cloud9 is a cloud-based integrated development environment (IDE) that lets you write, run, and debug your code with just a browser
- AWS CodeDeploy is a deployment service that automates application deployments to Amazon EC2 instances, on-premises instances, or serverless Lambda functions

**References:**

https://digitalcloud.training/certification-training/aws-certified-cloud-practitioner/additional-aws-services-tools/

https://aws.amazon.com/codecommit/

https://aws.amazon.com/codestar/

https://aws.amazon.com/cloud9/

https://docs.aws.amazon.com/codedeploy/latest/userguide/welcome.html

## 8. Question

**Which services can be used for asynchronous integration between application components? (choose 2)**

1. Amazon SQS
2. AWS CloudFormation
3. Amazon Step Functions
4. Amazon EC2 Auto Scaling
5. AWS Route 53

**Answer: 1,3**

**Explanation:**

- Asynchronous integration is a form of loose coupling between services. This model is suitable for any interaction that does not need an immediate response and where an acknowledgement that a request has been registered will suffice.
- Amazon Simple Queue Service (SQS) and Amazon Step Functions both provide asynchronous integration. SQS provides a durable message bus and Step Functions is an orchestrated workflow service.
- Amazon EC2 Auto Scaling helps with horizontal scaling of your EC2 instances. This is not an example of asynchronous integration.
- AWS CloudFormation automates the deployment of infrastructure based on templates.
- AWS Route 53 is a DNS service that resolves domain names to IP addresses.

**References:**

https://digitalcloud.training/certification-training/aws-certified-cloud-practitioner/architecting-for-the-cloud/

https://d1.awsstatic.com/whitepapers/AWS_Cloud_Best_Practices.pdf

## 9. Question

**What advantages does deploying Amazon CloudFront provide? (choose 2)**

1. Automated deployment of resources
2. Improved performance for end users
3. Reduced latency
4. Provides serverless compute services
5. A private network link to the AWS cloud

**Answer 2,3**

**Explanation:**

- CloudFront is a content delivery network (CDN) that allows you to store (cache) your content at "edge locations" located around the world
- This allows customers to access content more quickly and provides security against DDoS attacks
- CloudFront can be used for data, videos, applications, and APIs
- A private network link to the AWS cloud can be provisioned using AWS Direct Connect or an IPSec VPN
- Automated deployment of resources is performed using CloudFormation
- CloudFront is a CDN not a serverless compute service

**References:**

https://digitalcloud.training/certification-training/aws-certified-cloud-practitioner/content-delivery-and-dns-services/

## 10. Question

**Under the AWS shared responsibility model what is the customer responsible for? (choose 2)**

1. Physical security of the data center
2. Replacement and disposal of disk drives
3. Configuration of security groups
4. Patch management of infrastructure
5. Encryption of customer data

**Answer: 3,5**

**Explanation:**

- AWS are responsible for "Security of the Cloud"
- Customers are responsible for "Security in the Cloud"
- AWS are responsible for items such as the physical security of the DC, replacement of old disk drives, and patch management of the infrastructure

© 2020 Digital Cloud Training

- Customers are responsible for items such as configuring security groups, network ACLs, patching their operating systems and encrypting their data

**References:**

https://digitalcloud.training/certification-training/aws-certified-cloud-practitioner/aws-shared-responsibility-model/

## 11. Question

**Which tool enables you to visualize your usage patterns over time and to identify your underlying cost drivers?**

1. AWS Budgets
2. AWS Cost Explorer
3. Total Cost of Ownership (TCO) Calculator
4. AWS Simple Monthly Calculator

**Answer: 2**

**Explanation:**

- The AWS Cost Explorer is a free tool that allows you to view charts of your costs. You can view cost data for the past 13 months and forecast how much you are likely to spend over the next three months. Cost Explorer can be used to discover patterns in how much you spend on AWS resources over time and to identify cost problem area
- The TCO calculator is a free tool provided by AWS that allows you to estimate the cost savings of using the AWS Cloud vs. using an on-premised data center
- The AWS Simple Monthly Calculator helps customers and prospects estimate their monthly AWS bill more efficiently
- AWS Budgets gives you the ability to set custom budgets that alert you when your costs or usage exceed (or are forecasted to exceed) your budgeted amount

**References:**

https://digitalcloud.training/certification-training/aws-certified-cloud-practitioner/aws-billing-and-pricing/

https://aws.amazon.com/aws-cost-management/aws-budgets/

## 12. Question

**Which of the statements below is accurate regarding Amazon S3 buckets? (choose 2)**

1. Bucket names must be unique regionally
2. Buckets are region-specific
3. Buckets are replicated globally
4. Bucket names must be unique globally
5. Buckets can contain other buckets

**Answer: 2,4**

**Explanation:**

- S3 uses a universal (global) namespace, which means bucket names must be unique globally. However, you create the buckets in a region and the data never leaves that region unless explicitly configured to do so through cross-region replication (CRR)
- Objects within a bucket are replicated within a region across multiple AZs (except for the One-Zone IA class)
- You cannot create nested buckets

**References:**

https://digitalcloud.training/certification-training/aws-certified-cloud-practitioner/aws-storage/

https://digitalcloud.training/certification-training/aws-solutions-architect-associate/storage/amazon-s3/

## 13. Question

**Which AWS services are used for analytics? (choose 2)**

1. Amazon S3
2. Amazon Athena
3. Amazon RDS
4. Amazon EMR
5. Amazon ElastiCache

**Answer: 2,4**

**Explanation:**

- Amazon Elastic Map Reduce (EMR) provides a managed Hadoop framework that makes it easy, fast, and cost-effective to process vast amounts of data across dynamically scalable Amazon EC2 instance
- Amazon Athena is an interactive query service that makes it easy to analyze data in Amazon S3 using standard SQL
- ElastiCache is a data caching service that is used to help improve the speed/performance of web applications running on AWS
- Amazon RDS is Amazon's relational database and is primarily used for transactional workloads
- Amazon S3 is used for object storage

**References:**

https://digitalcloud.training/certification-training/aws-certified-cloud-practitioner/additional-aws-services-tools/

https://digitalcloud.training/certification-training/aws-certified-cloud-practitioner/additional-aws-services-tools/

## 14. Question

**Which service can be used for building and integrating loosely-coupled, distributed applications?**

1. Amazon EBS
2. Amazon SNS
3. Amazon EFS
4. Amazon RDS

**Answer: 2**

**Explanation:**

- Amazon Simple Notification Service (Amazon SNS) is a web service that makes it easy to set up, operate, and send notifications from the cloud
- Amazon SNS is used for building and integrating loosely-coupled, distributed applications
- Amazon Elastic Block Storage (EBS) provides storage volumes for EC2 instances
- Amazon Elastic File System (EFS) provides an NFS filesystem for usage by EC2 instances
- Amazon Relational Database Service (RDS) provides a managed relational database service

**References:**

https://digitalcloud.training/certification-training/aws-certified-cloud-practitioner/notification-services/

## 15. Question

**What is the term for describing the action of automatically running scripts on Amazon EC2 instances when launched to install software?**

1. Bootstrapping
2. Containerization
3. Golden Images
4. Workflow automation

**Answer: 1**

**Explanation:**

- Bootstrapping is the execution of automated actions to services such as EC2 and RDS. This is typically in the form of scripts that run when the instances are launched.
- Golden Images are snapshots of pre-configured EBS volumes that can be used to launch new instances. You do this using Amazon Machine Images (AMIs).
- Containerization is incorrect. Containers are packaged software that runs in a Docker image. Services such as Amazon ECS and Fargate can run Docker containers.
- Workflow automation is a process or orchestrating automated actions. This is associated with services such as Chef and Puppet or AWS OpsWorks.

**References:**

https://d1.awsstatic.com/whitepapers/AWS_Cloud_Best_Practices.pdf

## 16. Question

**Identify the services that have a global (rather than regional) scope? (choose 2)**

1. Amazon Route 53
2. AWS Lambda
3. Amazon S3
4. Amazon EC2
5. Amazon CloudFront

**Answer: 1,5**

**Explanation:**

- Amazon Route 53 and Amazon CloudFront have a global scope
- Amazon S3 uses a global namespace but buckets and objects are created within a region
- AWS Lambda is a regional service

**References:**

https://digitalcloud.training/certification-training/aws-certified-cloud-practitioner/content-delivery-and-dns-services/

## 17. Question

**How does AWS assist organizations with their capacity requirements?**

1. With AWS you don't pay for data centers
2. You don't own the infrastructure
3. You don't need to guess your capacity needs
4. With AWS you only pay for what you use

Answer: 3

**Explanation:**

- All of these statements are true; however, the question is specifically asking how AWS can assist with capacity requirements.
- i.e. how does AWS enable organizations to ensure they don't over or under-provision their resources.
- The ability to scale on demand is the key advantage that can help them here as they can deploy what they know they need today and scale it as they need to tomorrow.

**References:**

https://digitalcloud.training/certification-training/aws-certified-cloud-practitioner/cloud-computing-concepts/

https://d1.awsstatic.com/whitepapers/aws-overview.pdf

## 18. Question

**What strategy can assist with allocating metadata to AWS resources for cost tracking and visibility?**

1. Labelling
2. Tagging
3. Access Control
4. Categorizing

Answer: 2

**Explanation:**

- AWS allows customers to assign metadata to their AWS resources in the form of tags. Each tag is a simple label consisting of a customer-defined key and an optional value that can make it easier to manage, search for, and filter resources. AWS Cost Explorer and detailed billing reports support the ability to break down AWS costs by tag.

- The other options are incorrect as they are not methods of adding metadata to an AWS resource.

**References:**

https://digitalcloud.training/certification-training/aws-certified-cloud-practitioner/aws-billing-and-pricing/

https://aws.amazon.com/answers/account-management/aws-tagging-strategies/

## 19. Question

**Which AWS storage technology can be considered a "virtual hard disk in the cloud"?**

1. Amazon Elastic File Storage (EFS) filesystem
2. Amazon Elastic Block Storage (EBS) volume
3. Amazon Glacier archive
4. Amazon S3 object

Answer: 2

**Explanation:**

- An EBS volume is a block storage device that is most similar to a virtual hard disk in the cloud as when attached to an instance it appears as a local disk that can have an operating system installed on or be formatted and used for any other local storage purpose
- An EFS filesystem is mounted over the NFS protocol which is a file-level protocol. Therefore, it is a network filesystem not a virtual hard disk and cannot have an operating system installed or be formatted and used as a locally attached disk
- S3 is an object storage system and cannot be mounted and used as a virtual hard drive
- Glacier is an archiving solution where you can archive your S3 objects at extremely low cost

**References:**

https://digitalcloud.training/certification-training/aws-certified-cloud-practitioner/aws-storage/

## 20. Question

**A company plans to create a hybrid cloud architecture. What technology will allow them to create a hybrid cloud?**

1. Direct Connect
2. VPC Peering
3. Elastic Network Interface
4. Internet Gateway

Answer: 1

**Explanation:**

- Direct Connect provides a low-latency, high bandwidth connection to connect customer on-premise environments with the AWS cloud which allows them to create a "hybrid" cloud architecture
- VPC peering is a way of allowing routing between VPCs in different AWS accounts
- An Internet Gateway is used to connect public subnets to the Internet (egress)

- An Elastic Network Interface (ENI) is a logical networking component in a VPC that represents a virtual network card

**References:**

https://digitalcloud.training/certification-training/aws-certified-cloud-practitioner/aws-networking/

## 21. Question

**Which feature of Amazon Rekognition can assist with saving time?**

1. Identification of the language of text in a document
2. Identification of objects in images and videos
3. Adds automatic speech recognitions (ASR) to applications
4. Provides on-demand access to compliance-related information

**Answer: 2**

**Explanation:**

- Amazon Rekognition makes it easy to add image and video analysis to your applications. You just provide an image or video to the Rekognition API, and the service can identify the objects, people, text, scenes, and activities, as well as detect any inappropriate content
- Amazon Comprehend identifies the language of the text; extracts key phrases, places, people, brands, or events; understands how positive or negative the text is; analyzes text using tokenization and parts of speech; and automatically organizes a collection of text files by topic
- Amazon Transcribe is an automatic speech recognition (ASR) service that makes it easy for developers to add speech-to-text capability to their applications
- AWS Artifact is your go-to, central resource for compliance-related information that matters to you. It provides on-demand access to AWS' security and compliance reports and select online agreements

**References:**

https://digitalcloud.training/certification-training/aws-certified-cloud-practitioner/additional-aws-services-tools/

https://aws.amazon.com/rekognition/

## 22. Question

**Which AWS service can you use to install a third-party database?**

1. Amazon EMR
2. Amazon RDS
3. Amazon DynamoDB
4. Amazon EC2

**Answer: 4**

**Explanation:**

- All of these services are managed services except for Amazon EC2. EC2 is the only service in the list upon which you can manually install the database software of your choice

References:

https://digitalcloud.training/certification-training/aws-certified-cloud-practitioner/aws-compute/

https://digitalcloud.training/certification-training/aws-certified-cloud-practitioner/aws-databases/

## 23. Question

Which AWS service can be used to convert video and audio files from their source format into versions that will playback on devices like smartphones, tablets and PC?

1. Elastic Transcoder
2. Elastic Beanstalk
3. Auto Scaling
4. Elastic Load Balancer

Answer: 1

Explanation:

- Amazon Elastic Transcoder is a highly scalable, easy to use and cost-effective way for developers and businesses to convert (or "transcode") video and audio files from their source format into versions that will playback on devices like smartphones, tablets and PCs
- AWS Elastic Beanstalk can be used to quickly deploy and manage applications in the AWS Cloud
- ELB is used to distribute incoming connections to EC2 instances and Auto Scaling is used to automatically ensure the right number of EC2 instances are available to service current load

References:

https://digitalcloud.training/certification-training/aws-solutions-architect-associate/media-services/amazon-elastic-transcoder/

## 24. Question

Which type of Amazon Elastic Load Balancer operates at layer 7 of the OSI model?

1. F5 Load Balancer
2. Application Load Balancer
3. Classic Load Balancer
4. Network Load Balancer

Answer: 2

Explanation:

- Application Load Balancer (ALB) – layer 7 load balancer that routes connections based on the content of the request
- Network Load Balancer (NLB) – layer 4 load balancer that routes connections based on IP protocol data
- Classic Load Balancer (CLB) – this is the oldest of the three and provides basic load balancing at both layer 4 and layer 7
- An F5 load balancer is not an Amazon load balancer

References:

https://digitalcloud.training/certification-training/aws-certified-cloud-practitioner/elastic-load-balancing-and-auto-scaling/

## 25. Question

Which AWS service allows you to use block-based volumes on-premise that are then asynchronously backed up to Amazon S3?

1. AWS Storage Gateway Volume Gateway
2. Amazon S3 Transfer Acceleration
3. AWS Storage Gateway File Gateway
4. Amazon S3 Multi-Part upload

Answer: 1

Explanation:

- AWS Storage Gateway Volume Gateway represents the family of gateways that support block-based volumes, previously referred to as gateway-cached and gateway-stored mode
- AWS Storage Gateway Volume Gateway operates in 2 modes:
    - Stored Volume mode – the entire dataset is stored on-site and is asynchronously backed up to S3 (EBS point-in-time snapshots). Snapshots are incremental and compressed
    - Cached Volume mode – the entire dataset is stored on S3 and a cache of the most frequently accessed data is cached on-site
- AWS Storage Gateway File Gateway provides a virtual on-premises file server, which enables you to store and retrieve files as objects in Amazon S3
- Multi-part upload and transfer acceleration are features of S3 associated with uploading files directly to S3

References:

https://digitalcloud.training/certification-training/aws-certified-cloud-practitioner/additional-aws-services-tools/

https://digitalcloud.training/certification-training/aws-solutions-architect-associate/storage/aws-storage-gateway/

## 26. Question

Which AWS service allows you to connect to storage from on-premise servers using standard file protocols?

1. Amazon EBS
2. Amazon S3
3. Amazon EFS
4. Amazon Glacier

Answer: 3

Explanation:

- EFS is a fully-managed service that makes it easy to set up and scale file storage in the Amazon Cloud

- EFS filesystems are mounted using the NFS protocol (which is a file-level protocol)
- Access to EFS file systems from on-premises servers can be enabled via Direct Connect or AWS VPN
- You mount an EFS file system on your on-premises Linux server using the standard Linux mount command for mounting a file system via the NFSv4.1 protocol
- Amazon S3 is an object-level not file-level storage system
- Amazon Glacier is an archiving solution that is accessed through S3
- Amazon Elastic Block Storage (EBS) is block-level storage that can only be accessed by EC2 instances from the same AZ as the EBS volume

**References:**

https://digitalcloud.training/certification-training/aws-certified-cloud-practitioner/additional-aws-services-tools/

## 27. Question

**Which statement below is incorrect in relation to Network ACLs?**

1. Process rules in order
2. Support allow and deny rules
3. Operate at the Availability Zone level
4. Stateless

**Answer: 3**

**Explanation:**

- Network ACLS operate at the subnet level

**References:**

https://digitalcloud.training/certification-training/aws-certified-cloud-practitioner/aws-networking/

## 28. Question

**Which service can be used to help you to migrate databases to AWS quickly and securely?**

1. AWS Migration Hub
2. AWS DMS
3. AWS SMS
4. AWS KMS

**Answer: 2**

**Explanation:**

- AWS Database Migration Service helps you migrate databases to AWS quickly and securely
- AWS Server Migration Service (SMS) is an agentless service which makes it easier and faster for you to migrate thousands of on-premises workloads to AWS
- AWS Key Management Service (KMS) is used for managing encryption keys
- AWS Migration Hub provides a single location to track the progress of application migrations across multiple AWS and partner solutions

**References:**

https://digitalcloud.training/certification-training/aws-certified-cloud-practitioner/additional-aws-services-tools/

## 29. Question

**Which of the following statements is correct in relation to consolidated billing? (choose 2)**

1. One bill is provided per AWS organization
2. Only available to Enterprise customers
3. Volume pricing discounts cannot be applied to resources
4. Used to consolidate billing across organizations
5. Paying accounts are independent and cannot access resources of other accounts

**Answer: 1,5**

**Explanation:**

- AWS organizations allow you to consolidate multiple AWS accounts into an organization that you create and centrally manage
- Note that it allows you to consolidate billing across accounts within an organization not across organizations
- Volume pricing discounts can be applied to resources
- Consolidated billing is available to all customers

**References:**

https://digitalcloud.training/certification-training/aws-certified-cloud-practitioner/aws-billing-and-pricing/

## 30. Question

**Which AWS support plan should you use if you need a response time of < 15 minutes for a business-critical system failure?**

1. Basic
2. Developer
3. Business
4. Enterprise

**Answer: 4**

**Explanation:**

- Only the Enterprise plan provides a response time of < 15 minutes for the failure of a business-critical system
- Both Business and Enterprise offer < 1-hour response time for the failure of a production system

**References:**

https://digitalcloud.training/certification-training/aws-certified-cloud-practitioner/aws-billing-and-pricing/

## 31. Question

**Which feature of AWS allows you to deploy a new application for which the requirements may change over time?**

1. High availability
2. Disposable resources
3. Fault tolerance
4. Elasticity

**Answer: 4**

**Explanation:**

- Elasticity allows you to deploy your application without worrying about whether it will need more or less resources in the future. With elasticity, the infrastructure can scale on-demand
- Fault tolerance and high availability are mechanisms used for ensuring the availability of your application and protecting against the failure of hardware or software components
- Disposable resources is an architectural principle in which servers and other components are treated as temporary resources and are replaced rather than updated

**References:**

https://digitalcloud.training/certification-training/aws-certified-cloud-practitioner/architecting-for-the-cloud/

## 32. Question

**What is an availability zone composed of?**

1. A collection of VPCs
2. A collection of edge locations
3. One or more DCs in a location
4. One or more regions

**Answer: 3**

**Explanation:**

- Availability Zones are physically separate and isolated from each other
- AZ's have direct, low-latency, high throughput and redundant network connections between each other
- A region is a geographical area
- Each region consists of 2 or more availability zones

**References:**

https://digitalcloud.training/certification-training/aws-certified-cloud-practitioner/aws-global-infrastructure/

## 33. Question

**Which database service is a NoSQL type of database that is fully managed?**

1. Amazon RDS
2. Amazon DynamoDB
3. Amazon ElastiCache
4. Amazon RedShift

**Answer: 2**

**Explanation:**

- DynamoDB is Amazon's fully managed non-relational database service
- Amazon RDS is a relational (SQL) type of database
- Amazon RedShift is a data warehouse that can be analyzed using SQL tools
- Elasticache is a data caching service that is used to help improve performance

**References:**

https://digitalcloud.training/certification-training/aws-certified-cloud-practitioner/aws-databases/

## 34. Question

**Which service can you use to provision a preconfigured server with little to no AWS experience?**

1. Amazon Elastic Beanstalk
2. AWS Lambda
3. Amazon EC2
4. Amazon Lightsail

**Answer: 4**

**Explanation:**

- Lightsail provides developers compute, storage, and networking capacity and capabilities to deploy and manage websites, web applications, and databases in the cloud
- Lightsail provides preconfigured virtual private servers (instances) that include everything required to deploy an application or create a database
- Deploying a server on Lightsail is extremely easy and does not require knowledge of how to configure VPCs, security groups, network ACLs etc.
- AWS Elastic Beanstalk can be used to quickly deploy and manage applications in the AWS Cloud. It is considered a PaaS service. However, you do still need to deploy within a VPC so more AWS expertise is required
- Amazon EC2 also requires AWS expertise as it deploys within a VPC
- AWS Lambda provides serverless functions not preconfigured servers

**References:**

https://digitalcloud.training/certification-training/aws-certified-cloud-practitioner/aws-compute/

## 35. Question

**For which services does Amazon not charge customers? (choose 2)**

1. Amazon VPC
2. Amazon EBS

3. Amazon CloudFormation
4. Amazon S3
5. Amazon SNS

**Answer: 1,3**

**Explanation:**

- Amazon VPC and CloudFormation are free of charge, however in the case of CloudFormation you pay for the resources it creates
- All other listed services are chargeable

**References:**

https://digitalcloud.training/certification-training/aws-certified-cloud-practitioner/aws-billing-and-pricing/

## 36. Question

**What is the most cost-effective EC2 pricing option to use for a non-critical overnight workload?**

1. On-Demand
2. Spot
3. Reserved Instance
4. Dedicated Host

**Answer: 2**

**Explanation:**

- Spot instances are good for short term requirements as they can be very economical. Sometimes AWS may terminate your instance, e.g. when the market price exceeds your bid price. This is a good option for non-critical workloads that can be terminated
- On-Demand is not the most economical option
- Reserved instances are good for long-term, static requirements as you must lock-in for 1 or 3 years in return for a decent discount
- Dedicated hosts provide a full server dedicated to a single customer and is therefore expensive

**References:**

https://digitalcloud.training/certification-training/aws-certified-cloud-practitioner/aws-billing-and-pricing/

## 37. Question

**What benefits does Amazon EC2 provide over-using non-cloud servers? (choose 2)**

1. Fault tolerance
2. Inexpensive
3. High-availability with an SLA of 99.999%
4. Elastic web-scale computing
5. Complete control of the hypervisor layer

Answer: 2,4

Explanation:

- Elastic Web-Scale computing– you can increase or decrease capacity within minutes not hours and commission one to thousands of instances simultaneously
- Inexpensive – Amazon passes on the financial benefits of scale by charging very low rates and on a capacity consumed basis
- Amazon EC2 does not provide any control of the hypervisor or underlying hardware infrastructure
- Amazon does not offer fault tolerance for EC2, you need to design this into your application stack (and assume things will fail)
- AWS provide an SLA for EC2 that states that services will be available within each AWS region with a Monthly Uptime Percentage of at least 99.99%

References:

https://digitalcloud.training/certification-training/aws-certified-cloud-practitioner/cloud-computing-concepts/

https://digitalcloud.training/certification-training/aws-certified-cloud-practitioner/architecting-for-the-cloud/

## 38. Question

Which AWS service can an organization use to automate operational tasks on EC2 instances using existing Chef cookbooks?

1. AWS CodeDeploy
2. AWS Config
3. AWS Service Catalog
4. AWS OpsWorks

Answer: 4

Explanation:

- AWS OpsWorks is a configuration management service that provides managed instances of Chef and Puppet. With Chef, you use code templates, or cookbooks, to describe the desired configuration of instances or on-premises server
- AWS Service Catalog allows organizations to create and manage catalogs of IT services that are approved for use on AWS
- AWS Config is a service that enables you to assess, audit, and evaluate the configurations of your AWS resource
- AWS CodeDeploy is a fully managed deployment service that automates software deployments to a variety of compute services such as Amazon EC2, AWS Lambda, and your on-premises servers

References:

https://digitalcloud.training/certification-training/aws-certified-cloud-practitioner/additional-aws-services-tools/

https://aws.amazon.com/opsworks/chefautomate/features/

### 39. Question

**Which AWS service can be used to process a large amount of data using the Hadoop framework?**

1. Amazon EMR
2. Amazon Kinesis
3. AWS Glue
4. Amazon Athena

**Answer: 1**

**Explanation:**

- Amazon Elastic Map Reduce (EMR) provides a managed Hadoop framework that makes it easy, fast, and cost-effective to process vast amounts of data across dynamically scalable Amazon EC2 instances
- Amazon Kinesis makes it easy to collect, process, and analyze real-time, streaming data so you can get timely insights and react quickly to new information
- AWS Glue is a fully managed extract, transform, and load (ETL) service that makes it easy for customers to prepare and load their data for analytics
- Amazon Athena is an interactive query service that makes it easy to analyze data in Amazon S3 using standard SQL

**References:**

https://digitalcloud.training/certification-training/aws-certified-cloud-practitioner/additional-aws-services-tools/

### 40. Question

**Which statement below is incorrect in relation to Security Groups?**

1. Stateless
2. Evaluate all rules
3. Support allow rules only
4. Operate at the instance level

**Answer: 1**

**Explanation:**

- Security groups are stateful meaning that if traffic is allowed in one direction, the return traffic is automatically allowed regardless of whether there is a matching rule for the traffic

**References:**

https://digitalcloud.training/certification-training/aws-certified-cloud-practitioner/aws-networking/

### 41. Question

**How can an organization compare the cost of running applications in an on-premise or colocation environment against the AWS cloud?**

1. AWS Budgets
2. AWS Simple Monthly Calculator

3. TCO Calculator
4. AWS Cost Explorer

**Answer: 3**

**Explanation:**

- The TCO calculator is a free tool provided by AWS that allows you to estimate the cost savings of using the AWS Cloud vs. using an on-premised data center
- The AWS Cost Explorer is a free tool that allows you to view charts of your costs. You can view cost data for the past 13 months and forecast how much you are likely to spend over the next three months. Cost Explorer can be used to discover patterns in how much you spend on AWS resources over time and to identify cost problem area
- The AWS Simple Monthly Calculator helps customers and prospects estimate their monthly AWS bill more efficiently
- AWS Budgets gives you the ability to set custom budgets that alert you when your costs or usage exceed (or are forecasted to exceed) your budgeted amount

**References:**

https://digitalcloud.training/certification-training/aws-certified-cloud-practitioner/aws-billing-and-pricing/

## 42. Question

**Under the shared responsibility model, what are examples of shared controls? (choose 2)**

1. Patch management
2. Storage system patching
3. Service and Communications Protection
4. Physical and environmental
5. Configuration management

**Answer: 1,5**

**Explanation:**

- Shared Controls– Controls which apply to both the infrastructure layer and customer layers, but in completely separate contexts or perspectives
- Patch Management– AWS is responsible for patching and fixing flaws within the infrastructure, but customers are responsible for patching their guest OS and applications
- Configuration Management– AWS maintains the configuration of its infrastructure devices, but a customer is responsible for configuring their own guest operating systems, databases, and applications
- Service and Communications Protection is an example of a customer specific control
- Storage system patching is an AWS responsibility
- Physical and Environmental controls is an example of an inherited control (a customer fully inherits from AWS)

**References:**

https://digitalcloud.training/certification-training/aws-certified-cloud-practitioner/aws-shared-responsibility-model/

## 43. Question

**Which service can be used to track the CPU usage of an EC2 instance?**

1. Amazon CloudTrail
2. Amazon CloudFront
3. Amazon CloudFormation
4. Amazon CloudWatch

Answer: 4

**Explanation:**

- Amazon CloudWatch is a monitoring service for AWS cloud resources and the applications you run on AWS
- CloudWatch is for performance monitoring, whereas CloudTrail is for auditing
- AWS CloudTrail is a web service that records activity made on your account and delivers log files to an Amazon S3 bucket
- CloudFormation is used for automated provisioning of infrastructure
- CloudFront is a content delivery network (CDN) that caches content

**References:**

https://digitalcloud.training/certification-training/aws-certified-cloud-practitioner/monitoring-and-logging-services/

## 44. Question

**Which service allows you to automatically expand and shrink your application in response to demand?**

1. AWS Auto Scaling
2. Amazon Elastic Load Balancing
3. Amazon DynamoDB
4. AWS ElastiCache

Answer: 1

**Explanation:**

1. Auto Scaling automatically responds to demand by adding or removing EC2 instances to ensure the right amount of compute capacity is available at any time
2. Amazon ELB distributes incoming requests to EC2 instances. It can be used in conjunction with Auto Scaling
3. AWS Elasticache provides in-memory cache and database services
4. Amazon DynamoDB is a NoSQL database

**References:**

https://digitalcloud.training/certification-training/aws-certified-cloud-practitioner/elastic-load-balancing-and-auto-scaling/

## 45. Question

**Which of the following is a method of backup available in the AWS cloud?**

1. Route 53 Alias Record
2. EBS Snapshots
3. EFS File Systems
4. Availability Zones

Answer: 2

Explanation:

- Amazon Elastic Block Store (EBS) is a block-based storage system that provides a "virtual hard disk in the cloud". You can back up your EBS volumes using snapshots which are point-in-time copies of the data.
- Availability Zones are part of the AWS Global Infrastructure. AZs can be used for high availability and fault tolerance as you can architect your applications to be spread across them. However, they are not a backup solution.
- The Amazon Elastic File System (EFS) provides file-based storage that you access using the NFS v2 protocol. This is storage service but not a backup service. You can backup EFS using the AWS Backup service or using EFS-to-EFS backup.
- Amazon Route 53 provides a DNS service and an Alias record is a type of record that can map a public domain name to an AWS service target.

References:

https://digitalcloud.training/certification-training/aws-certified-cloud-practitioner/aws-storage/

https://docs.aws.amazon.com/AWSEC2/latest/UserGuide/EBSSnapshots.html

## 46. Question

Which type of cloud deployment enables customers to leverage the benefits of the public cloud and co-existing with on-premises infrastructure?

1. Public Cloud
2. Private Cloud
3. Hybrid Cloud
4. Legacy IT Infrastructure

Answer: 3

Explanation:

- A hybrid deployment is a way to connect infrastructure and applications between cloud-based resources and existing resources that are not located in the cloud. The most common method of hybrid deployment is between the cloud and existing on-premises infrastructure to extend, and grow, an organization's infrastructure into the cloud while connecting cloud resources to the internal system
- A cloud-based application is fully deployed in the cloud and all parts of the application run in the cloud. Applications in the cloud have either been created in the cloud or have been migrated from an existing infrastructure to take advantage of the benefits of cloud computing
- The deployment of resources on-premises, using virtualization and resource management tools, is sometimes called the "private cloud." On-premises deployment doesn't provide many of the benefits of cloud computing but is sometimes sought for its ability to provide dedicated resources

- Legacy IT infrastructure is not a cloud model. Typically, this includes systems that either not virtualized or do not have a cloud management layer

**References:**

https://digitalcloud.training/certification-training/aws-certified-cloud-practitioner/cloud-computing-concepts/

## 47. Question

**Which storage service allows you to connect multiple EC2 instances concurrently using file-level protocols?**

1. Amazon Glacier
2. Amazon S3
3. Amazon EBS
4. Amazon EFS

**Answer: 4**

**Explanation:**

- Amazon Elastic File System allows you to connect hundreds or thousands of EC2 instances concurrently and is accessed using the file-level NFS protocol
- Amazon Elastic Block Storage provides block-level volumes to individual EC2 instances (cannot connect multiple instances to a single EBS volume)
- Amazon S3 is an object storage system and Glacier is used for archiving S3 objects

**References:**

https://digitalcloud.training/certification-training/aws-certified-cloud-practitioner/aws-storage/

## 48. Question

**The AWS global infrastructure is composed of? (choose 2)**

1. Availability Zones
2. Fault Zones
3. Clusters
4. Regions
5. IP subnets

**Answer: 1,4**

**Explanation:**

- The AWS Global infrastructure is built around Regions and Availability Zones (AZs)
- A Region is a physical location in the world where AWS have multiple AZs
- AZs consist of one or more discrete data centers, each with redundant power, networking, and connectivity, housed in separate facilities

**References:**

https://digitalcloud.training/certification-training/aws-certified-cloud-practitioner/aws-global-infrastructure/

## 49. Question

**Which of the following are features of Amazon CloudWatch? (choose 2)**

1. Records account activity and service events from most AWS services
2. Used to gain system-wide visibility into resource utilization
3. Can be accessed via API, command-line interface, AWS SDKs, and the AWS Management Console
4. Provides visibility into user activity by recording actions taken on your account
5. Used for auditing of API calls

Answer: 2,3

Explanation:

- Amazon CloudWatch is a monitoring service for AWS cloud resources and the applications you run on AWS
- CloudWatch is for performance monitoring (CloudTrail is for auditing)
- CloudWatch is used to collect and track metrics, collect and monitor log files, and set alarms
- AWS CloudTrail is a web service that records activity made on your account and delivers log files to an Amazon S3 bucket
- CloudTrail is for auditing (CloudWatch is for performance monitoring)
- CloudTrail is about logging and saves a history of API calls for your AWS account
- CloudTrail records account activity and service events from most AWS services

References:

https://digitalcloud.training/certification-training/aws-certified-cloud-practitioner/monitoring-and-logging-services/

## 50. Question

**What considerations are there when choosing which region to use? (choose 2)**

1. Data sovereignty
2. Available compute capacity
3. Latency
4. Pricing in local currency
5. Available storage capacity

Answer: 1,3

Explanation:

- You may choose a region to reduce latency, minimize costs, or address regulatory requirements
- Available capacity is generally not a concern as AWS has a large pool of resources and does not disclose the available capacity in each region
- Pricing for AWS services is in USD

References:

https://docs.aws.amazon.com/emr/latest/ManagementGuide/emr-plan-region.html

https://digitalcloud.training/certification-training/aws-certified-cloud-practitioner/aws-global-infrastructure/

## 51. Question

Which pricing model should you use for EC2 instances that will be used in a lab environment for several hours on a weekend and must run uninterrupted?

1. On-Demand
2. Reserved
3. Spot
4. Dedicated Instance

Answer: 1

Explanation:

- Spot instances are good for short term requirements as they can be very economical. However, you may find that the instance is terminated if the spot market price moves
- On-Demand is the best choice for this situation as it is the most economical option that will ensure no interruptions
- Reserved instances are good for long-term, static requirements as you must lock-in for 1 or 3 years in return for a decent discount
- Dedicated instances are EC2 instances that run on hardware dedicated to a single customer

References:

https://digitalcloud.training/certification-training/aws-certified-cloud-practitioner/aws-billing-and-pricing/

## 52. Question

What benefits are provided by Amazon CloudFront? (choose 2)

1. Used to enable private subnet instances to access the Internet
2. Content is cached at Edge Locations for fast distribution to customers
3. Built-in Distributed Denial of Service (DDoS) attack protection
4. Provides a worldwide distributed DNS service
5. Allows you to register domain names

Answer: 2,3

Explanation:

- CloudFront is a content delivery network (CDN) that allows you to store (cache) your content at "edge locations" located around the world
- This allows customers to access content more quickly and provides security against DDoS attacks
- CloudFront can be used for data, videos, applications, and APIs

  Benefits include:

- Cache content at Edge Location for fast distribution to customers
- Built-in Distributed Denial of Service (DDoS) attack protection
- Integrates with many AWS services (S3, EC2, ELB, Route 53, Lambda)

References:

https://digitalcloud.training/certification-training/aws-certified-cloud-practitioner/content-delivery-and-dns-services/

## 53. Question

What method can you use to take a backup of an Amazon EC2 instance using AWS tools?

1. Take full and incremental file-level backups using the backup console
2. Take application-consistent backups using the EC2 API
3. Take a snapshot to capture the point-in-time state of the instance
4. Use Cross Region Replication (CRR) to copy the instance to another region

Answer: 3

Explanation:

- You can take snapshots of EC2 instances which creates a point-in-time copy of the instance. Snapshots are stored on S3
- If you make periodic snapshots of a volume, the snapshots are incremental, which means that only the blocks on the device that have changed after your last snapshot are saved in the new snapshot
- There is no backup console to take full and incremental backups
- There is no way of taking application-consistent backups using any AWS tools
- Cross Region Replication is used to replicate Amazon S3 buckets are across regions

References:

https://digitalcloud.training/certification-training/aws-certified-cloud-practitioner/aws-storage/

## 54. Question

Which service allows you to run code as functions without needing to provision or manage servers?

1. AWS Lambda
2. Amazon EKS
3. Amazon EC2
4. Amazon CodeDeploy

Answer: 1

Explanation:

- AWS Lambda is a serverless computing technology that allows you to run code without provisioning or managing servers
- Lambda is a serverless computing technology that allows you to run code without provisioning or managing servers
- AWS CodeDeploy is a fully managed deployment service that automates software deployments to a variety of compute services such as Amazon EC2, AWS Lambda, and your on-premises servers
- Amazon Elastic Container Service for Kubernetes (Amazon EKS) is a managed service that makes it easy for you to run Kubernetes on AWS without needing to stand up or maintain your own Kubernetes control plane

References:

https://digitalcloud.training/certification-training/aws-certified-cloud-practitioner/aws-compute/

## 55. Question

**What are two ways that moving to an AWS cloud can benefit an organization? (choose 2)**

1. Gain greater control of data center security
2. Depreciate assets over a longer timeframe
3. Stop guessing about capacity
4. Increase speed and agility
5. Switch to a CAPEX model

**Answer: 3,4**

**Explanation:**

- Eliminate guessing on your infrastructure capacity needs. When you make a capacity decision prior to deploying an application, you often end up either sitting on expensive idle resources or dealing with limited capacity. With cloud computing, these problems go away. You can access as much or as little capacity as you need, and scale up and down as required with only a few minutes' notice
- In a cloud computing environment, new IT resources are only a click away, which means that you reduce the time to make those resources available to your developers from weeks to just minutes. This results in a dramatic increase in agility for the organization, since the cost and time it takes to experiment and develop is significantly lower
- Cloud is based on an operational expenditure (OPEX) model, not a capital expenditure (CAPEX) model
- Cloud does not provide the ability to depreciate assets over a longer timeframe as you generally do not own the assets
- Though the AWS cloud does provide significant security standards for the data center, you do not get more control as this is an AWS responsibility

**References:**

https://digitalcloud.training/certification-training/aws-certified-cloud-practitioner/cloud-computing-concepts/

## 56. Question

**A company would like to maximize their potential volume and RI discounts across multiple accounts and also apply service control policies on member accounts. Which service or tool can they use to gain these benefits?**

1. AWS Budgets
2. AWS Cost Explorer
3. AWS IAM
4. AWS Organizations

**Answer: 4**

**Explanation:**

- AWS Organizations enables you to create groups of AWS accounts and then centrally manage policies across those accounts. AWS Organizations provides consolidated billing in both feature

sets, which allows you set up a single payment method in the organization's master account and still receive an invoice for individual activity in each member account. Volume pricing discounts can be applied to resources
- AWS Budgets gives you the ability to set custom budgets that alert you when your costs or usage exceed (or are forecasted to exceed) your budgeted amount
- AWS Identity and Access Management (IAM) enables you to manage access to AWS services and resources securely
- The AWS Cost Explorer is a free tool that allows you to view charts of your costs

**References:**

https://digitalcloud.training/certification-training/aws-certified-cloud-practitioner/aws-billing-and-pricing/

https://docs.aws.amazon.com/organizations/latest/userguide/orgs_getting-started_concepts.html

## 57. Question

Which AWS service is used to enable multi-factor authentication?

1. Amazon STS
2. AWS KMS
3. AWS IAM
4. Amazon EC2

**Answer: 3**

**Explanation:**

- IAM is used to securely control individual and group access to AWS resources
- IAM can be used to manage multi-factor authentication
- The AWS Security Token Service (STS) is a web service that enables you to request temporary, limited-privilege credentials for IAM users or for users that you authenticate (federated users)
- AWS Key Management Service (KMS) is a managed service that makes it easy for you to create and control the encryption keys used to encrypt your data
- Amazon EC2 is used for running operating systems instances in the cloud

**References:**

https://digitalcloud.training/certification-training/aws-certified-cloud-practitioner/identity-and-access-management/

## 58. Question

Which AWS database service supports complex queries and joins and is suitable for a transactional database deployment?

1. Amazon RDS
2. Amazon DynamoDB
3. Amazon EMR
4. Amazon RedShift

**Answer: 1**

**Explanation:**

- Amazon RDS supports complex queries and joins and is suitable for a transactional database deployment
- Amazon DynamoDB is a NoSQL database and does not support to complex queries and joins
- Amazon RedShift is a data warehouse used for analytic not transactional databases
- Amazon EMR is a Hadoop service that is not suitable for transactional databases

**References:**

https://digitalcloud.training/certification-training/aws-certified-cloud-practitioner/aws-databases/


## 59. Question

When instantiating compute resources, what are two techniques for using automated, repeatable processes that are fast and avoid human error? (choose 2)

1. Performance monitoring
2. Infrastructure as code
3. Bootstrapping
4. Fault tolerance
5. Snapshotting

**Answer: 2,3**

**Explanation:**

- With infrastructure as code AWS assets are programmable, so you can apply techniques, practices, and tools from software development to make your whole infrastructure reusable, maintainable, extensible, and testable
- With bootstrapping you can execute automated actions to modify default configurations. This includes scripts that install software or copy data to bring that resource to a particular state
- Snapshotting is about saving data, not instantiating resources. Fault tolerance is a method of increasing the availability of your system when components fail. Performance monitoring has nothing to do with instantiating resources

**References:**

https://digitalcloud.training/certification-training/aws-certified-cloud-practitioner/architecting-for-the-cloud/


## 60. Question

Which service supports the resolution of public domain names to IP addresses or AWS resources?

1. Amazon Route 53
2. Amazon CloudFront
3. Amazon SNS
4. Hosted Zones

**Answer: 1**

**Explanation:**

- Amazon Route 53 is a highly available and scalable Domain Name System (DNS) service
- A hosted zone is a collection of records for a specified domain in Route 53
- CloudFront is a content delivery network (CDN) that allows you to store (cache) your content at "edge locations" located around the world
- Simple Notification Service is used to send notifications over multiple transport protocols

**References:**

https://digitalcloud.training/certification-training/aws-certified-cloud-practitioner/content-delivery-and-dns-services/

## 61. Question

**Which feature can you use to grant read/write access to an Amazon S3 bucket?**

1. IAM Role
2. IAM User
3. IAM Policy
4. IAM Group

**Answer: 3**

**Explanation:**

- IAM Policies are documents that define permissions and can be applied to users, groups and roles
- IAM policies can be written to grant access to Amazon S3 buckets
- IAM Roles are created and then "assumed" by trusted entities and define a set of permissions for making AWS service requests
- IAM Groups are collections of users and have policies attached to them
- An IAM user is an entity that represents a person or service

**References:**

https://aws.amazon.com/blogs/security/writing-iam-policies-how-to-grant-access-to-an-amazon-s3-bucket/

## 62. Question

**Which services are integrated with KMS encryption? (choose 2)**

1. Amazon RDS
2. Amazon EC2
3. AWS CloudFormation
4. Amazon EBS
5. Amazon SWF

**Answer: 1,4**

**Explanation:**

- Not all services integrate with KMS. Review the reference below

**References:**

https://aws.amazon.com/kms/features/

## 63. Question

**What architectural best practice aims to reduce the interdependencies between services?**

1. Services, Not Servers
2. Removing Single Points of Failure
3. Automation
4. Loose Coupling

**Answer: 4**

**Explanation:**

- As application complexity increases, a desirable attribute of an IT system is that it can be broken into smaller, loosely coupled components. This means that IT systems should be designed in a way that reduces interdependencies—a change or a failure in one component should not cascade to other components
- The concept of loos coupling includes "well-defined interfaces" which reduce interdependencies in a system by enabling interaction only through specific, technology-agnostic interfaces (e.g. RESTful APIs)

**References:**

https://digitalcloud.training/certification-training/aws-certified-cloud-practitioner/architecting-for-the-cloud/

## 64. Question

**What is the most cost-effective support plan that should be selected to provide at least a 1-hour response time for a production system failure?**

1. Enterprise
2. Business
3. Developer
4. Basic

**Answer: 2**

**Explanation:**

- Basic does not provide any technical support
- Developer provides business hours access via email
- Business provides < 1-hour response times for a production system failure
- Enterprise provides < 1-hour response times for a production system failure but is a more expensive

**References:**

https://digitalcloud.training/certification-training/aws-certified-cloud-practitioner/aws-billing-and-pricing/

## 65. Question

**The IAM service can be used to manage which objects? (choose 2)**

1. Security groups
2. Key pairs
3. Roles
4. Access policies
5. Network ACLs

**Answer: 3,4**

**Explanation:**

- Access policies are objects that you attach to entities and resources to define their permissions
- Roles are created and then "assumed" by trusted entities and define a set of permissions for making AWS service requests
- Security groups and network ACLs are used as instance-level and subnet-level firewalls respectively
- Key pairs are created in EC2 and are used to login to EC2 instances. Don't confuse these with access keys and secret IDs which are used to grant programmatic access to resources

**References:**

https://digitalcloud.training/certification-training/aws-certified-cloud-practitioner/identity-and-access-management/

https://docs.aws.amazon.com/IAM/latest/UserGuide/access_policies.html

# SET 2: PRACTICE QUESTIONS ONLY

### 1. Question
**How can a security compliance officer retrieve AWS compliance documentation such as a SOC 2 report?**

1. Using AWS Artifact
2. Using AWS Trusted Advisor
3. Using the AWS Personal Health Dashboard
4. Using AWS Inspector

### 2. Question
**What is an example of using loose coupling when designing an information system?**

1. Proprietary interfaces
2. DNS name usage
3. Synchronous replication
4. Monolithic application architecture

### 3. Question
**Which AWS service can be used to run Docker containers?**

1. Amazon AMI
2. AWS Lambda
3. Amazon ECR
4. Amazon ECS

### 4. Question
**Which AWS service can be used to host a static website?**

1. AWS Lambda
2. Amazon EBS
3. Amazon S3
4. Amazon EFS

### 5. Question
**Which of the following services does Amazon Route 53 provide? (choose 2)**

1. Route tables
2. Auto Scaling
3. Domain registration
4. Domain Name Service (DNS)
5. Load balancing

## 6. Question

Which AWS network element allows you to assign a static IPv4 address to an EC2 instance?

1. Public IP
2. Dynamic IP
3. Elastic IP
4. Static IP


## 7. Question

What features does Amazon RDS provide to deliver scalability, availability and durability? (choose 2)

1. Multi-Subnet
2. Clustering
3. DB mirroring
4. Read Replicas
5. Multi-AZ


## 8. Question

A manager needs to keep a check on his AWS spend. How can the manager setup alarms that notify him when his bill reaches a certain amount?

1. Using AWS Trusted Advisor
2. By notifying AWS support
3. Using CloudTrail
4. Using CloudWatch


## 9. Question

What components can be managed in the Virtual Private Cloud (VPC) management console? (choose 2)

1. Elastic Load Balancers
2. Subnets
3. Auto Scaling
4. IP CIDR
5. Snapshots


## 10. Question

What is a Resource Group?

1. A collection of services within a region
2. A collection of services within a category
3. A collection of resources that share one or more tags
4. A collection of resources within a VPC


## 11. Question

A company is planning to migrate some resources into the cloud. What factors need to be considered when determining the cost of the AWS Cloud? (choose 2)

1. The number of VPCs created
2. The number of servers migrated into EC2
3. The number of IAM users created
4. The amount of egress data per month
5. The amount of ingress data per month

## 12. Question

**Which services are managed at a regional (rather than global) level? (choose 2)**

1. Amazon Route 53
2. Amazon CloudFront
3. AWS IAM
4. Amazon S3
5. Amazon EC2

## 13. Question

**To connect an on-premises network to an Amazon VPC using an Amazon Managed VPN connection, which components are required? (choose 2)**

1. Direct Connect
2. NAT Instance
3. Virtual Private Gateway
4. Customer Gateway
5. VPC Router

## 14. Question

**An application stores images which will be retrieved infrequently but must be available for retrieval immediately. Which is the most cost-effective storage option that meets these requirements?**

1. Amazon S3 Standard
2. Amazon EFS
3. Amazon S3 Standard-Infrequent Access
4. Amazon Glacier with expedited retrievals

## 15. Question

**Which AWS construct provides you with your own dedicated virtual network in the cloud?**

1. Amazon IAM
2. Amazon EC2
3. Amazon Workspaces
4. Amazon VPC

## 16. Question

**Which file format is used to write AWS Identity and Access Management (IAM) policies?**

1. DOC
2. XML

3. JBOD
4. JSON

## 17. Question

**Which services are involved with security? (choose 2)**

1. AWS SMS
2. AWS CloudHSM
3. Amazon ELB
4. AWS DMS
5. AWS KMS

## 18. Question

**Which of the following are AWS recommended best practices in relation to IAM? (choose 2)**

1. Enable MFA for all users
2. Embed access keys in application code
3. Assign permissions to users
4. Create individual IAM users
5. Grant greatest privilege

## 19. Question

**What are the names of two types of AWS Storage Gateway? (choose 2)**

1. Cached Gateway
2. File Gateway
3. Tape Gateway
4. S3 Gateway
5. Block Gateway

## 20. Question

**What kinds of routing policies are available in Amazon Route 53? (choose 2)**

1. Fault tolerant
2. Latency
3. Failback
4. Shortest Path First
5. Simple

## 21. Question

**To optimize pricing or ensure capacity is available reservations can be applied to which of the following services? (choose 2)**

1. Amazon S3
2. Amazon EC2
3. AWS Lambda
4. Amazon EBS

5. Amazon RDS

## 22. Question

**How can an organization assess applications for vulnerabilities and deviations from best practice?**

1. Use AWS WAF
2. Use AWS Artifact
3. Use AWS Inspector
4. Use AWS Shield

## 23. Question

**Which AWS service gives you centralized control over the encryption keys used to protect your data?**

1. AWS STS
2. Amazon EBS
3. AWS DMS
4. AWS KMS

## 24. Question

**What categories of Amazon Machine Image (AMI) are available? (choose 2)**

1. Enterprise AMIs
2. Shared AMIs
3. AWS Marketplace AMIs
4. Community AMIs
5. Partner AMIs

## 25. Question

**Which AWS services can be utilized at no cost? (choose 2)**

1. Amazon CloudFront
2. Identity and Access Management (IAM)
3. Amazon RedShift
4. Amazon VPC
5. Amazon S3

## 26. Question

**You need to ensure you have the right amount of compute available to service demand. Which AWS service can automatically scale the number of EC2 instances for your application?**

1. Amazon Elasticache
2. AWS Auto Scaling
3. Amazon Elastic Load Balancer
4. AWS RedShift

## 27. Question

Which cloud computing model gives the IT department the highest level of flexibility and management control?

1. On-premises cloud
2. Infrastructure as a Service (IaaS)
3. Software as a Service (SaaS)
4. Platform as a Service (PaaS)

## 28. Question

Which items should be included in a TCO analysis comparing on-premise to AWS Cloud? (choose 2)

1. Firewall management
2. Operating system patching
3. Data center security
4. Application licensing
5. Compute hardware

## 29. Question

Amazon S3 is typically used for which of the following use cases? (choose 2)

1. Install an operating system
2. In-memory data cache
3. Message queue
4. Host a static website
5. Media hosting

## 30. Question

Which AWS service protects against common exploits that could compromise application availability, compromise security or consume excessive resources?

1. AWS Shield
2. Network ACL
3. Security Group
4. AWS WAF

## 31. Question

Which tool can be used to create and manage a selection of AWS services that are approved for use on AWS?

1. AWS Service Catalog
2. AWS OpsWorks
3. AWS Organizations
4. Amazon Cloud Directory

## 32. Question

**What are the benefits of using the AWS Managed Services? (choose 2)**

1. Designed for small businesses
2. Baseline integration with ITSM tools
3. Managed applications so you can focus on infrastructure
4. Alignment with ITIL processes
5. Support for all AWS services

## 33. Question

**An architect needs to compare the cost of deploying an on-premise web server and an EC2 instance on the AWS cloud. Which tool can be used to assist the architect?**

1. AWS Budgets
2. AWS TCO Calculator
3. AWS Simple Monthly Calculator
4. AWS Cost Explorer

## 34. Question

**How should an organization deploy an application running on multiple EC2 instances to ensure that a power failure does not cause an application outage?**

1. Launch the EC2 instances into different VPCs
2. Launch the EC2 instances in separate regions
3. Launch the EC2 instances into Edge Locations
4. Launch the EC2 instances into different Availability Zones

## 35. Question

**Virtual servers such as EC2 instances are examples of services delivered under which cloud model?**

1. SaaS
2. DBaaS
3. PaaS
4. IaaS

## 36. Question

**Which of the facts below are accurate in relation to AWS Regions? (choose 2)**

1. Regions have direct, low-latency, high throughput and redundant network connections between each other
2. Each region is designed to be completely isolated from the other Amazon Regions
3. Each region consists of a collection of VPCs
4. Regions are Content Delivery Network (CDN) endpoints for CloudFront
5. Each region consists of 2 or more availability zones

## 37. Question

Which AWS service can assist with coordinating tasks across distributed application components?

1. Amazon STS
2. Amazon SQS
3. Amazon SWF
4. Amazon SNS

## 38. Question

Which database engines are supported by Amazon RDS? (choose 2)

1. DynamoDB
2. SQL Server
3. ElastiCache
4. Aurora
5. MongoDB

## 39. Question

Which of the following security operations tasks must be performed by AWS customers? (choose 2)

1. Installing security updates for server firmware
2. Issuing data center access keycards
3. Enabling multi-factor authentication (MFA) for privileged users
4. Collecting syslog messages from physical firewalls
5. Installing security updates on EC2 instances

## 40. Question

A Solutions Architect is designing an application stack that will be highly elastic. What AWS services can be used that don't require you to make any capacity decisions upfront? (choose 2)

1. AWS Lambda
2. Amazon EC2
3. Amazon RDS
4. Amazon S3
5. DynamoDB

## 41. Question

What type of storage is provided by Amazon EBS?

1. Relational
2. Object
3. File
4. Block

## 42. Question

Which types of AWS resource can be launched from a Golden Image? (choose 2)

1. Amazon DynamoDB tables
2. Amazon EC2 instances
3. Amazon RDS instances
4. Amazon S3 objects
5. AWS Lambda functions

### 43. Question

**Which AWS service provides elastic web-scale cloud computing allowing you to deploy operating system instances?**

1. Amazon EBS
2. AWS Lambda
3. Amazon RDS
4. Amazon EC2

### 44. Question

**Which of the following is NOT one of the five AWS Trusted Advisor categories?**

1. Performance
2. Application transformation
3. Cost Optimization
4. Security

### 45. Question

**Which configuration changes are associated with scaling horizontally? (choose 2)**

1. Adding additional EC2 instances through Auto Scaling
2. Changing an EC2 instance to a type that has more CPU and RAM
3. Adding additional hard drives to a storage array
4. Adding a larger capacity hard drive to a server
5. Changing the DB instance class on an RDS DB

### 46. Question

**You need to implement a hosted queue for storing messages in transit between application servers. Which service should you use?**

1. Amazon SWF
2. Amazon SNS
3. Amazon SQS
4. Amazon DynamoDB

### 47. Question

**How can you apply metadata to an EC2 instance that categorizes it according to its purpose, owner or environment?**

1. Tags
2. Stickers

3. Hostname
4. Labels

## 48. Question

An architect wants to find a tool for consistently deploying the same resources through a templated configuration. What AWS service can be used?

1. AWS CloudFormation
2. AWS Elastic Beanstalk
3. AWS CodeBuild
4. AWS CodeDeploy

## 49. Question

Which AWS service provides preconfigured virtual private servers (instances) that include everything required to deploy an application or create a database?

1. AWS Lambda
2. Amazon ECS
3. Amazon Lightsail
4. AWS CloudFormation

## 50. Question

What are two ways an AWS customer can reduce their monthly spend? (choose 2)

1. Use more power efficient instance types
2. Be efficient with usage of Security Groups
3. Turn off resources that are not being used
4. Reduce the amount of data ingress charges
5. Reserve capacity where suitable

## 51. Question

What type of database is fully managed and can be scaled without incurring downtime?

1. Amazon DynamoDB
2. Amazon S3
3. Amazon RDS
4. Amazon ElastiCache

## 52. Question

Which of the following compliance programs allows the AWS environment to process, maintain, and store protected health information?

1. HIPAA
2. PCI DSS
3. SOC 1
4. ISO 27001

### 53. Question

An organization would like to run managed desktops on the AWS cloud using the Windows 10 operating system. Which service can deliver these requirements?

1. Amazon does not provide desktop services
2. Amazon SWF
3. Amazon Workspaces
4. Amazon EC2

### 54. Question

What are two ways of connecting to an Amazon VPC from an on-premise data center? (choose 2)

1. VPC Router
2. Direct Connect
3. VPC Peering
4. VPN CloudHub
5. Internet Gateway

### 55. Question

Which AWS support plans provide support via email, chat and phone? (choose 2)

1. Basic
2. Enterprise
3. Business
4. Global
5. Developer

### 56. Question

Which of the statements below is correct in relation to Consolidated Billing? (choose 3)

1. You can combine usage and share volume pricing discounts
2. You receive one bill per AWS account
3. You receive a single bill for multiple accounts
4. You are not charged a fee
5. You pay a fee per linked account

### 57. Question

A new user is unable to access any AWS services, what is the most likely explanation?

1. The default limit for user logons has been reached
2. The services are currently unavailable
3. The user needs to login with a key pair
4. By default, new users are created without access to any AWS services

## 58. Question

Which AWS service can be used to load data from Amazon S3, transform it, and move it to another destination?

1. AWS Glue
2. Amazon RedShift
3. Amazon Kinesis
4. Amazon EMR

## 59. Question

Which statements are true about Amazon EBS volumes? (choose 2)

1. You can attach multiple EBS volumes to an instance
2. EBS volumes must be in the same AZ as the instances they are attached to
3. EBS volume data is ephemeral and is lost when an instance is stopped
4. You can attach EBS volumes to multiple instances
5. EBS volumes are object storage

## 60. Question

Which service provides visibility into user activity by recording actions taken on your account?

1. Amazon CloudWatch
2. Amazon CloudFormation
3. Amazon CloudHSM
4. Amazon CloudTrail

## 61. Question

At what level is a Network ACL applied?

1. Instance level
2. Region level
3. Availability Zone level
4. Subnet level

## 62. Question

Which of the following are valid types of Reserved Instance? (choose 2)

1. Convertible RI
2. Discounted RI
3. Long-Term RI
4. Special RI
5. Scheduled RI

## 63. Question

Using AWS terminology, which items can be created in an Amazon S3 bucket? (choose 2)

1. Objects

2. Folders
3. Queues
4. Files
5. Tables

## 64. Question

**Which of the below is Amazon's proprietary RDS database?**

1. MariaDB
2. DynamoDB
3. Aurora
4. MySQL

## 65. Question

**Which configuration changes are associated with scaling vertically? (choose 2)**

1. Adding additional EC2 instances through Auto Scaling
2. Adding additional hard drives to a storage array
3. Adding a larger capacity hard drive to a server
4. Changing an EC2 instance to a type that has more CPU and RAM
5. Distributed processing

# SET 2: PRACTICE QUESTIONS, ANSWERS & EXPLANATIONS

## 1. Question

How can a security compliance officer retrieve AWS compliance documentation such as a SOC 2 report?

1. Using AWS Artifact
2. Using AWS Trusted Advisor
3. Using the AWS Personal Health Dashboard
4. Using AWS Inspector

Answer: 1

Explanation:

- AWS Artifact, available in the console, is a self-service audit artifact retrieval portal that provides our customers with on-demand access to AWS' compliance documentation and AWS agreements
- You can use AWS Artifact Reports to download AWS security and compliance documents, such as AWS ISO certifications, Payment Card Industry (PCI), and System and Organization Control (SOC) reports
- AWS Trusted Advisor is an online resource to help you reduce cost, increase performance, and improve security by optimizing your AWS environment
- Inspector is an automated security assessment service that helps improve the security and compliance of applications deployed on AWS
- AWS Personal Health Dashboard provides alerts and remediation guidance when AWS is experiencing events that may impact you

References:

https://digitalcloud.training/certification-training/aws-certified-cloud-practitioner/cloud-security/

https://aws.amazon.com/artifact/

## 2. Question

What is an example of using loose coupling when designing an information system?

1. Proprietary interfaces
2. DNS name usage
3. Synchronous replication
4. Monolithic application architecture

Answer: 2

Explanation:

- DNS names are used for service discovery. In loose coupling disparate resources must have a way of discovering each other without prior knowledge of the network topology
- Asynchronous integration rather than synchronous replication is recommended so an interaction does not require an immediate response
- You should use standard, technology-agnostic interfaces rather than proprietary interfaces where possible

- A monolithic application architecture is not an example of loose coupling

**References:**

https://digitalcloud.training/certification-training/aws-certified-cloud-practitioner/architecting-for-the-cloud/

## 3. Question

**Which AWS service can be used to run Docker containers?**

1. Amazon AMI
2. AWS Lambda
3. Amazon ECR
4. Amazon ECS

**Answer: 4**

**Explanation:**

- Amazon Elastic Container Service (ECS) is a highly scalable, high performance container management service that supports Docker containers and allows you to easily run applications on a managed cluster of Amazon EC2 instances
- AWS Lambda is a serverless technology that lets you run code in response to events as functions
- Amazon Elastic Container Registry (ECR) is a fully-managed Docker container registry that makes it easy for developers to store, manage, and deploy Docker container images
- Amazon Machine Images (AMI) store configuration information for Amazon EC2 instances

**References:**

https://digitalcloud.training/certification-training/aws-certified-cloud-practitioner/aws-compute/

## 4. Question

**Which AWS service can be used to host a static website?**

1. AWS Lambda
2. Amazon EBS
3. Amazon S3
4. Amazon EFS

**Answer: 3**

**Explanation:**

- Amazon S3 can be used to host static websites. It is not possible to use dynamic content. You can use a custom domain name if you configure the bucket name to match
- The other services listed cannot be used to host a static website

**References:**

https://digitalcloud.training/certification-training/aws-solutions-architect-associate/storage/amazon-s3/

## 5. Question

**Which of the following services does Amazon Route 53 provide? (choose 2)**

1. Route tables
2. Auto Scaling
3. Domain registration
4. Domain Name Service (DNS)
5. Load balancing

**Answer: 3,4**

**Explanation:**

- Route 53 services include domain registration, DNS, health checking (availability monitoring) and traffic management

**References:**

https://digitalcloud.training/certification-training/aws-certified-cloud-practitioner/content-delivery-and-dns-services/

## 6. Question

**Which AWS network element allows you to assign a static IPv4 address to an EC2 instance?**

1. Public IP
2. Dynamic IP
3. Elastic IP
4. Static IP

**Answer: 3**

**Explanation:**

- An Elastic IP address is a static IPv4 address designed for dynamic cloud computing. An Elastic IP address is associated with your AWS account. With an Elastic IP address, you can mask the failure of an instance or software by rapidly remapping the address to another instance in your account
- An Elastic IP is a public IP however in the AWS cloud an elastic IP is the construct used to assign a public IP to an EC2 instance
- Static IP and dynamic IP are terms used to describe IP addresses (public or private) that are either statically defined or dynamically obtained (through DHCP)

**References:**

https://docs.aws.amazon.com/AWSEC2/latest/UserGuide/elastic-ip-addresses-eip.html

## 7. Question

**What features does Amazon RDS provide to deliver scalability, availability and durability? (choose 2)**

1. Multi-Subnet
2. Clustering
3. DB mirroring
4. Read Replicas

5. Multi-AZ

**Answer: 4,5**

**Explanation:**

- Multi-AZ RDS creates a replica in another AZ and synchronously replicates to it (DR only)
- Read replicas are used for read heavy DBs and replication is asynchronous
- DB mirroring, multi-subnet and clustering are not options provided by RDS

**References:**

https://digitalcloud.training/certification-training/aws-certified-cloud-practitioner/aws-databases/

https://digitalcloud.training/certification-training/aws-solutions-architect-associate/database/amazon-rds/

## 8. Question

A manager needs to keep a check on his AWS spend. How can the manager setup alarms that notify him when his bill reaches a certain amount?

1. Using AWS Trusted Advisor
2. By notifying AWS support
3. Using CloudTrail
4. Using CloudWatch

**Answer: 4**

**Explanation:**

- The best ways to do this is to use CloudWatch to configure alarms that deliver a notification when activated. The alarms can use cost metrics that trigger the alarm when a certain amount of spend has been reached

**References:**

https://digitalcloud.training/certification-training/aws-certified-cloud-practitioner/monitoring-and-logging-services/

https://docs.aws.amazon.com/AmazonCloudWatch/latest/monitoring/monitor_estimated_charges_with_cloudwatch.html

## 9. Question

What components can be managed in the Virtual Private Cloud (VPC) management console? (choose 2)

1. Elastic Load Balancers
2. Subnets
3. Auto Scaling
4. IP CIDR
5. Snapshots

**Answer: 2,4**

**Explanation:**

- Within the management console for VPC you can manage items such as subnets and the IP CIDR block for the VPC
- The other answers are all items that can be managed within the EC2 management console

**References:**

https://digitalcloud.training/certification-training/aws-certified-cloud-practitioner/aws-networking/

https://digitalcloud.training/certification-training/aws-certified-cloud-practitioner/aws-compute/

## 10. Question

**What is a Resource Group?**

1. A collection of services within a region
2. A collection of services within a category
3. A collection of resources that share one or more tags
4. A collection of resources within a VPC

**Answer: 3**

**Explanation:**

- A resource group is a collection of resources that share one or more tags or portions of tags. To create a resource group, you simply identify the tags that contain the items that members of the group should have in common

**References:**

https://docs.aws.amazon.com/awsconsolehelpdocs/latest/gsg/what-are-resource-groups.html

## 11. Question

**A company is planning to migrate some resources into the cloud. What factors need to be considered when determining the cost of the AWS Cloud? (choose 2)**

1. The number of VPCs created
2. The number of servers migrated into EC2
3. The number of IAM users created
4. The amount of egress data per month
5. The amount of ingress data per month

**Answer: 2,4**

**Explanation:**

AWS charge for EC2 instances and data egress. There are no charges for VPCs, IAM users or data ingress

**References:**

https://digitalcloud.training/certification-training/aws-certified-cloud-practitioner/cloud-computing-concepts/

## 12. Question

**Which services are managed at a regional (rather than global) level? (choose 2)**

1. Amazon Route 53
2. Amazon CloudFront
3. AWS IAM
4. Amazon S3
5. Amazon EC2

**Answer: 4,5**

**Explanation:**

- Both Amazon EC2 and Amazon S3 are managed at a regional level. Note: Amazon S3 is a global namespace but you still create your buckets within a region
- CloudFront, Route 53 and IAM are managed at a global level

**References:**

https://digitalcloud.training/certification-training/aws-certified-cloud-practitioner/aws-global-infrastructure/

https://aws.amazon.com/about-aws/global-infrastructure/regional-product-services/

## 13. Question

**To connect an on-premises network to an Amazon VPC using an Amazon Managed VPN connection, which components are required? (choose 2)**

1. Direct Connect
2. NAT Instance
3. Virtual Private Gateway
4. Customer Gateway
5. VPC Router

**Answer: 3,4**

**Explanation:**

- Two of the components you need to connect to your VPC with a VPN connection are a virtual private gateway on the VPC side and a customer gateway on the on-premise network side
- VPC routers are not part of the VPN configuration
- NAT instances are not used for VPN, they are used by EC2 instances in private subnets to access the Internet
- Direct Connect can be used to connect an on-premise network to the cloud however it is not part of the configuration of an Amazon Managed VPN connection

**References:**

https://docs.aws.amazon.com/vpc/latest/userguide/VPC_VPN.html

## 14. Question

An application stores images which will be retrieved infrequently but must be available for retrieval immediately. Which is the most cost-effective storage option that meets these requirements?

1. Amazon S3 Standard
2. Amazon EFS
3. Amazon S3 Standard-Infrequent Access
4. Amazon Glacier with expedited retrievals

Answer: 3

Explanation:

- Amazon Glacier with expedited retrievals is fast (1-5 minutes) but not immediate
- Amazon S3 Standard-Infrequent Access is the most cost-effective choice
- Amazon EFS is a high-performance file system and not ideally suited to this scenario, it is also not the most cost-effective option
- Amazon S3 Standard provides immediate retrieval but is not less cost-effective compared to Standard-Infrequent access

References:

https://digitalcloud.training/certification-training/aws-certified-cloud-practitioner/aws-storage/

## 15. Question

Which AWS construct provides you with your own dedicated virtual network in the cloud?

1. Amazon IAM
2. Amazon EC2
3. Amazon Workspaces
4. Amazon VPC

Answer: 4

Explanation:

- A virtual private cloud (VPC) is a virtual network dedicated to your AWS account. A VPC is analogous to having your own DC inside AWS. It is logically isolated from other virtual networks in the AWS Cloud
- Amazon WorkSpaces is a managed desktop computing service running on the AWS cloud
- IAM is used to securely control individual and group access to AWS resources
- Amazon Elastic Compute Cloud (Amazon EC2) is a web service that provides secure, resizable compute capacity in the cloud

References:

https://digitalcloud.training/certification-training/aws-certified-cloud-practitioner/aws-networking/

## 16. Question

Which file format is used to write AWS Identity and Access Management (IAM) policies?

1. DOC
2. XML
3. JBOD
4. JSON

**Answer: 4**

**Explanation:**

- You manage access in AWS by creating policies and attaching them to IAM identities or AWS resources. A policy is an object in AWS that, when associated with an entity or resource, defines their permissions. AWS evaluates these policies when a principal, such as a user, makes a request. Permissions in the policies determine whether the request is allowed or denied. Most policies are stored in AWS as JSON documents

**References:**

https://docs.aws.amazon.com/IAM/latest/UserGuide/access_policies.html

## 17. Question

**Which services are involved with security? (choose 2)**

1. AWS SMS
2. AWS CloudHSM
3. Amazon ELB
4. AWS DMS
5. AWS KMS

**Answer: 2,5**

**Explanation:**

- AWS Key Management Service gives you centralized control over the encryption keys used to protect your data
- AWS CloudHSM is a cloud-based hardware security module (HSM) that enables you to easily generate and use your own encryption keys on the AWS Cloud
- AWS Database Migration Service and Server Migration Service are used for migration
- Amazon Elastic Load Balancing is used for distributing incoming connections to pools of EC2 instances

**References:**

https://digitalcloud.training/certification-training/aws-certified-cloud-practitioner/cloud-security/

## 18. Question

**Which of the following are AWS recommended best practices in relation to IAM? (choose 2)**

1. Enable MFA for all users
2. Embed access keys in application code
3. Assign permissions to users
4. Create individual IAM users
5. Grant greatest privilege

Answer: 1,4

Explanation:

- AWS recommend creating individual IAM users and assigning the least privilege necessary for them to perform their role
- You should use groups to assign permissions to IAM users and should avoid embedding access keys in application code
- For extra security, AWS recommend that you require multi-factor authentication (MFA) for all users in your account. For privileged IAM users who are allowed to access sensitive resources or API operations, AWS recommend using U2F or hardware MFA devices

References:

https://docs.aws.amazon.com/IAM/latest/UserGuide/best-practices.html

## 19. Question

**What are the names of two types of AWS Storage Gateway? (choose 2)**

1. Cached Gateway
2. File Gateway
3. Tape Gateway
4. S3 Gateway
5. Block Gateway

Answer: 2,3

Explanation:

- The AWS Storage Gateway service enables hybrid storage between on-premises environments and the AWS Cloud. It provides low-latency performance by caching frequently accessed data on premises, while storing data securely and durably in Amazon cloud storage services. AWS Storage Gateway supports three storage interfaces: file, volume, and tape
- File gateway provides a virtual on-premises file server, which enables you to store and retrieve files as objects in Amazon S3
- The volume gateway represents the family of gateways that support block-based volumes, previously referred to as gateway-cached and gateway-stored modes
- Tape Gateway (formerly known as Gateway Virtual Tape Library) is used for backup with popular backup software
- All other answers are bogus and use terms that are associated with Storage Gateways (S3, block, cached)

References:

https://digitalcloud.training/certification-training/aws-solutions-architect-associate/storage/aws-storage-gateway/

## 20. Question

**What kinds of routing policies are available in Amazon Route 53? (choose 2)**

1. Fault tolerant

2. Latency
3. Failback
4. Shortest Path First
5. Simple

**Answer: 2,5**

**Explanation:**

- Route 53 routing policies include Simple, Weighted, Latency based, Failover, Geo-location, Geo-Proximity, Multi-Value and Traffic Flow

**References:**

https://digitalcloud.training/certification-training/aws-certified-cloud-practitioner/content-delivery-and-dns-services/

https://digitalcloud.training/certification-training/aws-solutions-architect-associate/networking-and-content-delivery/amazon-route-53/

## 21. Question

**To optimize pricing or ensure capacity is available reservations can be applied to which of the following services? (choose 2)**

1. Amazon S3
2. Amazon EC2
3. AWS Lambda
4. Amazon EBS
5. Amazon RDS

**Answer: 2,5**

**Explanation:**

- Reservations apply to various services, including: EC2, DynamoDB, ElastiCache, RDS and RedShift

**References:**

https://digitalcloud.training/certification-training/aws-certified-cloud-practitioner/aws-billing-and-pricing/

## 22. Question

**How can an organization assess applications for vulnerabilities and deviations from best practice?**

1. Use AWS WAF
2. Use AWS Artifact
3. Use AWS Inspector
4. Use AWS Shield

**Answer: 3**

**Explanation:**

- Inspector is an automated security assessment service that helps improve the security and compliance of applications deployed on AWS. Inspector automatically assesses applications for vulnerabilities or deviations from best practices
- AWS Artifact is your go-to, central resource for compliance-related information that matters to you
- AWS Shield is a managed Distributed Denial of Service (DDoS) protection service
- AWS WAF is a web application firewall

**References:**

https://digitalcloud.training/certification-training/aws-certified-cloud-practitioner/cloud-security/

## 23. Question

**Which AWS service gives you centralized control over the encryption keys used to protect your data?**

1. AWS STS
2. Amazon EBS
3. AWS DMS
4. AWS KMS

**Answer: 4**

**Explanation:**

- AWS Key Management Service gives you centralized control over the encryption keys used to protect your data. You can create, import, rotate, disable, delete, define usage policies for, and audit the use of encryption keys used to encrypt your data
- The AWS Security Token Service (STS) is a web service that enables you to request temporary, limited-privilege credentials for AWS Identity and Access Management (IAM) users
- AWS Database Migration Service (DMS) helps you migrate databases to AWS quickly and securely
- Amazon Elastic Block Store (Amazon EBS) provides persistent block storage volumes for use with Amazon EC2instances in the AWS Cloud

**References:**

https://digitalcloud.training/certification-training/aws-certified-cloud-practitioner/cloud-security/

## 24. Question

**What categories of Amazon Machine Image (AMI) are available? (choose 2)**

1. Enterprise AMIs
2. Shared AMIs
3. AWS Marketplace AMIs
4. Community AMIs
5. Partner AMIs

**Answer: 3,4**

**Explanation:**

- AMIs come in three main categories:

- Community AMIs– free to use, generally you just select the operating system you want
- AWS Marketplace AMIs– pay to use, generally come packaged with additional, licensed software
- My AMIs– AMIs that you create yourself

**References:**

https://digitalcloud.training/certification-training/aws-certified-cloud-practitioner/aws-compute/

## 25. Question

**Which AWS services can be utilized at no cost? (choose 2)**

1. Amazon CloudFront
2. Identity and Access Management (IAM)
3. Amazon RedShift
4. Amazon VPC
5. Amazon S3

**Answer: 2,4**

**Explanation:**

- The only services that do not incur cost in this list are IAM and VPC

**References:**

https://digitalcloud.training/certification-training/aws-certified-cloud-practitioner/aws-billing-and-pricing/

## 26. Question

**You need to ensure you have the right amount of compute available to service demand. Which AWS service can automatically scale the number of EC2 instances for your application?**

1. Amazon Elasticache
2. AWS Auto Scaling
3. Amazon Elastic Load Balancer
4. AWS RedShift

**Answer: 2**

**Explanation:**

- Auto Scaling automates the process of adding (scaling up) OR removing (scaling down) EC2 instances based on the traffic demand for your application
- ELB automatically distributes incoming application traffic across multiple targets, such as Amazon EC2 instances, containers, and IP addresses
- Amazon Redshift is a fast, scalable data warehouse that makes it simple and cost-effective to analyze all your data across your data warehouse and data lake
- Amazon ElastiCache offers fully managed Redis and Memcached

**References:**

https://digitalcloud.training/certification-training/aws-certified-cloud-practitioner/elastic-load-balancing-and-auto-scaling/

## 27. Question

Which cloud computing model gives the IT department the highest level of flexibility and management control?

1. On-premises cloud
2. Infrastructure as a Service (IaaS)
3. Software as a Service (SaaS)
4. Platform as a Service (PaaS)

Answer: 2

Explanation:

- With IaaS the IT department have the most flexibility and management control over resources as only the infrastructure layer is provided by the Cloud Provider. Everything else is managed by the end customer. This means more control and more responsibility for management.
- With PaaS and SaaS, the Cloud Provider manages up to a higher level in the stack. This means that as an organization using the service you have less control (and less responsibility).
- On-premises cloud is a cloud deployment model, not a cloud computing model. Other cloud deployment models are Private, Public and Hybrid.

References:

https://digitalcloud.training/certification-training/aws-certified-cloud-practitioner/cloud-computing-concepts/

https://d1.awsstatic.com/whitepapers/aws-overview.pdf

## 28. Question

Which items should be included in a TCO analysis comparing on-premise to AWS Cloud? (choose 2)

1. Firewall management
2. Operating system patching
3. Data center security
4. Application licensing
5. Compute hardware

Answer: 3,5

Explanation:

- You need to identify the items that have a cost on-premise and that will be rolled into the service in the cloud. Compute hardware costs and data center security costs will be rolled in the service cost in the cloud so you need to include them in the model so you can really understand the true TCO on-premise vs. the cloud
- Firewall management, application licensing and operating system patching need to be paid for on-premise and in the cloud so there is little difference

References:

https://media.amazonwebservices.com/AWS_TCO_Web_Applications.pdf

## 29. Question

**Amazon S3 is typically used for which of the following use cases? (choose 2)**

1. Install an operating system
2. In-memory data cache
3. Message queue
4. Host a static website
5. Media hosting

**Answer: 4,5**

**Explanation:**

- Amazon S3 is an object storage system. Typical use cases include: Backup and storage, application hosting, media hosting, software delivery and hosting a static website.
- You cannot install an operating system on an object-based storage system. Instead, you need a block-based storage system such as Amazon EBS.
- You cannot use Amazon S3 as an in-memory data cache; for this you need a service such as Amazon ElastiCache.
- You cannot use Amazon S3 as a message queue (or at least it is not a typical use case). You should use a services such as Amazon SQS or Amazon MQ.

**References:**

https://digitalcloud.training/certification-training/aws-certified-cloud-practitioner/aws-storage/

https://aws.amazon.com/s3/getting-started/

## 30. Question

**Which AWS service protects against common exploits that could compromise application availability, compromise security or consume excessive resources?**

1. AWS Shield
2. Network ACL
3. Security Group
4. AWS WAF

**Answer: 4**

**Explanation:**

- AWS WAF is a web application firewall that protects against common exploits that could compromise application availability, compromise security or consume excessive resources
- AWS Shield is a managed Distributed Denial of Service (DDoS) protection service
- Security groups and Network ACLs are firewalls protecting at the instance and subnet level respectively

**References:**

https://digitalcloud.training/certification-training/aws-certified-cloud-practitioner/cloud-security/

## 31. Question

Which tool can be used to create and manage a selection of AWS services that are approved for use on AWS?

1. AWS Service Catalog
2. AWS OpsWorks
3. AWS Organizations
4. Amazon Cloud Directory

Answer: 1

Explanation:

- AWS Service Catalog allows organizations to create and manage catalogs of IT services that are approved for use on AWS. These IT services can include everything from virtual machine images, servers, software, and databases to complete multi-tier application architectures
- AWS OpsWorks is a configuration management service that provides managed instances of Chef and Puppet
- Amazon Cloud Directory enables you to build flexible cloud-native directories for organizing hierarchies of data along multiple dimensions
- AWS Organizations offers policy-based management for multiple AWS accounts

References:

https://aws.amazon.com/servicecatalog/

## 32. Question

What are the benefits of using the AWS Managed Services? (choose 2)

1. Designed for small businesses
2. Baseline integration with ITSM tools
3. Managed applications so you can focus on infrastructure
4. Alignment with ITIL processes
5. Support for all AWS services

Answer: 2,4

Explanation:

- AWS Managed Services manages the daily operations of your AWS infrastructure in alignment with ITIL processes
- AWS Managed Services provides a baseline integration with IT Service Management (ITSM) tools such as the ServiceNow platform
- AWS Managed Services provides ongoing management of your AWS infrastructure so you can focus on your applications. By implementing best practices to maintain your infrastructure, AWS Managed Services helps to reduce your operational overhead and risk
- AWS Managed Services currently supports the 20+ services most critical for Enterprises, and will continue to expand our list of integrated AWS services
- AWS Managed Services is designed to meet the needs of Enterprises that require stringent SLAs, adherence to corporate compliance, and integration with their systems and ITIL®-based processes

References:

https://aws.amazon.com/managed-services/

## 33. Question

An architect needs to compare the cost of deploying an on-premise web server and an EC2 instance on the AWS cloud. Which tool can be used to assist the architect?

1. AWS Budgets
2. AWS TCO Calculator
3. AWS Simple Monthly Calculator
4. AWS Cost Explorer

Answer: 2

Explanation:

- The TCO calculator is a free tool provided by AWS that allows you to estimate the cost savings of using the AWS Cloud vs. using an on-premised data center
- The AWS Cost Explorer is a free tool that allows you to view charts of your costs
- The AWS Simple Monthly Calculator helps customers and prospects estimate their monthly AWS bill more efficiently
- AWS Budgets gives you the ability to set custom budgets that alert you when your costs or usage exceed

References:

https://digitalcloud.training/certification-training/aws-certified-cloud-practitioner/aws-billing-and-pricing/

## 34. Question

How should an organization deploy an application running on multiple EC2 instances to ensure that a power failure does not cause an application outage?

1. Launch the EC2 instances into different VPCs
2. Launch the EC2 instances in separate regions
3. Launch the EC2 instances into Edge Locations
4. Launch the EC2 instances into different Availability Zones

Answer: 4

Explanation:

- If you have multiple EC2 instances that are part of an application, you should deploy them into separate availability zones (AZs). Each AZ has redundant power and is also fed from a different grid. AZs also have low-latency network links which is often advantageous for most applications.
- You do not need to deploy into separate regions to prevent a power outage bringing your application down. AZs have redundant power and grids so you are safe deploying your applications into multiple AZs. If you split your applications across regions you introduce latency which may impact your application. You may also run into data sovereignty issues in some cases.
- Deploying your EC2 instances into different VPCs is not required and would complicate your application deployment. Also, bear in mind that VPCs within a region use the same underlying

infrastructure so deploying into different VPCs may still result in your EC2 instances being deployed into the same AZs. It is a best practice to deploy into separate AZs.

**References:**

https://digitalcloud.training/certification-training/aws-certified-cloud-practitioner/aws-global-infrastructure/

https://aws.amazon.com/about-aws/global-infrastructure/

## 35. Question

**Virtual servers such as EC2 instances are examples of services delivered under which cloud model?**

1. SaaS
2. DBaaS
3. PaaS
4. IaaS

**Answer: 4**

**Explanation:**

- Infrastructure as a Service (IaaS) contains the basic building blocks for cloud IT and typically provide access to networking features, computers (virtual or on dedicated hardware), and data storage space
- Platform as a Service (PaaS) removes the need for your organization to manage the underlying infrastructure (usually hardware and operating systems) and allows you to focus on the deployment and management of your applications
- Software as a Service (SaaS) provides you with a completed product that is run and managed by the service provider. In most cases, people referring to Software as a Service are referring to end-user applications
- Database as a Service (DBaaS) is a type of PaaS in which a managed database is offered for consumption

**References:**

https://digitalcloud.training/certification-training/aws-certified-cloud-practitioner/cloud-computing-concepts/

## 36. Question

**Which of the facts below are accurate in relation to AWS Regions? (choose 2)**

1. Regions have direct, low-latency, high throughput and redundant network connections between each other
2. Each region is designed to be completely isolated from the other Amazon Regions
3. Each region consists of a collection of VPCs
4. Regions are Content Delivery Network (CDN) endpoints for CloudFront
5. Each region consists of 2 or more availability zones

**Answer: 2,5**

**Explanation:**

- A region is not a collection of VPCs, it is composed of at least 2 AZs. VPCs exist within accounts on a per region basis
- Availability Zones (not regions) have direct, low-latency, high throughput and redundant network connections between each other
- Edge locations are (not regions) are Content Delivery Network (CDN) endpoints for CloudFront

**References:**

https://digitalcloud.training/certification-training/aws-certified-cloud-practitioner/aws-global-infrastructure/

## 37. Question

**Which AWS service can assist with coordinating tasks across distributed application components?**

1. Amazon STS
2. Amazon SQS
3. Amazon SWF
4. Amazon SNS

**Answer: 3**

**Explanation:**

- Amazon Simple Workflow Service (SWF) is a web service that makes it easy to coordinate work across distributed application components. SWF enables applications for a range of use cases, including media processing, web application back-ends, business process workflows, and analytics pipelines, to be designed as a coordination of tasks
- Amazon Security Token Service (STS) is used for requesting temporary credentials
- Amazon Simple Queue Service (SQS) is a message queue used for decoupling application components
- Amazon Simple Notification Service (SNS) is a web service that makes it easy to set up, operate, and send notifications from the cloud
- SNS supports notifications over multiple transports including HTTP/HTTPS, Email/Email-JSON, SQS and SMS

**References:**

https://digitalcloud.training/certification-training/aws-certified-cloud-practitioner/additional-aws-services-tools/

https://digitalcloud.training/certification-training/aws-solutions-architect-associate/application-integration/amazon-swf/

## 38. Question

**Which database engines are supported by Amazon RDS? (choose 2)**

1. DynamoDB
2. SQL Server
3. ElastiCache
4. Aurora
5. MongoDB

Answer: 2,4

Explanation:

- RDS supports the following engines: SQL Server, Oracle, MySQL Server, PostgreSQL, Aurora, MariaDB
- DynamoDB is Amazon's NoSQL database
- MongoDB is a NoSQL database
- ElastiCache is not a type of RDS database

References:

https://digitalcloud.training/certification-training/aws-certified-cloud-practitioner/aws-databases/

## 39. Question

Which of the following security operations tasks must be performed by AWS customers? (choose 2)

1. Installing security updates for server firmware
2. Issuing data center access keycards
3. Enabling multi-factor authentication (MFA) for privileged users
4. Collecting syslog messages from physical firewalls
5. Installing security updates on EC2 instances

Answer: 3,5

Explanation:

- The customer is responsible for installing security updates on EC2 instances and enabling MFA. AWS is responsible for security of the physical data center and the infrastructure upon which customer services run

References:

https://digitalcloud.training/certification-training/aws-certified-cloud-practitioner/aws-shared-responsibility-model/

## 40. Question

A Solutions Architect is designing an application stack that will be highly elastic. What AWS services can be used that don't require you to make any capacity decisions upfront? (choose 2)

1. AWS Lambda
2. Amazon EC2
3. Amazon RDS
4. Amazon S3
5. DynamoDB

Answer: 1,4

Explanation:

- With Amazon S3 you don't need to specify any capacity at any time, the service scales in both capacity and performance as required
- AWS Lambda lets you run code without provisioning or managing servers. You pay only for the compute time you consume – there is no charge when your code is not running
- With Amazon EC2 you need to select your instance sizes and number of instances
- With RDS you need to select the instance size for the DB
- With DynamoDB you need to specify the read/write capacity of the DB

**References:**

https://digitalcloud.training/certification-training/aws-certified-cloud-practitioner/aws-storage/

https://digitalcloud.training/certification-training/aws-certified-cloud-practitioner/aws-compute/

## 41. Question

**What type of storage is provided by Amazon EBS?**

1. Relational
2. Object
3. File
4. Block

**Answer: 4**

**Explanation:**

- Amazon Elastic Block Storage (EBS) is block storage. This means you can mount the volume for operating systems and format and partition as if it is a local disk
- File and object are other types of storage that you can use with AWS. File storage is provided by EFS and object storage is provided by Amazon S3
- Relational is not a type of storage, it is typically used to describe a type of database such as RDS

**References:**

https://digitalcloud.training/certification-training/aws-certified-cloud-practitioner/aws-storage/

## 42. Question

**Which types of AWS resource can be launched from a Golden Image? (choose 2)**

1. Amazon DynamoDB tables
2. Amazon EC2 instances
3. Amazon RDS instances
4. Amazon S3 objects
5. AWS Lambda functions

**Answer: 2,3**

**Explanation:**

- Some resource types can be launched from a golden image. A golden image is a snapshot of a particular state for that resource. Examples are EC2 instances, RDS instances and EBS volumes

**References:**

https://digitalcloud.training/certification-training/aws-certified-cloud-practitioner/architecting-for-the-cloud/

## 43. Question

Which AWS service provides elastic web-scale cloud computing allowing you to deploy operating system instances?

1. Amazon EBS
2. AWS Lambda
3. Amazon RDS
4. Amazon EC2

Answer: 4

Explanation:

- Amazon EC2 provides elastic web-scale computing in the cloud allowing you to deploy Windows and Linux
- AWS Lambda lets you run code without provisioning or managing server operating systems
- Amazon Elastic Block Store (Amazon EBS) provides persistent block storage volumes for use with Amazon EC2instances in the AWS Cloud
- Amazon Relational Database Service (Amazon RDS) makes it easy to set up, operate, and scale a relational database in the cloud

References:

https://digitalcloud.training/certification-training/aws-certified-cloud-practitioner/aws-compute/

## 44. Question

Which of the following is NOT one of the five AWS Trusted Advisor categories?

1. Performance
2. Application transformation
3. Cost Optimization
4. Security

Answer: 2

Explanation:

- The five categories are cost optimization, performance, security, fault tolerance and service limits

References:

https://digitalcloud.training/certification-training/aws-certified-cloud-practitioner/cloud-security/

## 45. Question

Which configuration changes are associated with scaling horizontally? (choose 2)

1. Adding additional EC2 instances through Auto Scaling
2. Changing an EC2 instance to a type that has more CPU and RAM

3. Adding additional hard drives to a storage array
4. Adding a larger capacity hard drive to a server
5. Changing the DB instance class on an RDS DB

**Answer: 1,3**

**Explanation:**

- Scaling horizontally takes place through an increase in the number of resources (e.g., adding more hard drives to a storage array or adding more servers to support an application)
- Scaling vertically takes place through an increase in the specifications of an individual resource (e.g., upgrading a server with a larger hard drive or a faster CPU). On Amazon EC2, this can easily be achieved by stopping an instance and resizing it to an instance type that has more RAM, CPU, IO, or networking capabilities

**References:**

https://digitalcloud.training/certification-training/aws-certified-cloud-practitioner/architecting-for-the-cloud/

## 46. Question

You need to implement a hosted queue for storing messages in transit between application servers. Which service should you use?

1. Amazon SWF
2. Amazon SNS
3. Amazon SQS
4. Amazon DynamoDB

**Answer: 3**

**Explanation:**

- Amazon Simple Queue Service (Amazon SQS) is a web service that gives you access to message queues that store messages waiting to be processed. SQS offers a reliable, highly-scalable, hosted queue for storing messages in transit between computers. SQS is used for distributed/decoupled application
- Amazon SWF helps developers build, run, and scale background jobs that have parallel or sequential steps
- Amazon Simple Notification Service (SNS) is a highly available, durable, secure, fully managed pub/sub messaging service that enables you to decouple microservices, distributed systems, and serverless applications
- Amazon DynamoDB is a nonrelational database that delivers reliable performance at any scale

**References:**

https://digitalcloud.training/certification-training/aws-solutions-architect-associate/application-integration/amazon-sqs/

## 47. Question

How can you apply metadata to an EC2 instance that categorizes it according to its purpose, owner or environment?

1. Tags
2. Stickers
3. Hostname
4. Labels

Answer: 1

Explanation:

- A tag is a label that you assign to an AWS resource. Each tag consists of a key and an optional value, both of which you define. Tags enable you to categorize your AWS resources in different ways, for example, by purpose, owner, or environment

References:

https://docs.aws.amazon.com/AWSEC2/latest/UserGuide/Using_Tags.html

## 48. Question

An architect wants to find a tool for consistently deploying the same resources through a templated configuration. What AWS service can be used?

1. AWS CloudFormation
2. AWS Elastic Beanstalk
3. AWS CodeBuild
4. AWS CodeDeploy

Answer: 1

Explanation:

- AWS CloudFormation provides a common language for you to describe and provision all the infrastructure resources in your cloud environment. CloudFormation allows you to use a simple text file to model and provision, in an automated and secure manner, all the resources needed for your applications across all regions and accounts
- AWS CodeDeploy is a fully managed deployment service that automates software deployments to a variety of compute services such as Amazon EC2, AWS Lambda, and your on-premises servers
- AWS CodeBuild is a fully managed continuous integration service that compiles source code, runs tests, and produces software packages that are ready to deploy
- AWS Elastic Beanstalk is the fastest and simplest way to get web applications up and running on AWS

References:

https://digitalcloud.training/certification-training/aws-certified-cloud-practitioner/additional-aws-services-tools/

## 49. Question

**Which AWS service provides preconfigured virtual private servers (instances) that include everything required to deploy an application or create a database?**

1. AWS Lambda
2. Amazon ECS
3. Amazon Lightsail
4. AWS CloudFormation

Answer: 3

Explanation:

- Lightsail provides developers compute, storage, and networking capacity and capabilities to deploy and manage websites, web applications, and databases in the cloud
- Lightsail includes everything you need to launch your project quickly – a virtual machine, SSD-based storage, data transfer, DNS management, and a static IP
- Lightsail provides preconfigured virtual private servers (instances) that include everything required to deploy an application or create a database
- CloudFormation is used to deploy resources through code, as a service it does not include preconfigured servers
- Amazon Elastic Container Service (ECS) is a highly scalable, high performance container management service that supports Docker containers and allows you to easily run applications on a managed cluster of Amazon EC2 instances
- Lambda is a serverless computing technology that allows you to run code without provisioning or managing servers

References:

https://digitalcloud.training/certification-training/aws-certified-cloud-practitioner/aws-compute/

## 50. Question

**What are two ways an AWS customer can reduce their monthly spend? (choose 2)**

1. Use more power efficient instance types
2. Be efficient with usage of Security Groups
3. Turn off resources that are not being used
4. Reduce the amount of data ingress charges
5. Reserve capacity where suitable

Answer: 3,5

Explanation:

- Turning of resources that are not used can reduce spend. You can also use reserved instances to reduce the monthly spend at the expense of having to lock into a 1 or 3-year contract – good for stable workloads
- You don't pay for power, security groups, or data ingress to the AWS cloud so these answers are all incorrect

References:

https://digitalcloud.training/certification-training/aws-certified-cloud-practitioner/aws-billing-and-pricing/

## 51. Question

What type of database is fully managed and can be scaled without incurring downtime?

1. Amazon DynamoDB
2. Amazon S3
3. Amazon RDS
4. Amazon ElastiCache

Answer 1:

Explanation:

- DynamoDB is fully managed and can be scaled without incurring downtime
- S3 is not a fully managed database, it is an object store
- Both RDS and ElastiCache use EC2 instances and therefore scaling (vertically) requires downtime

References:

https://digitalcloud.training/certification-training/aws-certified-cloud-practitioner/aws-databases/

## 52. Question

Which of the following compliance programs allows the AWS environment to process, maintain, and store protected health information?

1. HIPAA
2. PCI DSS
3. SOC 1
4. ISO 27001

Answer: 1

Explanation:

- AWS enables covered entities and their business associates subject to the U.S. Health Insurance Portability and Accountability Act of 1996 (HIPAA) to use the secure AWS environment to process, maintain, and store protected health information

References:

https://aws.amazon.com/compliance/hipaa-compliance/

## 53. Question

An organization would like to run managed desktops on the AWS cloud using the Windows 10 operating system. Which service can deliver these requirements?

1. Amazon does not provide desktop services
2. Amazon SWF
3. Amazon Workspaces

4. Amazon EC2

**Answer: 3**

**Explanation:**

- Amazon WorkSpaces is a managed desktop computing service running on the AWS cloud
- WorkSpaces allows customers to easily provision cloud-based desktops that allow end-users to access documents and applications
- WorkSpaces offers bundles that come with a Windows 7 or Windows 10 desktop experience, powered by Windows Server 2008 R2 and Windows Server 2016 respectively

**References:**

https://digitalcloud.training/certification-training/aws-solutions-architect-associate/desktop-app-streaming/amazon-workspaces/

## 54. Question

**What are two ways of connecting to an Amazon VPC from an on-premise data center? (choose 2)**

1. VPC Router
2. Direct Connect
3. VPC Peering
4. VPN CloudHub
5. Internet Gateway

**Answer: 2,4**

**Explanation:**

- You can connect from your on-premise data center to a VPC via Direct Connect or VPN CloudHub
- AWS Direct Connect is a network service that provides an alternative to using the Internet to connect a customer's on-premise sites to AWS
- If you have multiple VPN connections, you can provide secure communication between sites using the AWS VPN CloudHub
- Internet gateways and VPC routers are components of a VPC and are not used for connecting from external locations

**References:**

https://digitalcloud.training/certification-training/aws-certified-cloud-practitioner/aws-networking/

https://docs.aws.amazon.com/vpc/latest/userguide/VPN_CloudHub.html

## 55. Question

**Which AWS support plans provide support via email, chat and phone? (choose 2)**

1. Basic
2. Enterprise
3. Business
4. Global
5. Developer

Answer: 2,3

Explanation:

- Only the business and enterprise plans provide support via email, chat and phone

References:

https://digitalcloud.training/certification-training/aws-certified-cloud-practitioner/aws-billing-and-pricing/

## 56. Question

Which of the statements below is correct in relation to Consolidated Billing? (choose 3)

1. You can combine usage and share volume pricing discounts
2. You receive one bill per AWS account
3. You receive a single bill for multiple accounts
4. You are not charged a fee
5. You pay a fee per linked account

Answer: 1,3,4

Explanation:

Consolidated billing has the following benefits:

- One bill – You get one bill for multiple accounts.
- Easy tracking – You can track the charges across multiple accounts and download the combined cost and usage data.
- Combined usage – You can combine the usage across all accounts in the organization to share the volume pricing discounts and Reserved Instance discounts. This can result in a lower charge for your project, department, or company than with individual standalone accounts.
- No extra fee – Consolidated billing is offered at no additional cost.

References:

https://digitalcloud.training/certification-training/aws-certified-cloud-practitioner/aws-billing-and-pricing/

https://docs.aws.amazon.com/awsaccountbilling/latest/aboutv2/consolidated-billing.html

## 57. Question

A new user is unable to access any AWS services, what is the most likely explanation?

1. The default limit for user logons has been reached
2. The services are currently unavailable
3. The user needs to login with a key pair
4. By default, new users are created without access to any AWS services

Answer: 4

Explanation:

- By default, new users are created with NO access to any AWS services – they can only login to the AWS console

**References:**

https://digitalcloud.training/certification-training/aws-certified-cloud-practitioner/identity-and-access-management/

## 58. Question

**Which AWS service can be used to load data from Amazon S3, transform it, and move it to another destination?**

1. AWS Glue
2. Amazon RedShift
3. Amazon Kinesis
4. Amazon EMR

**Answer: 1**

**Explanation:**

- AWS Glue is an Extract, Transform, and Load (ETL) service. You can use AWS Glue with data sources on Amazon S3, RedShift and other databases. With AWS Glue you transform and move the data to various destinations. It is used to prepare and load data for analytics
- Amazon RedShift is a data warehouse. With a data warehouse you load data from other databases such as transactional SQL databases and run analysis. You can analyze data using SQL and Business Intelligence tools.
- Amazon EMR is a managed Hadoop framework running on EC2 and S3. It is used for analyzing data, not for ETL
- Amazon Kinesis is used for collecting, processing and analyzing real-time streaming data.

**References:**

https://digitalcloud.training/certification-training/aws-certified-cloud-practitioner/aws-analytics/

https://aws.amazon.com/glue/

## 59. Question

**Which statements are true about Amazon EBS volumes? (choose 2)**

1. You can attach multiple EBS volumes to an instance
2. EBS volumes must be in the same AZ as the instances they are attached to
3. EBS volume data is ephemeral and is lost when an instance is stopped
4. You can attach EBS volumes to multiple instances
5. EBS volumes are object storage

**Answer: 1,2**

**Explanation:**

- EBS volumes must be in the same AZ as the instances they are attached to
- You can attach multiple EBS volumes to an instance

- You cannot attach an EBS volume to multiple instances (use Elastic File Store instead)
- EBS volume data persists independently of the life of the instance
- EBS volumes are block storage

**References:**

https://digitalcloud.training/certification-training/aws-certified-cloud-practitioner/aws-storage/

## 60. Question

**Which service provides visibility into user activity by recording actions taken on your account?**

1. Amazon CloudWatch
2. Amazon CloudFormation
3. Amazon CloudHSM
4. Amazon CloudTrail

**Answer: 4**

**Explanation:**

- CloudTrail is a web service that records activity made on your account and delivers log files to an Amazon S3 bucket
- CloudTrail is for auditing (CloudWatch is for performance monitoring)
- CloudFormation is used for deploying infrastructure through code
- CloudHSM is a hardware security module for generating, managing and storing encryption keys

**References:**

https://digitalcloud.training/certification-training/aws-certified-cloud-practitioner/monitoring-and-logging-services/

## 61. Question

**At what level is a Network ACL applied?**

1. Instance level
2. Region level
3. Availability Zone level
4. Subnet level

**Answer: 4**

**Explanation:**

- Network Access Control Lists (ACLs) provide a firewall/security layer at the subnet level
- Security Groups provide a firewall/security layer at the instance level

**References:**

https://digitalcloud.training/certification-training/aws-certified-cloud-practitioner/aws-networking/

### 62. Question

**Which of the following are valid types of Reserved Instance? (choose 2)**

1. Convertible RI
2. Discounted RI
3. Long-Term RI
4. Special RI
5. Scheduled RI

**Answer: 1,5**

**Explanation:**

- Standard RIs: These provide the most significant discount (up to 75% off On-Demand) and are best suited for steady-state usage
- Convertible RIs: These provide a discount (up to 54% off On-Demand) and the capability to change the attributes of the RI as long as the exchange results in the creation of Reserved Instances of equal or greater value. Like Standard RIs, Convertible RIs are best suited for steady-state usage
- Scheduled RIs: These are available to launch within the time windows you reserve. This option allows you to match your capacity reservation to a predictable recurring schedule that only requires a fraction of a day, a week, or a month

**References:**

https://digitalcloud.training/certification-training/aws-certified-cloud-practitioner/aws-billing-and-pricing/

https://aws.amazon.com/ec2/pricing/reserved-instances/

### 63. Question

**Using AWS terminology, which items can be created in an Amazon S3 bucket? (choose 2)**

1. Objects
2. Folders
3. Queues
4. Files
5. Tables

**Answer: 1,2**

**Explanation:**

- You can create folders within buckets and can also upload objects
- As S3 is an object store you create objects not files
- Tables and queues cannot be created on S3

**References:**

https://digitalcloud.training/certification-training/aws-certified-cloud-practitioner/aws-storage/

### 64. Question

**Which of the below is Amazon's proprietary RDS database?**

1. MariaDB
2. DynamoDB
3. Aurora
4. MySQL

Answer: 3

Explanation:

- Aurora is Amazon's proprietary database
- MariaDB and MySQL can be used on RDS but they are not Amazon proprietary
- DynamoDB is an Amazon proprietary DB but it is not an RDS DB

References:

https://digitalcloud.training/certification-training/aws-certified-cloud-practitioner/aws-databases/

## 65. Question

Which configuration changes are associated with scaling vertically? (choose 2)

1. Adding additional EC2 instances through Auto Scaling
2. Adding additional hard drives to a storage array
3. Adding a larger capacity hard drive to a server
4. Changing an EC2 instance to a type that has more CPU and RAM
5. Distributed processing

Answer: 3,4

Explanation:

- Scaling vertically takes place through an increase in the specifications of an individual resource (e.g., upgrading a server with a larger hard drive or a faster CPU). On Amazon EC2, this can easily be achieved by stopping an instance and resizing it to an instance type that has more RAM, CPU, IO, or networking capabilities
- Scaling horizontally takes place through an increase in the number of resources (e.g., adding more hard drives to a storage array or adding more servers to support an application)

References:

https://digitalcloud.training/certification-training/aws-certified-cloud-practitioner/architecting-for-the-cloud/

# SET 3: PRACTICE QUESTIONS ONLY

### 1. Question

**To gain greater discounts, which services can be reserved? (choose 2)**

1. Amazon DynamoDB
2. Amazon RedShift
3. Amazon S3
4. AWS Lambda
5. Amazon CloudWatch

### 2. Question

**Which service can an organization use to track API activity within their account?**

1. Amazon CloudHSM
2. Amazon IAM
3. Amazon CloudWatch
4. AWS CloudTrail

### 3. Question

**Which AWS support plan comes with a Technical Account Manager (TAM)?**

1. Basic
2. Developer
3. Business
4. Enterprise

### 4. Question

**Which of the below is a fully managed Amazon search service based on open source software?**

1. Amazon Elasticsearch
2. Amazon CloudSearch
3. AWS OpsWorks
4. Amazon Elastic Beanstalk

### 5. Question

**What are the charges for using Amazon Glacier? (choose 2)**

1. Data storage
2. Retrieval requests
3. Minimum storage fees
4. Enhanced networking
5. Data transferred into Glacier

## 6. Question

Which pricing options are available when using Amazon EC2 Reserved Instances? (choose 2)

1. Partial upfront
2. Capacity upfront
3. Enterprise upfront
4. All upfront
5. Mainly upfront

## 7. Question

Which of the options below are recommendations in the security pillar of the well-architected framework? (choose 2)

1. Enable traceability
2. Apply security at the application layer
3. Expect to be secure
4. Automate security best practices
5. Protect data when it is at rest only

## 8. Question

Which of the following represent economic advantages of moving to the AWS cloud? (choose 2)

1. Reduce the need to manage infrastructure
2. Reduce the need to manage applications
3. Increase efficiencies through automation
4. Reduce the rate of change
5. Increase time to market for new applications

## 9. Question

Which service provides the ability to simply upload applications and have AWS handle the deployment details of capacity provisioning, load balancing, auto-scaling, and application health monitoring?

1. AWS Auto Scaling
2. AWS OpsWorks
3. Amazon Elastic Beanstalk
4. Amazon EC2

## 10. Question

What is the best way for an organization to transfer hundreds of terabytes of data from their on-premise data center into Amazon S3 with limited bandwidth available?

1. Use S3 Transfer Acceleration
2. Use Amazon CloudFront
3. Apply compression before uploading
4. Use AWS Snowball

## 11. Question

Which service can be used to create sophisticated, interactive graph applications?

1. Amazon Neptune
2. AWS X-Ray
3. Amazon Athena
4. Amazon RedShift

## 12. Question

Which AWS database service provides a fully managed data warehouse that can be analyzed using SQL tools and business intelligence tools?

1. Amazon ElastiCache
2. Amazon DynamoDB
3. Amazon RDS
4. Amazon RedShift

## 13. Question

Which descriptions are correct regarding cloud deployment models? (choose 2)

1. With the public cloud the consumer organization typically incurs OPEX costs for usage
2. With the public cloud the consumer organization typically owns and manages the infrastructure
3. With the private cloud the consumer organization typically owns and manages the infrastructure
4. With the private cloud the consumer organization typically incurs OPEX costs for usage
5. With the hybrid cloud, multiple private clouds are connected

## 14. Question

You are concerned that you may be getting close to some of the default service limits for several AWS services. What AWS tool can be used to display current usage and limits?

1. AWS Systems Manager
2. AWS Trusted Advisor
3. AWS Personal Health Dashboard
4. AWS CloudWatch

## 15. Question

How can an organization track resource inventory and configuration history for the purpose of security and regulatory compliance?

1. Create an Amazon CloudTrail trail
2. Configure AWS Config with the resource types
3. Implement Amazon GuardDuty
4. Run a report with AWS Artifact

## 16. Question

When deploying resources using AWS CloudFormation, what are you charged for? (choose 2)

1. AWS Auto Scaling Groups
2. Provisioned EBS volumes
3. Provisioned route tables
4. Provisioned EC2 instances
5. Per-usage costs for CloudFormation

## 17. Question

Which IAM entity can be used for assigning permissions to multiple users?

1. IAM User
2. IAM Group
3. IAM Role
4. IAM password policy

## 18. Question

Where is the information stored that defines an EC2 instance such as the template for the root volume, launch permissions and block device mappings?

1. EBS
2. ARN
3. AMI
4. EFS

## 19. Question

Which service provides a way to convert video and audio files from their source format into versions that will playback on devices like smartphones, tablets and PCs?

1. Amazon Rekognition
2. AWS Glue
3. Amazon Elastic Transcoder
4. Amazon Comprehend

## 20. Question

You have been running an on-demand Amazon EC2 instance running Linux for 4hrs, 5 minutes and 6 seconds. How much time will you be billed for?

1. 5hrs
2. 4hrs, 6mins
3. 4hrs, 5mins, and 6 seconds
4. 4hrs

## 21. Question

Which service allows an organization to view operational data from multiple AWS services through a unified user interface and automate operational tasks?

1. AWS Systems Manager
2. AWS Config

3. AWS CloudWatch
4. AWS OpsWorks

## 22. Question

**A security operations engineer needs to implement threat detection and monitoring for malicious or unauthorized behavior. Which service should be used?**

1. AWS GuardDuty
2. AWS Shield
3. AWS CloudHSM
4. AWS KMS

## 23. Question

**What tool provides real time guidance to help you provision your resources following best practices in the areas of cost optimization, performance, security and fault tolerance?**

1. AWS Inspector
2. AWS Personal Health Dashboard
3. Amazon IAM
4. AWS Trusted Advisor

## 24. Question

**Which AWS service is known as a "serverless" service and runs code as functions triggered by events?**

1. Amazon ECS
2. Amazon Cognito
3. AWS Lambda
4. Amazon CodeDeploy

## 25. Question

**Which Amazon EC2 Reserved Instance type enables you to match your capacity reservation to predictable recurring dates and times?**

1. Standard RI
2. Customized RI
3. Convertible RI
4. Scheduled RI

## 26. Question

**Which IAM entity can be used for assigning permissions to AWS services?**

1. IAM Access Key ID and Secret Access Key
2. IAM Policy
3. IAM Role
4. Security Token Service (STS)

## 27. Question

Which service can be used to easily create multiple accounts?

1. AWS Organizations
2. AWS CloudFormation
3. Amazon IAM
4. Amazon Connect


## 28. Question

What speeds is AWS Direct Connect offered at by AWS? (choose 2)

1. 50 Mbps
2. 10 Gbps
3. 100 Gbps
4. 1 Gbps


## 29. Question

What are the benefits of using reserved instances? (choose 2)

1. Reduced cost
2. More flexibility
3. High availability
4. Uses dedicated hardware
5. Reserve capacity


## 30. Question

Which AWS service lets you use Chef and Puppet to automate how servers are configured, deployed, and managed across your Amazon EC2 instances or on-premises compute environments?

1. AWS OpsWorks
2. AWS Systems Manager
3. AWS CloudFormation
4. AWS Elastic Beanstalk


## 31. Question

Which IAM entity is associated with an access key ID and secret access key?

1. IAM User
2. IAM Role
3. IAM Group
4. IAM Policy


## 32. Question

What is required to enable an EC2 instance in a public subnet to access the Internet? (choose 2)

1. A VPN connection
2. A public IP address

3. A NAT Gateway
4. A NAT Instance
5. A route to an Internet Gateway

## 33. Question

**How does Amazon EC2 Auto Scaling help with resiliency?**

1. By changing instance types to increase capacity
2. By launching and terminating instances as needed
3. By automating the failover of applications
4. By distributing connections to EC2 instances

## 34. Question

**What are the benefits of using Amazon Rekognition with image files?**

1. Can be used to resize images
2. Can help with image compression
3. Can be used to transcode audio
4. Can be used to identify objects in an image

## 35. Question

**An Amazon EC2 instance running the Amazon Linux 2 AMI is billed in what increment?**

1. Per CPU
2. Per hour
3. Per GB
4. Per second

## 36. Question

**Which of the following statements are correct about the benefits of AWS Direct Connect? (choose 2)**

1. Uses redundant paths across the Internet
2. Quick to implement
3. Increased bandwidth (predictable bandwidth)
4. Increased reliability (predictable performance)
5. Lower cost than a VPN

## 37. Question

**Which service can be used to cost-effectively move exabytes of data into AWS?**

1. S3 Cross-Region Replication (CRR)
2. S3 Transfer Acceleration
3. AWS Snowball
4. AWS Snowmobile

## 38. Question

Which services provide protection measures against distributed denial of service (DDoS) attacks? (choose 2)

1. Managed VPN
2. Internet Gateway
3. Amazon CloudFront
4. AWS CloudHSM
5. AWS WAF

## 39. Question

Which statement best describes elasticity in the cloud?

1. The ability to scale resources up or down and only pay for what you use
2. The ability for a system to recover from the failure of a single component
3. A flexible model of code development that results in faster deployment times
4. A pricing model that allows upfront payments and term commitments to reduce cost

## 40. Question

Which AWS service does API Gateway integrate with to enable users from around the world to achieve the lowest possible latency for API requests and responses?

1. AWS Direct Connect
2. Amazon S3 Transfer Acceleration
3. Amazon CloudFront
4. AWS Lambda

## 41. Question

Which of the options below are recommendations in the reliability pillar of the well-architected framework? (choose 2)

1. Use ad-hoc recovery procedures
2. Automatically recover from failure
3. Scale vertically to increase aggregate system availability
4. Manage change in automation
5. Attempt to accurately estimate capacity requirements

## 42. Question

What are the advantages of Availability Zones? (choose 2)

1. They are connected by low-latency network connections
2. They enable the caching of data for faster delivery to end users
3. They allow regional disaster recovery
4. They provide fault isolation
5. They enable you to connect your on-premises networks to AWS to form a hybrid cloud

### 43. Question

**Which statement best describes Amazon Route 53?**

1. Amazon Route 53 is a service that enables routing within VPCs in an account
2. Amazon Route 53 is a highly available and scalable Domain Name System (DNS) service
3. Amazon Route 53 enables hybrid cloud models by extending an organization's on-premise networks into the AWS cloud
4. Amazon Route 53 is a service for distributing incoming connections between a fleet of registered EC2 instances

### 44. Question

**Your CTO wants to move to cloud. What cost advantages are there to moving to cloud?**

1. You get free data transfer into and out of the cloud
2. You don't need to pay for application licensing
3. You can reduce your marketing costs
4. You provision only what you need and adjust to peak load

### 45. Question

**How is data protected by default in Amazon S3?**

1. Buckets are replicated across all regions
2. Objects are redundantly stored on multiple devices across multiple facilities within a region
3. Objects are redundantly stored on multiple devices across multiple facilities across all regions
4. Objects are copied across at least two Availability Zones per region

### 46. Question

**Which of the below AWS services supports automated backups as a default configuration?**

1. Amazon EBS
2. Amazon S3
3. Amazon RDS
4. Amazon EC2

### 47. Question

**Which AWS tools can be used for automation? (choose 2)**

1. AWS CloudFormation
2. Elastic Load Balancing
3. AWS Lambda
4. Amazon Elastic File System (EFS)
5. AWS Elastic Beanstalk

### 48. Question

**Which of the below is an example of an architectural benefit of moving to the cloud?**

1. Proprietary hardware

2. Monolithic services
3. Elasticity
4. Vertical scalability

## 49. Question

When using Amazon IAM, what authentication methods are available to use? (choose 2)

1. Amazon KMS
2. Access keys
3. AES 256
4. Client certificates
5. Server certificates

## 50. Question

Under the AWS shared responsibility model what is AWS responsible for? (choose 2)

1. Replacement and disposal of disk drives
2. Encryption of customer data
3. Configuration of security groups
4. Patch management of operating systems
5. Physical security of the data center

## 51. Question

Which feature enables fast, easy, and secure transfers of files over long distances between a client and an Amazon S3 bucket?

1. S3 Static Websites
2. S3 Copy
3. Multipart Upload
4. S3 Transfer Acceleration

## 52. Question

Which of the options below are recommendations in the cost optimization pillar of the well-architected framework? (choose 2)

1. Adopt a capital expenditure model
2. Adopt a consumption model
3. Start spending money on data center operations
4. Manage your services independently
5. Analyze and attribute expenditure

## 53. Question

What is a specific benefit of an Enterprise Support plan?

1. Included Cloud Support Associate
2. Included Technical Support Manager
3. Included AWS Solutions Architect

4. Included Technical Account Manager

## 54. Question

**What advantages do NAT Gateways have over NAT Instances? (choose 2)**

1. Can be scaled up manually
2. Managed for you by AWS
3. Highly available within each AZ
4. Can be used as a bastion host
5. Can be assigned to security groups

## 55. Question

**What is the best way to apply an organizational system to EC2 instances so they can be identified by descriptors such as purpose or department?**

1. Apply tags
2. Use the instance meta-data
3. Use descriptive hostnames
4. Organize the instances into separate subnets

## 56. Question

**Which authentication method is used to authenticate programmatic calls to AWS services?**

1. Console password
2. Key pair
3. Server certificate
4. Access keys

## 57. Question

**What is a benefit of moving an on-premises database to Amazon Relational Database Service (RDS)?**

1. There is no need to manage operating systems
2. You can scale vertically without downtime
3. There is no database administration required
4. You can run any database engine

## 58. Question

**To ensure the security of your AWS account, what are two AWS best practices for managing access keys? (choose 2)**

1. Don't generate an access key for the root account user
2. Where possible, use IAM roles with temporary security credentials
3. Don't create any access keys, use IAM roles instead
4. Rotate access keys daily
5. Use MFA for access keys

## 59. Question

How does the consolidated billing feature of AWS Organizations treat Reserved Instances that were purchased by another account in the organization?

1. All accounts in the organization are treated as one account so any account can receive the hourly cost benefit
2. Only the master account can benefit from the hourly cost benefit of the reserved instances
3. AWS Organizations does not support any volume or reserved instance benefits across accounts, it is just a method of aggregating bills
4. All accounts in the organization are treated as one account for volume discounts but not for reserved instances

## 60. Question

Which database allows you to scale at the push of a button without incurring any downtime?

1. Amazon RDS
2. Amazon EMR
3. Amazon DynamoDB
4. Amazon RedShift

## 61. Question

When using AWS Organizations with consolidated billing what are two valid best practices? (choose 2)

1. Never exceed the limit of 20 linked accounts
2. Always enable multi-factor authentication (MFA) on the root account
3. Always use a straightforward password on the root account
4. The paying account should be used for billing purposes only
5. Use the paying account for deploying resources

## 62. Question

Which AWS services are associated with Edge Locations? (choose 2)

1. AWS Config
2. Amazon EBS
3. Amazon CloudFront
4. AWS Shield
5. AWS Direct Connect

## 63. Question

Which of the options below are recommendations in the performance efficiency pillar of the well-architected framework? (choose 2)

1. Go global in days
2. Rarely experiment
3. Democratize advanced technologies
4. Mechanical complexity
5. Use serverless architectures

### 64. Question

**What are Edge locations used for?**

1. They are used by regions for inter-region connectivity
2. They are the public-facing APIs for Amazon S3
3. They host a CDN called CloudFront
4. They are used for terminating VPN connections

### 65. Question

**You need to run a production process that will use several EC2 instances and run constantly on an ongoing basis. The process cannot be interrupted or restarted without issue. What EC2 pricing model would be best for this workload?**

1. Reserved instances
2. Spot instances
3. Flexible instances
4. On-demand instances

# SET 3: PRACTICE QUESTIONS, ANSWERS & EXPLANATIONS

## 1. Question

To gain greater discounts, which services can be reserved? (choose 2)

1. Amazon DynamoDB
2. Amazon RedShift
3. Amazon S3
4. AWS Lambda
5. Amazon CloudWatch

Answer: 1,2

Explanation:

- Reservations provide you with greater discounts, up to 75%, by paying for capacity ahead of time. Some of the services you can reserve include: EC2, DynamoDB, ElastiCache, RDS, and RedShift.
- You cannot reserve Amazon S3, you pay for what you use
- AWS Lambda is a service that provides functions and cannot be reserved.
- You cannot reserve Amazon CloudWatch which is a monitoring service.

References:

https://digitalcloud.training/certification-training/aws-certified-cloud-practitioner/aws-billing-and-pricing/

https://d1.awsstatic.com/whitepapers/aws_pricing_overview.pdf

## 2. Question

Which service can an organization use to track API activity within their account?

1. Amazon CloudHSM
2. Amazon IAM
3. Amazon CloudWatch
4. AWS CloudTrail

Answer: 4

Explanation:

- AWS CloudTrail is a web service that records activity made on your account and delivers log files to an Amazon S3 bucket. CloudTrail is for auditing (CloudWatch is for performance monitoring). CloudTrail is about logging and saves a history of API calls for your AWS account. Provides visibility into user activity by recording actions taken on your account. API history enables security analysis, resource change tracking, and compliance auditing
- Amazon CloudWatch is a monitoring service for AWS cloud resources and the applications you run on AWS. CloudWatch is for performance monitoring (CloudTrail is for auditing). Used to collect and track metrics, collect and monitor log files, and set alarms
- Amazon Identity and Access Management is an identity service that provide authentication and authorization services

- AWS CloudHSM is a cloud-based hardware security module (HSM) that enables you to easily generate and use your own encryption keys on the AWS Cloud

**References:**

https://digitalcloud.training/certification-training/aws-certified-cloud-practitioner/monitoring-and-logging-services/

## 3. Question

**Which AWS support plan comes with a Technical Account Manager (TAM)?**

1. Basic
2. Developer
3. Business
4. Enterprise

**Answer: 4**

**Explanation:**

- Only the Enterprise plan comes with a TAM

**References:**

https://digitalcloud.training/certification-training/aws-certified-cloud-practitioner/aws-billing-and-pricing/

## 4. Question

**Which of the below is a fully managed Amazon search service based on open source software?**

1. Amazon Elasticsearch
2. Amazon CloudSearch
3. AWS OpsWorks
4. Amazon Elastic Beanstalk

**Answer: 1**

**Explanation:**

- Amazon Elasticsearch Service, is a fully managed service that makes it easy for you to deploy, secure, operate, and scale Elasticsearch to search, analyze, and visualize data in real-time. Elasticsearch is based on open source software
- Amazon CloudSearch is a managed service in the AWS Cloud that makes it simple and cost-effective to set up, manage, and scale a search solution for your website or application
- AWS OpsWorks is a configuration management service that provides managed instances of Chef and Puppet
- AWS Elastic Beanstalk is the fastest and simplest way to get web applications up and running on AWS. Developers simply upload their application code and the service automatically handles all the details such as resource provisioning, load balancing, auto-scaling, and monitoring

**References:**

https://digitalcloud.training/certification-training/aws-certified-cloud-practitioner/additional-aws-services-tools/

## 5. Question

What are the charges for using Amazon Glacier? (choose 2)

1. Data storage
2. Retrieval requests
3. Minimum storage fees
4. Enhanced networking
5. Data transferred into Glacier

Answer: 1,2

Explanation:

- With Amazon Glacier you pay for storage on a per GB / month basis, retrieval requests and quantity (based on expedited, standard, or bulk), and data transfer out of Glacier
- You do not pay for data transferred in and there are no minimum storage fees
- Enhanced networking is a feature of EC2

References:

https://digitalcloud.training/certification-training/aws-certified-cloud-practitioner/aws-billing-and-pricing/

https://aws.amazon.com/glacier/pricing/

## 6. Question

Which pricing options are available when using Amazon EC2 Reserved Instances? (choose 2)

1. Partial upfront
2. Capacity upfront
3. Enterprise upfront
4. All upfront
5. Mainly upfront

Answer: 1,4

Explanation:

- Amazon EC2 Reserved Instances (RI) provide a significant discount (up to 75%) compared to On-Demand pricing and provide a capacity reservation when used in a specific Availability Zone
- Payment options include All Upfront, Partial Upfront, and No Upfront

References:

https://aws.amazon.com/ec2/pricing/reserved-instances/

## 7. Question

**Which of the options below are recommendations in the security pillar of the well-architected framework? (choose 2)**

1. Enable traceability
2. Apply security at the application layer
3. Expect to be secure
4. Automate security best practices
5. Protect data when it is at rest only

**Answer: 1,4**

**Explanation:**

- The security pillar includes the ability to protect information, systems, and assets while delivering business value through risk assessments and mitigation strategies
- There are six design principles for security in the cloud:
    - Implement a strong identity foundation
    - Enable traceability
    - Apply security at all layers
    - Automate security best practices
    - Protect data in transit and at rest
    - Prepare for security events

**References:**

https://aws.amazon.com/blogs/apn/the-5-pillars-of-the-aws-well-architected-framework/

https://digitalcloud.training/certification-training/aws-certified-cloud-practitioner/architecting-for-the-cloud/

## 8. Question

**Which of the following represent economic advantages of moving to the AWS cloud? (choose 2)**

1. Reduce the need to manage infrastructure
2. Reduce the need to manage applications
3. Increase efficiencies through automation
4. Reduce the rate of change
5. Increase time to market for new applications

**Answer: 1,3**

**Explanation:**

- With the AWS Cloud you can increase efficiency through the use of automation and reduce the need to manage infrastructure, allowing you to concentrate on managing applications instead
- You do not reduce the need to manage applications in most cases.
- Reducing the rate of change is not something organizations strive for in the cloud (usually faster development cycles are preferred) so it does not represent a valid economic advantage
- You want to reduce not increase time to market for new applications

**References:**

https://d1.awsstatic.com/whitepapers/introduction-to-aws-cloud-economics-final.pdf

## 9. Question

Which service provides the ability to simply upload applications and have AWS handle the deployment details of capacity provisioning, load balancing, auto-scaling, and application health monitoring?

1. AWS Auto Scaling
2. AWS OpsWorks
3. Amazon Elastic Beanstalk
4. Amazon EC2

Answer: 3

Explanation:

- AWS Elastic Beanstalk can be used to quickly deploy and manage applications in the AWS Cloud. Developers upload applications and Elastic Beanstalk handles the deployment details of capacity provisioning, load balancing, auto-scaling, and application health monitoring. Considered a Platform as a Service (PaaS) solution. Supports Java, .NET, PHP, Node.js, Python, Ruby, Go, and Docker web applications
- Amazon EC2 is an IaaS solution that provides unmanaged instances that you can deploy with a variety of operating systems
- AWS Auto Scaling provides elasticity for your applications by automatically launching or terminating EC2 instances according to application load or schedules you define
- AWS OpsWorks provides a managed service for Chef and Puppet

References:

https://digitalcloud.training/certification-training/aws-certified-cloud-practitioner/additional-aws-services-tools/

## 10. Question

What is the best way for an organization to transfer hundreds of terabytes of data from their on-premise data center into Amazon S3 with limited bandwidth available?

1. Use S3 Transfer Acceleration
2. Use Amazon CloudFront
3. Apply compression before uploading
4. Use AWS Snowball

Answer: 4

Explanation:

- Snowball is a petabyte-scale data transport solution that uses devices designed to be secure to transfer large amounts of data into and out of the AWS Cloud. Using Snowball addresses common challenges with large-scale data transfers including high network costs, long transfer times, and security concerns
- Amazon S3 Transfer Acceleration enables fast, easy, and secure transfers of files over long distances between your client and an S3 bucket. Transfer Acceleration takes advantage of Amazon

CloudFront's globally distributed edge locations. However, for these volumes of data Snowball is a better choice

**References:**

https://digitalcloud.training/certification-training/aws-certified-cloud-practitioner/aws-storage/

## 11. Question

**Which service can be used to create sophisticated, interactive graph applications?**

1. Amazon Neptune
2. AWS X-Ray
3. Amazon Athena
4. Amazon RedShift

Answer: 1

**Explanation:**

- Amazon Neptune is a fast, reliable, fully-managed graph database service that makes it easy to build and run applications that work with highly connected datasets. With Amazon Neptune, you can create sophisticated, interactive graph applications that can query billions of relationships in milliseconds
- Amazon Redshift is a fast, scalable data warehouse that makes it simple and cost-effective to analyze all your data across your data warehouse and data lake
- AWS X-Ray helps developers analyze and debug production, distributed applications, such as those built using a microservices architecture
- Amazon Athena is an interactive query service that makes it easy to analyze data in Amazon S3 using standard SQL

**References:**

https://digitalcloud.training/certification-training/aws-certified-cloud-practitioner/additional-aws-services-tools/

## 12. Question

**Which AWS database service provides a fully managed data warehouse that can be analyzed using SQL tools and business intelligence tools?**

1. Amazon ElastiCache
2. Amazon DynamoDB
3. Amazon RDS
4. Amazon RedShift

Answer: 4

**Explanation:**

- RedShift is a fully managed data warehouse service designed to handle petabytes of data for analysis. Data can be analyzed with standard SQL tools and business intelligence tools. RedShift allows you to run complex analytic queries against petabytes of structured data
- RDS is Amazon's transactional relational database

- DynamoDB is Amazon's non-relational database service
- ElastiCache is a data caching service that is used to help improve the speed/performance of web applications running on AWS

**References:**

https://digitalcloud.training/certification-training/aws-certified-cloud-practitioner/aws-databases/

## 13. Question

**Which descriptions are correct regarding cloud deployment models? (choose 2)**

1. With the public cloud the consumer organization typically incurs OPEX costs for usage
2. With the public cloud the consumer organization typically owns and manages the infrastructure
3. With the private cloud the consumer organization typically owns and manages the infrastructure
4. With the private cloud the consumer organization typically incurs OPEX costs for usage
5. With the hybrid cloud, multiple private clouds are connected

**Answer: 1,3**

**Explanation:**

- With public cloud the consumer organization typically incurs OPEX costs as they do not own the infrastructure and just pay usage costs
- With the private cloud the consumer organization typically owns the infrastructure and will often manage it themselves or use a third-party organization to manage it for them. This model is largely CAPEX driven
- Hybrid clouds are created when you connect private and public clouds together

**References:**

https://digitalcloud.training/certification-training/aws-certified-cloud-practitioner/cloud-computing-concepts/

## 14. Question

**You are concerned that you may be getting close to some of the default service limits for several AWS services. What AWS tool can be used to display current usage and limits?**

1. AWS Systems Manager
2. AWS Trusted Advisor
3. AWS Personal Health Dashboard
4. AWS CloudWatch

**Answer: 2**

**Explanation:**

- Trusted Advisor is an online resource to help you reduce cost, increase performance, and improve security by optimizing your AWS environment. Trusted Advisor provides real time guidance to help you provision your resources following AWS best practices. Offers a Service Limits check (in the Performance category) that displays your usage and limits for some aspects of some services
- Amazon CloudWatch is a monitoring and management service built for developers, system operators, site reliability engineers (SRE), and IT managers

- AWS Personal Health Dashboard provides alerts and remediation guidance when AWS is experiencing events that may impact you
- AWS Systems Manager gives you visibility and control of your infrastructure on AWS

**References:**

https://docs.aws.amazon.com/general/latest/gr/aws_service_limits.html

## 15. Question

**How can an organization track resource inventory and configuration history for the purpose of security and regulatory compliance?**

1. Create an Amazon CloudTrail trail
2. Configure AWS Config with the resource types
3. Implement Amazon GuardDuty
4. Run a report with AWS Artifact

**Answer: 2**

**Explanation:**

- AWS Config is a fully-managed service that provides you with an AWS resource inventory, configuration history, and configuration change notifications to enable security and regulatory compliance.
- CloudTrail tracks API activity. This means it is used to monitor who does what on Amazon. It does not provide a resource inventory or configuration history.
- Amazon GuardDuty offers threat detection and continuous security monitoring for malicious or unauthorized behavior to help you protect your AWS accounts and workloads.
- AWS Artifact is used for obtaining on-demand security and compliance reports and select online agreements. This service provides access to AWS security and compliance reports such as SOC and PCI. You don't use Artifact to track your own resource inventory and configuration history.

**References:**

https://digitalcloud.training/certification-training/aws-certified-cloud-practitioner/cloud-security/

https://docs.aws.amazon.com/config/latest/developerguide/gs-console.html

## 16. Question

**When deploying resources using AWS CloudFormation, what are you charged for? (choose 2)**

1. AWS Auto Scaling Groups
2. Provisioned EBS volumes
3. Provisioned route tables
4. Provisioned EC2 instances
5. Per-usage costs for CloudFormation

**Answer: 2,4**

**Explanation:**

- You do not pay for AWS CloudFormation, just for the chargeable resources that it provisions

- EC2 instances and EBS volumes both incur costs
- Route tables and Auto Scaling Groups do not incur costs

**References:**

https://digitalcloud.training/certification-training/aws-certified-cloud-practitioner/additional-aws-services-tools/

https://digitalcloud.training/certification-training/aws-solutions-architect-associate/management-tools/aws-cloudformation/

## 17. Question

Which IAM entity can be used for assigning permissions to multiple users?

1. IAM User
2. IAM Group
3. IAM Role
4. IAM password policy

**Answer: 2**

**Explanation:**

- Groups are collections of users and have policies attached to them. You can use groups to assign permissions to multiple users. To do this place the users in the group and then create an IAM policy with the correct permissions and attach it to the group.
- You do not use an IAM User, Role, or password policy to assign permissions to multiple users.

**References:**

https://digitalcloud.training/certification-training/aws-certified-cloud-practitioner/identity-and-access-management/

## 18. Question

Where is the information stored that defines an EC2 instance such as the template for the root volume, launch permissions and block device mappings?

1. EBS
2. ARN
3. AMI
4. EFS

**Answer: 3**

**Explanation:**

- An Amazon Machine Image (AMI) provides the information required to launch an instance, which is a virtual server in the cloud. You must specify a source AMI when you launch an instance. You can launch multiple instances from a single AMI when you need multiple instances with the same configuration. You can use different AMIs to launch instances when you need instances with different configurations
- EBS is the Elastic Block Store

- ARN is the Amazon Resource Name which uniquely identifies AWS resources

**References:**

https://docs.aws.amazon.com/AWSEC2/latest/UserGuide/AMIs.html

## 19. Question

**Which service provides a way to convert video and audio files from their source format into versions that will playback on devices like smartphones, tablets and PCs?**

1. Amazon Rekognition
2. AWS Glue
3. Amazon Elastic Transcoder
4. Amazon Comprehend

Answer: 3

**Explanation:**

- Amazon Elastic Transcoder is a highly scalable, easy to use and cost-effective way for developers and businesses to convert (or "transcode") video and audio files from their source format into versions that will playback on devices like smartphones, tablets and PCs
- AWS Glue is a fully managed extract, transform, and load (ETL) service that makes it easy for customers to prepare and load their data for analytics
- Amazon Rekognition makes it easy to add image and video analysis to your applications
- Amazon Comprehend is a natural language processing (NLP) service that uses machine learning to find insights and relationships in text

**References:**

https://digitalcloud.training/certification-training/aws-certified-cloud-practitioner/additional-aws-services-tools/

https://digitalcloud.training/certification-training/aws-solutions-architect-associate/media-services/amazon-elastic-transcoder/

## 20. Question

**You have been running an on-demand Amazon EC2 instance running Linux for 4hrs, 5 minutes and 6 seconds. How much time will you be billed for?**

1. 5hrs
2. 4hrs, 6mins
3. 4hrs, 5mins, and 6 seconds
4. 4hrs

Answer: 3

**Explanation:**

- On-demand, Reserved and Spot Amazon EC2 Linux instances are charged per second with a minimum charge of 1 minute. Therefore, as the minimum has been exceeded, exactly 4hrs, 5mins and 6 seconds will be charged.

**References:**

https://digitalcloud.training/certification-training/aws-certified-cloud-practitioner/aws-billing-and-pricing/

https://aws.amazon.com/blogs/aws/new-per-second-billing-for-ec2-instances-and-ebs-volumes/

## 21. Question

Which service allows an organization to view operational data from multiple AWS services through a unified user interface and automate operational tasks?

1. AWS Systems Manager
2. AWS Config
3. AWS CloudWatch
4. AWS OpsWorks

**Answer: 1**

**Explanation:**

- AWS Systems Manager gives you visibility and control of your infrastructure on AWS. Systems Manager provides a unified user interface so you can view operational data from multiple AWS services and allows you to automate operational tasks across your AWS resources.
- AWS OpsWorks is a configuration management service that provides managed instances of Chef and Puppet.
- AWS Config is a fully-managed service that provides you with an AWS resource inventory, configuration history, and configuration change notifications to enable security and regulatory compliance.
- Amazon CloudWatch is a monitoring service for AWS cloud resources and the applications you run on AWS. You use CloudWatch for performance monitoring, not automating operational tasks.

**References:**

https://aws.amazon.com/systems-manager/

## 22. Question

A security operations engineer needs to implement threat detection and monitoring for malicious or unauthorized behavior. Which service should be used?

1. AWS GuardDuty
2. AWS Shield
3. AWS CloudHSM
4. AWS KMS

**Answer: 1**

**Explanation:**

- Amazon GuardDuty offers threat detection and continuous security monitoring for malicious or unauthorized behavior to help you protect your AWS accounts and workloads.
- AWS Shield is a managed Distributed Denial of Service (DDoS) protection service.

- AWS Key Management Service gives you centralized control over the encryption keys used to protect your data.
- AWS CloudHSM is a cloud-based hardware security module (HSM) that enables you to easily generate and use your own encryption keys on the AWS Cloud.

**References:**

https://digitalcloud.training/certification-training/aws-certified-cloud-practitioner/cloud-security/

https://aws.amazon.com/guardduty/

## 23. Question

**What tool provides real time guidance to help you provision your resources following best practices in the areas of cost optimization, performance, security and fault tolerance?**

1. AWS Inspector
2. AWS Personal Health Dashboard
3. Amazon IAM
4. AWS Trusted Advisor

**Answer: 4**

**Explanation:**

- Trusted Advisor is an online resource that helps to reduce cost, increase performance and improve security by optimizing your AWS environment. Trusted Advisor provides real time guidance to help you provision your resources following best practices. Advisor will advise you on Cost Optimization, Performance, Security, and Fault Tolerance
- Inspector is an automated security assessment service that helps improve the security and compliance of applications deployed on AWS
- AWS Personal Health Dashboard provides alerts and remediation guidance when AWS is experiencing events that may impact you
- Amazon Identity and Access Management is an identity service that provide authentication and authorization services

**References:**

https://digitalcloud.training/certification-training/aws-certified-cloud-practitioner/cloud-security/

## 24. Question

**Which AWS service is known as a "serverless" service and runs code as functions triggered by events?**

1. Amazon ECS
2. Amazon Cognito
3. AWS Lambda
4. Amazon CodeDeploy

**Answer: 3**

**Explanation:**

- AWS Lambda lets you run code as functions without provisioning or managing servers. Lambda-based applications (also referred to as serverless applications) are composed of functions triggered by events. With serverless computing, your application still runs on servers, but all the server management is done by AWS
- Amazon Elastic Container Service (ECS) is a highly scalable, high performance container management service that supports Docker containers and allows you to easily run applications on a managed cluster of Amazon EC2 instances
- AWS CodeDeploy is a fully managed deployment service that automates software deployments to a variety of compute services such as Amazon EC2, AWS Lambda, and your on-premises servers
- Amazon Cognito lets you add user sign-up, sign-in, and access control to your web and mobile apps quickly and easily

**References:**

https://digitalcloud.training/certification-training/aws-certified-cloud-practitioner/aws-compute/

## 25. Question

Which Amazon EC2 Reserved Instance type enables you to match your capacity reservation to predictable recurring dates and times?

1. Standard RI
2. Customized RI
3. Convertible RI
4. Scheduled RI

**Answer: 4**

**Explanation:**

- With RIs, you can choose the type that best fits your applications needs.
- Standard RIs: These provide the most significant discount (up to 75% off On-Demand) and are best suited for steady-state usage
- Convertible RIs: These provide a discount (up to 54% off On-Demand) and the capability to change the attributes of the RI as long as the exchange results in the creation of Reserved Instances of equal or greater value. Like Standard RIs, Convertible RIs are best suited for steady-state usage
- Scheduled RIs: These are available to launch within the time windows you reserve. This option allows you to match your capacity reservation to a predictable recurring schedule that only requires a fraction of a day, a week, or a month

**References:**

https://aws.amazon.com/ec2/pricing/reserved-instances/

## 26. Question

Which IAM entity can be used for assigning permissions to AWS services?

1. IAM Access Key ID and Secret Access Key
2. IAM Policy
3. IAM Role
4. Security Token Service (STS)

Answer: 3

Explanation:

- With IAM Roles you can delegate permissions to resources for users and services without using permanent credentials (e.g. username and password). To do so you can create a role and assign an IAM policy to the role that has the permissions required.
- An access key ID and secret access key are assigned to IAM users and used for programmatic access using the API or CLI.
- An IAM policy is a policy document that is used to define permissions that can be applied to users, groups and roles. You don't apply the policy to the service, you apply it to the role. The role is then used to assign permissions to the AWS service.

References:

https://digitalcloud.training/certification-training/aws-certified-cloud-practitioner/identity-and-access-management/

https://docs.aws.amazon.com/IAM/latest/UserGuide/id_roles_create_for-service.html

## 27. Question

**Which service can be used to easily create multiple accounts?**

1. AWS Organizations
2. AWS CloudFormation
3. Amazon IAM
4. Amazon Connect

Answer: 1

Explanation:

- AWS Organizations can be used for automating AWS account creation via the Organizations API.
- You cannot use IAM for creating accounts.
- You could theoretically use AWS CloudFormation to automate the account creation along with some scripting, but that is certainly not an easy way to reach this result.
- Amazon Connect is a self-service, cloud-based contact center service that makes it easy for businesses to deliver better customer service at a lower cost.

References:

https://docs.aws.amazon.com/organizations/latest/userguide/orgs_manage_accounts_create.html

https://aws.amazon.com/blogs/security/how-to-use-aws-organizations-to-automate-end-to-end-account-creation/

https://digitalcloud.training/certification-training/aws-certified-cloud-practitioner/aws-billing-and-pricing/

## 28. Question

**What speeds is AWS Direct Connect offered at by AWS? (choose 2)**

1. 50 Mbps

2. 10 Gbps
3. 100 Gbps
4. 1 Gbps

**Answer: 2,4**

**Explanation:**

- AWS Direct Connect is a network service that provides an alternative to using the Internet to connect a customer's on-premise sites to AWS. Data is transmitted through a private network connection between AWS and a customer's data center or corporate network
- Available in 1Gbps and 10Gbps
- Speeds of 50Mbps, 100Mbps, 200Mbps, 300Mbps, 400Mbps, and 500Mbps can be purchased through AWS Direct Connect Partners

**References:**

https://digitalcloud.training/certification-training/aws-certified-cloud-practitioner/aws-networking/

## 29. Question

**What are the benefits of using reserved instances? (choose 2)**

1. Reduced cost
2. More flexibility
3. High availability
4. Uses dedicated hardware
5. Reserve capacity

**Answer: 1,5**

**Explanation:**

- With reserved instances you commit to a 1- or 3-year term and get a significant discount from the on-demand rate. You can also reserve capacity in an availability zone with reserved instances.
- You don't get more flexibility with reserved instances. If you need flexibility on-demand is better but more costly.
- Reserved instances are different to dedicated instances. Dedicates instances and dedicates hosts use dedicated hardware but reserved instances do not.
- You do not get high availability with reserved instances; this is a pricing model.

**References:**

https://aws.amazon.com/ec2/pricing/reserved-instances/

https://digitalcloud.training/certification-training/aws-certified-cloud-practitioner/aws-billing-and-pricing/

## 30. Question

**Which AWS service lets you use Chef and Puppet to automate how servers are configured, deployed, and managed across your Amazon EC2 instances or on-premises compute environments?**

1. AWS OpsWorks

2. AWS Systems Manager
3. AWS CloudFormation
4. AWS Elastic Beanstalk

**Answer: 1**

**Explanation:**

- AWS OpsWorks is a configuration management service that provides managed instances of Chef and Puppet
- OpsWorks lets you use Chef and Puppet to automate how servers are configured, deployed, and managed across your Amazon EC2 instances or on-premises compute environments
- OpsWorks is an automation platform that transforms infrastructure into code
- Automates how applications are configured, deployed and managed

**References:**

https://digitalcloud.training/certification-training/aws-certified-cloud-practitioner/additional-aws-services-tools/

https://digitalcloud.training/certification-training/aws-solutions-architect-associate/management-tools/aws-opsworks/

## 31. Question

**Which IAM entity is associated with an access key ID and secret access key?**

1. IAM User
2. IAM Role
3. IAM Group
4. IAM Policy

**Answer: 1**

**Explanation:**

- An access key ID and secret access key are used to sign programmatic requests to AWS. They are associated with an IAM user.
- You cannot associate an access key ID and secret access key with an IAM Group, Role or Policy.

**References:**

https://digitalcloud.training/certification-training/aws-certified-cloud-practitioner/identity-and-access-management/

https://docs.aws.amazon.com/general/latest/gr/aws-sec-cred-types.html#access-keys-and-secret-access-keys

## 32. Question

**What is required to enable an EC2 instance in a public subnet to access the Internet? (choose 2)**

1. A VPN connection
2. A public IP address
3. A NAT Gateway

4. A NAT Instance
5. A route to an Internet Gateway

**Answer: 2,5**

**Explanation:**

- A public subnet is a subnet that is configured to assign public IP addresses to instances and which has a route to an Internet Gateway (which is created at the VPC level) configured in the route table
- NAT instances and NAT gateways are used by EC2 instances in private subnets (without public IPs) to access the Internet
- A VPN connection is used to establish a secure connection between the AWS cloud and an on-premise data center or other cloud location. They are not used to access the Internet

**References:**

https://digitalcloud.training/certification-training/aws-certified-cloud-practitioner/aws-networking/

## 33. Question

How does Amazon EC2 Auto Scaling help with resiliency?

1. By changing instance types to increase capacity
2. By launching and terminating instances as needed
3. By automating the failover of applications
4. By distributing connections to EC2 instances

**Answer: 2**

**Explanation:**

- Amazon EC2 Auto Scaling launches and terminates instances as demand changes. This helps with resiliency and high availability as it can also be set to ensure a minimum number of instances are always available.
- Auto Scaling is not responsible for distributing connections to EC2 instances, that is a job for an Elastic Load Balancer (ELB).
- Auto Scaling does not change the instance type. You have to create a new launch configuration if you need to increase your instance size, this is not automatic.
- Auto Scaling does not do application failover.

**References:**

https://digitalcloud.training/certification-training/aws-certified-cloud-practitioner/elastic-load-balancing-and-auto-scaling/

## 34. Question

What are the benefits of using Amazon Rekognition with image files?

1. Can be used to resize images
2. Can help with image compression
3. Can be used to transcode audio
4. Can be used to identify objects in an image

**Answer: 4**

**Explanation:**

- Rekognition Image is a deep learning powered image recognition service that detects objects, scenes, and faces; extracts text; recognizes celebrities; and identifies inappropriate content in images. It also allows you to search and compare faces
- You cannot use Rekognition to resize or compress images.
- You should use the Elastic Transcoder service to transcode audio.

**References:**

https://aws.amazon.com/rekognition/image-features/

## 35. Question

**An Amazon EC2 instance running the Amazon Linux 2 AMI is billed in what increment?**

1. Per CPU
2. Per hour
3. Per GB
4. Per second

**Answer: 4**

**Explanation:**

- Amazon EC2 instances running Linux are billed in one second increments, with a minimum of 60 seconds.
- You do not pay per hour anymore (since October 2017).
- Per CPU and per GB are incorrect answers. You do pay for Amazon EBS on a per GB of provisioned storage basis.

**References:**

https://digitalcloud.training/certification-training/aws-certified-cloud-practitioner/aws-billing-and-pricing/

https://aws.amazon.com/about-aws/whats-new/2017/10/announcing-amazon-ec2-per-second-billing/

https://d1.awsstatic.com/whitepapers/aws_pricing_overview.pdf

## 36. Question

**Which of the following statements are correct about the benefits of AWS Direct Connect? (choose 2)**

1. Uses redundant paths across the Internet
2. Quick to implement
3. Increased bandwidth (predictable bandwidth)
4. Increased reliability (predictable performance)
5. Lower cost than a VPN

**Answer: 3,4**

**Explanation:**

- AWS Direct Connect is a network service that provides an alternative to using the Internet to connect customers' on-premise sites to AWS
- Data is transmitted through a private network connection between AWS and a customer's datacenter or corporate network
- Benefits:
    - Reduce cost when using large volumes of traffic
    - Increase reliability (predictable performance)
    - Increase bandwidth (predictable bandwidth)
    - Decrease latency
- Direct Connect is not fast to implement as it can take weeks to months to setup (use VPN for fast deployment times)
- Direct Connect is more expensive than VPN
- Direct Connect uses private network connections, it does not use redundant paths over the Internet

**References:**

- https://digitalcloud.training/certification-training/aws-certified-cloud-practitioner/aws-networking/

## 37. Question

Which service can be used to cost-effectively move exabytes of data into AWS?

1. S3 Cross-Region Replication (CRR)
2. S3 Transfer Acceleration
3. AWS Snowball
4. AWS Snowmobile

**Answer: 4**

**Explanation:**

- With AWS Snowmobile you can move 100PB per snowmobile. AWS call this an "Exabyte-scale data transfer service".
- With AWS Snowball you can move up to 80TB per device. AWS call this a "petabyte-scale data transfer service".
- S3 Transfer Acceleration is meant speed up uploads to Amazon S3 but would not be used for exabytes of data.
- S3 Cross-Region Replication is used for copying data between regions, not into AWS. It is also unsuitable for moving such as huge amount of data.

**References:**

https://aws.amazon.com/snowmobile/

## 38. Question

Which services provide protection measures against distributed denial of service (DDoS) attacks? (choose 2)

1. Managed VPN

2. Internet Gateway
3. Amazon CloudFront
4. AWS CloudHSM
5. AWS WAF

**Answer: 3,5**

**Explanation:**

- AWS offers globally distributed, high network bandwidth and resilient services that, when used in conjunction with application-specific strategies, are key to mitigating DDoS attacks
- AWS WAF is a web application firewall that helps protect web applications from common web exploits that could affect application availability, compromise security, or consume excessive resources
- Amazon CloudFront distributes traffic across multiple edge locations and filters requests to ensure that only valid HTTP(S) requests will be forwarded to backend hosts. CloudFront also supports geoblocking, which you can use to prevent requests from particular geographic locations from being served
- Internet Gateways, Managed VPN and CloudHSM do not help to mitigate DDoS attacks

**References:**

https://aws.amazon.com/answers/networking/aws-ddos-attack-mitigation/

https://digitalcloud.training/certification-training/aws-certified-cloud-practitioner/cloud-security/

## 39. Question

**Which statement best describes elasticity in the cloud?**

1. The ability to scale resources up or down and only pay for what you use
2. The ability for a system to recover from the failure of a single component
3. A flexible model of code development that results in faster deployment times
4. A pricing model that allows upfront payments and term commitments to reduce cost

**Answer: 1**

**Explanation:**

- Elasticity is the ability to scale resources up or down and only pay for what you use. A great example is Auto Scaling which adds and removes EC2 instances based on the amount of load

**References:**

https://digitalcloud.training/certification-training/aws-certified-cloud-practitioner/architecting-for-the-cloud/

## 40. Question

**Which AWS service does API Gateway integrate with to enable users from around the world to achieve the lowest possible latency for API requests and responses?**

1. AWS Direct Connect
2. Amazon S3 Transfer Acceleration

3. Amazon CloudFront
4. AWS Lambda

**Answer: 3**

**Explanation:**

- CloudFront is used as the public endpoint for API Gateway. Provides reduced latency and distributed denial of service protection through the use of CloudFront
- AWS Direct Connect is a cloud service solution that makes it easy to establish a dedicated network connection from your premises to AWS
- Amazon S3 Transfer Acceleration is a bucket-level feature that enables faster data transfers to and from Amazon S3
- AWS Lambda lets you run code without provisioning or managing servers

**References:**

https://digitalcloud.training/certification-training/aws-certified-cloud-practitioner/additional-aws-services-tools/

https://digitalcloud.training/certification-training/aws-solutions-architect-associate/networking-and-content-delivery/amazon-api-gateway/

## 41. Question

Which of the options below are recommendations in the reliability pillar of the well-architected framework? (choose 2)

1. Use ad-hoc recovery procedures
2. Automatically recover from failure
3. Scale vertically to increase aggregate system availability
4. Manage change in automation
5. Attempt to accurately estimate capacity requirements

**Answer: 2,4**

**Explanation:**

- The reliability pillar includes the ability of a system to recover from infrastructure or service disruptions, dynamically acquire computing resources to meet demand, and mitigate disruptions such as misconfigurations or transient network issues
- There are five design principles for reliability in the cloud:
    - Test recovery procedures
    - Automatically recover from failure
    - Scale horizontally to increase aggregate system availability
    - Stop guessing capacity
    - Manage change in automation

**References:**

https://aws.amazon.com/blogs/apn/the-5-pillars-of-the-aws-well-architected-framework/

https://digitalcloud.training/certification-training/aws-certified-cloud-practitioner/architecting-for-the-cloud/

## 42. Question

**What are the advantages of Availability Zones? (choose 2)**

1. They are connected by low-latency network connections
2. They enable the caching of data for faster delivery to end users
3. They allow regional disaster recovery
4. They provide fault isolation
5. They enable you to connect your on-premises networks to AWS to form a hybrid cloud

**Answer: 1,4**

**Explanation:**

- Each AWS region contains multiple distinct locations called Availability Zones (AZs). Each AZ is engineered to be isolated from failures in other AZs. An AZ is a data center, and in some cases, an AZ consists of multiple data centers. AZs within a region provide inexpensive, low-latency network connectivity to other zones in the same region. This allows you to replicate your data across data centers in a synchronous manner so that failover can be automated and be transparent for your users
- An AZ enables fault tolerance and high availability for your applications within a region not across regions
- CloudFront is the technology that is used to enable caching of data for faster delivery to end users
- Direct Connect is the technology that is used to connect your on-premises network to AWS to form a hybrid cloud

**References:**

https://digitalcloud.training/certification-training/aws-certified-cloud-practitioner/architecting-for-the-cloud/

## 43. Question

**Which statement best describes Amazon Route 53?**

1. Amazon Route 53 is a service that enables routing within VPCs in an account
2. Amazon Route 53 is a highly available and scalable Domain Name System (DNS) service
3. Amazon Route 53 enables hybrid cloud models by extending an organization's on-premise networks into the AWS cloud
4. Amazon Route 53 is a service for distributing incoming connections between a fleet of registered EC2 instances

**Answer: 2**

**Explanation:**

- Amazon Route 53 is a highly available and scalable Domain Name System (DNS) service
- The VPC router performs routing within a VPC
- Direct Connect enables hybrid cloud models by extending an organization's on-premise networks into the AWS cloud
- Auto Scaling is a service for distributing incoming connections between a fleet of registered EC2 instances

**References:**

https://digitalcloud.training/certification-training/aws-certified-cloud-practitioner/content-delivery-and-dns-services/

https://digitalcloud.training/certification-training/aws-solutions-architect-associate/networking-and-content-delivery/amazon-route-53/

## 44. Question

**Your CTO wants to move to cloud. What cost advantages are there to moving to cloud?**

1. You get free data transfer into and out of the cloud
2. You don't need to pay for application licensing
3. You can reduce your marketing costs
4. You provision only what you need and adjust to peak load

Answer: 4

**Explanation:**

- One of the best benefits of cloud is that you can launch what you need to and automatically adjust your resources as demand changes. This means you only ever pay for what you're using.
- You don't reduce marketing costs when moving to the cloud, your organization still needs to do the same amount of marketing.
- It is not true that you don't need to pay for application licensing in the cloud. You still pay for your application licenses when running on Amazon EC2.
- You do not get free bi-directional data transfer into and out of the cloud. AWS charge for outbound data transfer.

**References:**

https://digitalcloud.training/certification-training/aws-certified-cloud-practitioner/aws-billing-and-pricing/

https://aws.amazon.com/pricing/

## 45. Question

**How is data protected by default in Amazon S3?**

1. Buckets are replicated across all regions
2. Objects are redundantly stored on multiple devices across multiple facilities within a region
3. Objects are redundantly stored on multiple devices across multiple facilities across all regions
4. Objects are copied across at least two Availability Zones per region

Answer: 2

**Explanation:**

- Amazon S3 provides a highly durable storage infrastructure designed for mission-critical and primary data storage. Objects are redundantly stored on multiple devices across multiple facilities in an Amazon S3 region
- Amazon does not specify how data is replicated across AZs, they use the term facilities instead

**References:**

https://digitalcloud.training/certification-training/aws-certified-cloud-practitioner/aws-storage/

https://docs.aws.amazon.com/AmazonS3/latest/dev/DataDurability.html

## 46. Question

**Which of the below AWS services supports automated backups as a default configuration?**

1. Amazon EBS
2. Amazon S3
3. Amazon RDS
4. Amazon EC2

**Answer: 3**

**Explanation:**

- RDS automated backups allow point in time recovery to any point within the retention period down to a second. When automated backups are turned on for your DB Instance, Amazon RDS automatically performs a full daily snapshot of your data (during your preferred backup window) and captures transaction logs (as updates to your DB Instance are made). Automated backups are enabled by default and data is stored on S3 and is equal to the size of the DB
- EC2 instances using EBS volumes can be backed up by creating a snapshot of the EBS volume
- Amazon S3 objects are replicated across multiple facilities. You can also archive data onto Amazon Glacier and use versioning to maintain copies of older versions of objects

**References:**

https://digitalcloud.training/certification-training/aws-certified-cloud-practitioner/aws-databases/

https://digitalcloud.training/certification-training/aws-solutions-architect-associate/database/amazon-rds/

## 47. Question

**Which AWS tools can be used for automation? (choose 2)**

1. AWS CloudFormation
2. Elastic Load Balancing
3. AWS Lambda
4. Amazon Elastic File System (EFS)
5. AWS Elastic Beanstalk

**Answer: 1,5**

**Explanation:**

- AWS Elastic Beanstalk and AWS CloudFormation are both examples of automation. Beanstalk is a platform service that leverages the automation capabilities of CloudFormation to build out application architectures.
- Elastic Load Balancing (ELB) is used for distributing incoming connections to Amazon EC2 instances. This is not an example of automation; it is load balancing.
- Amazon EFS is a file system.
- AWS Lambda is a compute service, not an automation service.

References:

https://aws.amazon.com/elasticbeanstalk/

https://aws.amazon.com/cloudformation/

## 48. Question

Which of the below is an example of an architectural benefit of moving to the cloud?

1. Proprietary hardware
2. Monolithic services
3. Elasticity
4. Vertical scalability

Answer: 3

Explanation:

- A key architectural benefit of moving to the cloud is that you get elasticity. This means your applications can scale as demand increases and scale back as demand decreases. This reduces cost as you only pay for what you use, when you need it.
- Monolithic services are not a design patter of the public cloud. Developers and architects prefer service oriented or micro-service architectures instead.
- You do not get to choose your hardware in AWS as the infrastructure on which your services run is managed and operated by AWS. So, you cannot use proprietary hardware.
- Vertical scalability is not unique to the cloud, nor is it something we aspire to as architects. Most of the time horizontal scalability is preferred and is something that the AWS cloud provides for many services.

References:

https://digitalcloud.training/certification-training/aws-certified-cloud-practitioner/architecting-for-the-cloud/

## 49. Question

When using Amazon IAM, what authentication methods are available to use? (choose 2)

1. Amazon KMS
2. Access keys
3. AES 256
4. Client certificates
5. Server certificates

Answer: 2,5

Explanation:

- Supported authentication methods include console passwords, access keys and server certificates
- Access keys are a combination of an access key ID and a secret access key and can be used to make programmatic calls to AWS
- Server certificates are SSL/TLS certificates that you can use to authenticate with some AWS services

- Client certificates are not a valid IAM authentication method
- Amazon Key Management Service (KMS) is used for managing encryption keys and is not used for authentication
- AES 256 is an encryption algorithm, not an authentication method

**References:**

https://digitalcloud.training/certification-training/aws-certified-cloud-practitioner/identity-and-access-management/

## 50. Question

**Under the AWS shared responsibility model what is AWS responsible for? (choose 2)**

1. Replacement and disposal of disk drives
2. Encryption of customer data
3. Configuration of security groups
4. Patch management of operating systems
5. Physical security of the data center

**Answer: 1,5**

**Explanation:**

- AWS are responsible for "Security of the Cloud"
- Customers are responsible for "Security in the Cloud"
- AWS are responsible for items such as the physical security of the DC, replacement of old disk drives, and patch management of the infrastructure
- Customers are responsible for items such as configuring security groups, network ACLs, patching their operating systems and encrypting their data

**References:**

https://digitalcloud.training/certification-training/aws-certified-cloud-practitioner/aws-shared-responsibility-model/

## 51. Question

**Which feature enables fast, easy, and secure transfers of files over long distances between a client and an Amazon S3 bucket?**

1. S3 Static Websites
2. S3 Copy
3. Multipart Upload
4. S3 Transfer Acceleration

**Answer: 4,**

**Explanation:**

- Amazon S3 Transfer Acceleration enables fast, easy, and secure transfers of files over long distances between your client and your Amazon S3 bucket. S3 Transfer Acceleration leverages Amazon CloudFront's globally distributed AWS Edge Locations

- With S3 copy you can create a copy of objects up to 5GB in size in a single atomic operation
- Multipart upload can be used to speed up uploads to S3
- S3 can also be used to host static websites

**References:**

https://digitalcloud.training/certification-training/aws-certified-cloud-practitioner/aws-storage/


## 52. Question

**Which of the options below are recommendations in the cost optimization pillar of the well-architected framework? (choose 2)**

1. Adopt a capital expenditure model
2. Adopt a consumption model
3. Start spending money on data center operations
4. Manage your services independently
5. Analyze and attribute expenditure

**Answer: 2,5**

**Explanation:**

- The cost optimization pillar includes the ability to avoid or eliminate unneeded cost or suboptimal resource
- There are five design principles for cost optimization in the cloud:
    - Adopt a consumption model
    - Measure overall efficiency
    - Stop spending money on data center operations
    - Analyze and attribute expenditure
    - Use managed services to reduce cost of ownership

**References:**

https://aws.amazon.com/blogs/apn/the-5-pillars-of-the-aws-well-architected-framework/

https://digitalcloud.training/certification-training/aws-certified-cloud-practitioner/architecting-for-the-cloud/


## 53. Question

**What is a specific benefit of an Enterprise Support plan?**

1. Included Cloud Support Associate
2. Included Technical Support Manager
3. Included AWS Solutions Architect
4. Included Technical Account Manager

**Answer: 4**

**Explanation:**

- Only the Enterprise Support plan gets a Technical Account Manager (TAM).
- You do not get an AWS Solutions Architect with any plan.

- Cloud Support Associates are provided in the Developer plan.
- There's no such thing as a Technical Support Manager in the AWS support plans.

**References:**

https://digitalcloud.training/certification-training/aws-certified-cloud-practitioner/aws-billing-and-pricing/

## 54. Question

**What advantages do NAT Gateways have over NAT Instances? (choose 2)**

1. Can be scaled up manually
2. Managed for you by AWS
3. Highly available within each AZ
4. Can be used as a bastion host
5. Can be assigned to security groups

**Answer: 2,3**

**Explanation:**

- NAT gateways are managed for you by AWS. NAT gateways are highly available in each AZ into which they are deployed. They are not associated with any security groups and can scale automatically up to 45Gbps
- NAT instances are managed by AWS. They must be scaled manually and do not provide HA. NAT Instances can be used as bastion hosts and can be assigned to security groups

**References:**

https://digitalcloud.training/certification-training/aws-certified-cloud-practitioner/aws-networking/

## 55. Question

**What is the best way to apply an organizational system to EC2 instances so they can be identified by descriptors such as purpose or department?**

1. Apply tags
2. Use the instance meta-data
3. Use descriptive hostnames
4. Organize the instances into separate subnets

**Answer: 1**

**Explanation:**

- To help you manage your instances, images, and other Amazon EC2 resources, you can optionally assign your own metadata to each resource in the form of a tag which is a label that you assign to an AWS resource. Each tag consists of a key and an optional value, both of which you define. Tags enable you to categorize your AWS resources in different ways, for example, by purpose, owner, or environment
- Using descriptive hostnames or organizing instances into separate subnets is a messy way to try and organize resources and lacks the power and flexibility of tagging

- Storing information in instance meta-data is possible but you need to retrieve the information, tags enable you to do this more easily

**References:**

https://docs.aws.amazon.com/AWSEC2/latest/UserGuide/Using_Tags.html

## 56. Question

**Which authentication method is used to authenticate programmatic calls to AWS services?**

1. Console password
2. Key pair
3. Server certificate
4. Access keys

**Answer: 4**

**Explanation:**

- Access keys are a combination of an access key ID and a secret access key. They are used to make programmatic calls to AWS using the API.
- Console passwords are used for signing users into the AWS Management Console, not for making programmatic calls to AWS services.
- Server certificates can be used to authenticate to some AWS services using HTTPS/
- Key pairs should not be confused with access keys. Key pairs are used for authenticating to Amazon EC2 instances.

**References:**

https://digitalcloud.training/certification-training/aws-certified-cloud-practitioner/identity-and-access-management/

https://docs.aws.amazon.com/IAM/latest/UserGuide/id_credentials_access-keys.html

## 57. Question

**What is a benefit of moving an on-premises database to Amazon Relational Database Service (RDS)?**

1. There is no need to manage operating systems
2. You can scale vertically without downtime
3. There is no database administration required
4. You can run any database engine

**Answer: 1**

**Explanation:**

- With Amazon RDS, which is a managed service, you do not need to manage operating systems. This reduces operational costs.
- You cannot scale vertically without downtime. When scaling with RDS you must change the instance type, and this requires a short period of downtime while the instances' operating system reboots.

- There is still database administration required in the cloud. You don't manage the underlying operating system but still need to manage your own tables and data within the DB.
- You cannot run any database engine with RDS. The options are MySQL, Microsoft SQL, MariaDB, Oracle, PostgreSQL and Aurora.

**References:**

https://digitalcloud.training/certification-training/aws-certified-cloud-practitioner/aws-databases/

https://aws.amazon.com/rds/features/

## 58. Question

To ensure the security of your AWS account, what are two AWS best practices for managing access keys? (choose 2)

1. Don't generate an access key for the root account user
2. Where possible, use IAM roles with temporary security credentials
3. Don't create any access keys, use IAM roles instead
4. Rotate access keys daily
5. Use MFA for access keys

**Answer: 1,2**

**Explanation:**

- Best practices include:
    - Don't generate an access key for the root account user
    - Use Temporary Security Credentials (IAM Roles) Instead of Long-Term Access Keys
    - Manage IAM User Access Keys Properly
- Rotating access keys is a recommended practice, but doing it daily would be excessive and hard to manage
- You can use MFA for securing privileged accounts, but it does not secure access keys
- You should use IAM roles where possible, but AWS do not recommend that you don't create any access keys as they also have a purpose

**References:**

https://digitalcloud.training/certification-training/aws-certified-cloud-practitioner/identity-and-access-management/

https://docs.aws.amazon.com/general/latest/gr/aws-access-keys-best-practices.html

## 59. Question

How does the consolidated billing feature of AWS Organizations treat Reserved Instances that were purchased by another account in the organization?

1. All accounts in the organization are treated as one account so any account can receive the hourly cost benefit
2. Only the master account can benefit from the hourly cost benefit of the reserved instances
3. AWS Organizations does not support any volume or reserved instance benefits across accounts, it is just a method of aggregating bills
4. All accounts in the organization are treated as one account for volume discounts but not for reserved instances

Answer: 1

Explanation:
- For billing purposes, the consolidated billing feature of AWS Organizations treats all the accounts in the organization as one account. This means that all accounts in the organization can receive the hourly cost benefit of Reserved Instances that are purchased by any other account

References:

https://docs.aws.amazon.com/awsaccountbilling/latest/aboutv2/ri-behavior.html


## 60. Question

Which database allows you to scale at the push of a button without incurring any downtime?

1. Amazon RDS
2. Amazon EMR
3. Amazon DynamoDB
4. Amazon RedShift


Answer: 3

Explanation:
- Amazon Dynamo DB is a fully managed NoSQL database service that provides fast and predictable performance with seamless scalability. Push button scaling means that you can scale the DB at any time without incurring downtime
- All other databases are based on EC2 instances and therefore you must increase the instance size to scale which will incur downtime

References:

https://digitalcloud.training/certification-training/aws-certified-cloud-practitioner/aws-databases/

https://digitalcloud.training/certification-training/aws-solutions-architect-associate/database/amazon-dynamodb/


## 61. Question

When using AWS Organizations with consolidated billing what are two valid best practices? (choose 2)

1. Never exceed the limit of 20 linked accounts
2. Always enable multi-factor authentication (MFA) on the root account
3. Always use a straightforward password on the root account
4. The paying account should be used for billing purposes only
5. Use the paying account for deploying resources


Answer: 2,4

Explanation:
- Best practices include:
    - Always enable multi-factor authentication (MFA) on the root account

- Always use a strong and complex password on the root account
- The Paying account should be used for billing purposes only. Do not deploy resources into the Paying account
• There is a default limit of 20 linked accounts but this can be extended and there is no reason why you should stick to a maximum of 20 accounts

**References:**

https://digitalcloud.training/certification-training/aws-certified-cloud-practitioner/aws-billing-and-pricing/

## 62. Question

**Which AWS services are associated with Edge Locations? (choose 2)**

1. AWS Config
2. Amazon EBS
3. Amazon CloudFront
4. AWS Shield
5. AWS Direct Connect

**Answer: 3,4**

**Explanation:**

- Edge Locations are parts of the Amazon CloudFront content delivery network (CDN) that are all around the world and are used to get content closer to end-users for better performance. AWS Shield which protects against Distributed Denial of Service (DDoS) attacks is available globally on Amazon CloudFront Edge Locations.
- AWS Direct Connect is a networking service used for creating a hybrid cloud between on-premises and AWS Cloud using a private network connection.
- Amazon EBS is a storage service.
- AWS Config is used for evaluating the configuration state of AWS resources.

**References:**

https://aws.amazon.com/shield/

https://aws.amazon.com/cloudfront/

https://digitalcloud.training/certification-training/aws-certified-cloud-practitioner/content-delivery-and-dns-services/

## 63. Question

**Which of the options below are recommendations in the performance efficiency pillar of the well-architected framework? (choose 2)**

1. Go global in days
2. Rarely experiment
3. Democratize advanced technologies
4. Mechanical complexity
5. Use serverless architectures

Answer: 3,5

Explanation:

- The performance efficiency pillar includes the ability to use computing resources efficiently to meet system requirements and to maintain that efficiency as demand changes and technologies evolve
- There are five design principles for performance efficiency in the cloud:
    - Democratize advanced technologies
    - Go global in minutes
    - Use serverless architectures
    - Experiment more often
    - Mechanical sympathy

References:

https://aws.amazon.com/blogs/apn/the-5-pillars-of-the-aws-well-architected-framework/

https://digitalcloud.training/certification-training/aws-certified-cloud-practitioner/architecting-for-the-cloud/

## 64. Question

**What are Edge locations used for?**

1. They are used by regions for inter-region connectivity
2. They are the public-facing APIs for Amazon S3
3. They host a CDN called CloudFront
4. They are used for terminating VPN connections

Answer: 3

Explanation:

- An edge location is used by CloudFront as is the location where content is cached (separate to AWS regions/AZs). Requests are automatically routed to the nearest edge location. Edge locations are not tied to Availability Zones or regions

References:

https://digitalcloud.training/certification-training/aws-certified-cloud-practitioner/content-delivery-and-dns-services/

## 65. Question

**You need to run a production process that will use several EC2 instances and run constantly on an ongoing basis. The process cannot be interrupted or restarted without issue. What EC2 pricing model would be best for this workload?**

1. Reserved instances
2. Spot instances
3. Flexible instances
4. On-demand instances

**Answer: 1**

**Explanation:**

- RIs provide you with a significant discount (up to 75%) compared to On-Demand instance pricing
- You have the flexibility to change families, OS types, and tenancies while benefitting from RI pricing when you use Convertible RIs
- In this scenario for a stable process that will run constantly on an ongoing basis RIs will be the most affordable solution

**References:**

https://aws.amazon.com/ec2/pricing/reserved-instances/

https://digitalcloud.training/certification-training/aws-certified-cloud-practitioner/aws-billing-and-pricing/

# SET 4: PRACTICE QUESTIONS ONLY

### 1. Question
Which statement is true in relation to data stored within an AWS Region?

1. Data is automatically archived after 90 days
2. Data is always automatically replicated to at least one other availability zone
3. Data is not replicated outside of a region unless you configure it
4. Data is always replicated to another region

### 2. Question
What are the fundamental charges for an Amazon EC2 instance? (choose 2)

1. Basic monitoring
2. Server uptime
3. Data storage
4. Private IP address
5. AMI

### 3. Question
When using Amazon RDS databases, which items are you charged for? (choose 2)

1. Inbound data transfer
2. Multi AZ
3. Backup up to the DB size
4. Outbound data transfer
5. Single AZ

### 4. Question
Which of the following is an advantage of cloud computing compared to deploying your own infrastructure on-premise?

1. Flexibility to choose your own hardware
2. Ability to choose bespoke infrastructure configurations
3. Paying only for what you use
4. Spend using a CAPEX model

### 5. Question
What is the main benefit of the principle of "loose coupling"?

1. Reduce operational complexity
2. Reduce interdependencies so a failure in one component does not cascade to other components
3. Automate the deployment of infrastructure using code
4. Enables applications to scale automatically based on current demand

### 6. Question

Where can resources be launched when configuring AWS Auto Scaling?

1. Multiple VPCs
2. Multiple AZs and multiple regions
3. Multiple AZs within a region
4. A single subnet

### 7. Question

When performing a total cost of ownership (TCO) analysis between on-premises and the AWS Cloud, which factors are only relevant to on-premises deployments? (choose 2)

1. Hardware procurement teams
2. Database administration
3. Application licensing
4. Operating system licensing
5. Facility operations costs

### 8. Question

What are two examples of the advantages of cloud computing? (choose 2)

1. Trade operating costs for capital costs
2. Benefit from massive economies of scale
3. Increase speed and agility
4. Secure data centers
5. Trade variable expense for capital expense

### 9. Question

Which Amazon EC2 feature provides a static IPv4 public IP address that does not change when the instance is rebooted?

1. Elastic IP
2. Dynamic IP
3. Elastic Network
4. Static IP

### 10. Question

Which of the following are architectural best practices for the AWS Cloud? (choose 2)

1. Deploy into multiple Availability Zones
2. Design for fault tolerance
3. Create monolithic architectures
4. Deploy into a single availability zone
5. Close coupling

## 11. Question

Which tool can be used to provide real time guidance on provisioning resources following AWS best practices?

1. AWS Trusted Advisor
2. AWS Simple Monthly Calculator
3. AWS Personal Health Dashboard
4. AWS Inspector

## 12. Question

Which Amazon EC2 pricing option provides significant discounts for fixed term contracts?

1. Reserved Instances
2. Dedicated Instances
3. Dedicated Hosts
4. Spot Instances

## 13. Question

What do Amazon S3 objects consist of? (choose 2)

1. Key
2. Userdata
3. Value
4. ARN
5. AMI

## 14. Question

Which of the following is an architectural best practice recommended by AWS?

1. Design for success
2. Use manual operational processes
3. Think servers, not services
4. Design for failure

## 15. Question

Which Amazon RDS deployment type is best used to enable fault tolerance in the event of the failure of an availability zone?

1. Multiple Availability Zones
2. Write Replicas
3. Multiple Regions
4. Read Replicas

## 16. Question

Which service can be used to manage configuration versions?

1. AWS Service Catalog

2. AWS Artifact
3. AWS Config
4. Amazon Inspector

## 17. Question

**How does "elasticity" benefit an application design?**

1. By selecting the correct storage tier for your workload
2. By reserving capacity to reduce cost
3. By reducing interdependencies between application components
4. By automatically scaling resources based on demand

## 18. Question

**What are two components of Amazon S3? (choose 2)**

1. Buckets
2. Directories
3. Block devices
4. Objects
5. File systems

## 19. Question

**What is the benefit of using fully managed services compared to deploying 3rd party software on EC2?**

1. You have greater control and flexibility
2. Reduced operational overhead
3. Improved security
4. You don't need to back-up your data

## 20. Question

**Which of the advantages of cloud listed below is most closely addressed by the capabilities of AWS Auto Scaling?**

1. Benefit from massive economies of scale
2. Go global in minutes
3. Stop guessing about capacity
4. Stop spending money running and maintaining data centers

## 21. Question

**Which AWS service allows you to automate the evaluation of recorded configurations against desired configuration?**

1. AWS OpsWorks
2. AWS Service Catalog
3. AWS Config
4. AWS CloudFormation

## 22. Question
Which of the below are components that can be configured in the VPC section of the AWS management console? (choose 2)

1. Elastic Load Balancer
2. EBS volumes
3. Subnet
4. DNS records
5. Endpoints


## 23. Question
Which of the following is a benefit of moving to the AWS Cloud?

1. Pay for what you use
2. Outsource all IT operations
3. Capital purchases
4. Long term commitments


## 24. Question
Which Amazon namespace is used to uniquely identify AWS resources?

1. AMI
2. API
3. ARN
4. ACL


## 25. Question
Which service can be used to assign a policy to a group?

1. AWS Shield
2. Amazon STS
3. Amazon Cognito
4. AWS IAM


## 26. Question
The AWS acceptable use policy for penetration testing allows?

1. Authorized security assessors to perform penetration tests against any AWS customer without authorization
2. AWS to perform penetration testing against customer resources without notification
3. Customers to carry out security assessments or penetration tests against their AWS infrastructure after obtaining authorization from AWS
4. Customers to carry out security assessments or penetration tests against their AWS infrastructure without prior approval for selected services

## 27. Question

Which type of connection should be used to connect an on-premises data center with the AWS cloud that is high speed, low latency and does not use the Internet?

1. VPC Endpoints
2. IPSec VPN
3. AWS Managed VPN
4. Direct Connect

## 28. Question

An organization has multiple AWS accounts and uses a mixture of on-demand and reserved instances. One account has a considerable amount of unused reserved instances. How can the organization reduce their costs? (choose 2)

1. Redeem their reserved instances
2. Switch to using placement groups
3. Create an AWS Organization configuration linking the accounts
4. Use Spot instances instead
5. Setup consolidated billing between the accounts

## 29. Question

Which feature of AWS IAM enables you to identify unnecessary permissions that have been assigned to users?

1. Role Advisor
2. Group Advisor
3. Access Advisor
4. Permissions Advisor

## 30. Question

Which Amazon EC2 billing option gives you low cost, maximum flexibility, no upfront costs or commitment, and you only pay for what you use?

1. On-Demand Instances
2. Reserved Instances
3. Spot Instances
4. Dedicated Host

## 31. Question

What is the scope of an Amazon Virtual Private Cloud (VPC)?

1. It spans multiple subnets
2. It spans a single CIDR block
3. It spans all Availability Zones within a region
4. It spans all Availability Zones in all regions

## 32. Question

You would like to collect custom metrics from a production application every 1 minute. What type of monitoring should you use?

1. CloudWatch with detailed monitoring
2. CloudWatch with basic monitoring
3. CloudTrail with basic monitoring
4. CloudTrail with detailed monitoring

## 33. Question

To reduce the price of your Amazon EC2 instances, which term lengths are available for reserved instances? (choose 2)

1. 1 year
2. 2 years
3. 3 years
4. 4 years
5. 5 years

## 34. Question

Which Compute service should be used for running a Linux operating system upon which you will install custom software?

1. Amazon EC2
2. AWS Lambda
3. Amazon EKS
4. Amazon ECS

## 35. Question

Which of the following security related activities are AWS customers responsible for? (choose 2)

1. Installing patches on network devices
2. Installing patches on Windows operating systems
3. Secure disposal of faulty disk drives
4. Implementing data center access controls
5. Implementing IAM password policies

## 36. Question

Your organization is looking to expand into the cloud for their web presence and development and test environments. Production systems will remain on-premises. What cloud computing deployment model will best suit the organization?

1. PaaS
2. Hybrid
3. Public
4. Private

### 37. Question

**What does an organization need to do to move to another AWS region?**

1. Just start deploying resources in the additional region
2. Submit an application to extend their account to the additional region
3. Create a separate IAM account for that region
4. Apply for another AWS account in that region


### 38. Question

**Which of the following need to be included in a total cost of ownership (TCO) analysis? (choose 2)**

1. Facility equipment installation
2. IT Manager salary
3. Application development
4. Company-wide marketing
5. Data center security costs


### 39. Question

**Which of the below are good use cases for a specific Amazon EC2 pricing model? (choose 2)**

1. Spot for consistent load over a long term
2. On-demand for ad-hoc requirements that cannot be interrupted
3. Reserved instances for applications with flexible start and end times
4. Reserved instances for steady state predictable usage
5. On-demand for regulatory requirements that do not allow multi-tenant virtualization


### 40. Question

**Which AWS service lets you add user sign up, sign-in and access control to web and mobile apps?**

1. AWS Directory Service
2. AWS Cognito
3. AWS Artifact
4. AWS CloudHSM


### 41. Question

**How are AWS Lambda functions triggered?**

1. Metrics
2. Schedules
3. Counters
4. Events


### 42. Question

**What types of monitoring can Amazon CloudWatch be used for? (choose 2)**

1. Infrastructure
2. Operational health

3. Application performance
4. API access
5. Data center

## 43. Question

**What billing timeframes are available for Amazon EC2 on-demand instances? (choose 2)**

1. Per second
2. Per minute
3. Per hour
4. Per day
5. Per week

## 44. Question

**Which aspects of security on AWS are customer responsibilities? (choose 2)**

1. Availability of AWS regions
2. Physical access controls
3. Setting up account password policies
4. Patching of storage systems
5. Server-side encryption

## 45. Question

**Which service can be added to a database to provide improved performance for some requests?**

1. Amazon RedShift
2. Amazon EFS
3. Amazon ElastiCache
4. Amazon RDS

## 46. Question

**Which AWS service uses a highly secure hardware storage device to store encryption keys?**

1. Amazon Cloud Directory
2. AWS WAF
3. AWS IAM
4. AWS CloudHSM

## 47. Question

**Which statement is correct in relation to the AWS Shared Responsibility Model?**

1. Customers are responsible for security of the cloud
2. AWS are responsible for encrypting customer data
3. AWS are responsible for the security of regions and availability zones
4. Customers are responsible for patching storage systems

## 48. Question

Which service can be used to improve performance for users around the world?

1. AWS LightSail
2. Amazon CloudFront
3. Amazon ElastiCache
4. Amazon Connect

## 49. Question

Which type of security control can be used to deny network access from a specific IP address?

1. Security Group
2. AWS Shield
3. Network ACL
4. AWS WAF

## 50. Question

Which AWS service enables hybrid cloud storage between on-premises and the AWS Cloud?

1. Amazon CloudFront
2. AWS Storage Gateway
3. Amazon S3 Cross Region Replication (CRR)
4. Amazon Elastic File System (EFS)

## 51. Question

Which team is available to support AWS customers on an Enterprise support plan with account issues?

1. AWS Technical Account Manager
2. AWS Concierge
3. AWS Billing and Accounts
4. AWS Technical Support

## 52. Question

Which type of AWS Storage Gateway can be used to backup data with popular backup software?

1. File Gateway
2. Volume Gateway
3. Gateway Virtual Tape Library
4. Backup Gateway

## 53. Question

Which security service only requires a rule to be created in one direction as it automatically allows return traffic?

1. Network ACL
2. VPC Router
3. Security Group

4. AWS Shield

## 54. Question
**What is the difference between an EBS volume and an Instance store?**

1. Instance store volumes can be used with all EC2 instance types whereas EBS cannot
2. EBS volumes are file-level storage devices whereas Instance store volumes are object-based
3. Instance store volumes are ephemeral whereas EBS volumes are persistent storage
4. EBS volumes are object storage devices whereas Instance store volume are block based

## 55. Question
**Which of the options below are recommendations in the reliability pillar of the well-architected framework? (choose 2)**

1. Stop guessing about capacity
2. Scale vertically using big systems
3. Manually recover from failure
4. Test recovery procedures
5. Manage change in manual processes

## 56. Question
**In addition to DNS services, what other services does Amazon Route 53 provide? (choose 2)**

1. DHCP
2. Traffic flow
3. Caching
4. Domain registration
5. IP Routing

## 57. Question
**What is the most cost-effective Amazon S3 storage tier for data that is not often accessed but requires high availability?**

1. Amazon S3 Standard-IA
2. Amazon Glacier
3. Amazon S3 Standard
4. Amazon S3 One Zone-IA

## 58. Question
**What does an organization need to do in Amazon IAM to enable user access to services being launched in new region?**

1. Nothing, IAM is global
2. Enable global mode in IAM to provision the required access
3. Create new user accounts in the new region
4. Update the user accounts to allow access from another region

### 59. Question

**Which types of root storage devices are available for Amazon EC2 instances? (choose 2)**

1. Instance Store
2. EBS volume
3. RAM
4. EFS file system
5. S3 Bucket


### 60. Question

**What are the fundamental charges for Elastic Block Store (EBS) volumes? (choose 2)**

1. Provisioned IOPS
2. The amount of data storage provisioned
3. Inbound data transfer
4. Number of snapshots
5. The amount of data storage consumed


### 61. Question

**What can be assigned to an IAM user? (choose 2)**

1. A password for access to the management console
2. A password for logging into Linux
3. An access key ID and secret access key
4. A key pair
5. An SSL/TLS certificate


### 62. Question

**An organization has an on-premises cloud and accesses their AWS Cloud over the Internet. How can they create a private hybrid cloud connection?**

1. AWS VPC Endpoint
2. AWS Managed VPN
3. AWS VPN CloudHub
4. AWS Direct Connect


### 63. Question

**Which AWS service provides a single location to track the progress of application migrations across multiple AWS and partner solutions?**

1. AWS Database Migration Service
2. AWS Batch
3. AWS Server Migration Service
4. AWS Migration Hub

## 64. Question

**Which read/write capacity modes are available for DynamoDB? (choose 2)**

1. Reserved capacity mode
2. On-demand capacity mode
3. Dedicated capacity mode
4. Spot capacity mode
5. Provisioned capacity mode

## 65. Question

**Which storage type can be mounted using the NFS protocol to many EC2 instances simultaneously?**

1. Amazon S3
2. Amazon EFS
3. Amazon EBS
4. Amazon Instance Store

# SET 4: PRACTICE QUESTIONS, ANSWERS & EXPLANATIONS

## 1. Question

Which statement is true in relation to data stored within an AWS Region?

1. Data is automatically archived after 90 days
2. Data is always automatically replicated to at least one other availability zone
3. Data is not replicated outside of a region unless you configure it
4. Data is always replicated to another region

Answer: 3

Explanation:

- Data stored within an AWS region is not replicated outside of that region automatically. It is up to customers of AWS to determine whether they want to replicate their data to other regions. You must always consider compliance and network latency when making this decision.
- Data is not automatically replicated to at least one availability zone – this is specific to each service and you must check how your data is stored and whether the availability and durability is acceptable.
- Data is never automatically archived. You must configure data to be archived.

References:

https://d1.awsstatic.com/whitepapers/Security/AWS_Security_Best_Practices.pdf

## 2. Question

What are the fundamental charges for an Amazon EC2 instance? (choose 2)

1. Basic monitoring
2. Server uptime
3. Data storage
4. Private IP address
5. AMI

Answer: 2,3

Explanation:

- When using EC2 instances you are charged for the compute uptime of the instance based on the family and type you chose. You are also charged for the amount of data provisioned.
- Basic monitoring is free for EC2, detailed monitoring is charged.
- Amazon Machine Images (AMIs) are not chargeable. You can purchase chargeable AMIs via the marketplace but you are not charged for any you create.
- You do not pay for private IP addresses.

References:

https://digitalcloud.training/certification-training/aws-certified-cloud-practitioner/aws-billing-and-pricing/

## 3. Question

**When using Amazon RDS databases, which items are you charged for? (choose 2)**

1. Inbound data transfer
2. Multi AZ
3. Backup up to the DB size
4. Outbound data transfer
5. Single AZ

Answer: 2,4

Explanation:

- With Amazon RDS you are charged for the type and size of database, the uptime, any additional storage of backup (above the DB size), requests, deployment type (e.g. you pay for multi AZ), and data transfer outbound

References:

https://digitalcloud.training/certification-training/aws-certified-cloud-practitioner/aws-billing-and-pricing/

## 4. Question

**Which of the following is an advantage of cloud computing compared to deploying your own infrastructure on-premise?**

1. Flexibility to choose your own hardware
2. Ability to choose bespoke infrastructure configurations
3. Paying only for what you use
4. Spend using a CAPEX model

Answer: 3

Explanation:

- With AWS you only pay for what you use. However, you cannot choose your own hardware/infrastructure and the payment model is operational (OPEX) not capital (CAPEX)

References:

https://digitalcloud.training/certification-training/aws-certified-cloud-practitioner/cloud-computing-concepts/

## 5. Question

**What is the main benefit of the principle of "loose coupling"?**

1. Reduce operational complexity
2. Reduce interdependencies so a failure in one component does not cascade to other components
3. Automate the deployment of infrastructure using code
4. Enables applications to scale automatically based on current demand

Answer: 2

Explanation:

- As application complexity increases, a desirable attribute of an IT system is that it can be broken into smaller, loosely coupled components. This means that IT systems should be designed in a way that reduces interdependencies—a change or a failure in one component should not cascade to other components.
- Enabling an application to scale automatically based on current demand is an examples of Elasticity.
- Automating the deployment of infrastructure using code is an example of "Infrastructure as code" – services such as CloudFormation provide this functionality.
- Loose coupling does not reduce operational complexity. In fact, it may increase complexity as you have more services running and more interactions.

References:

https://digitalcloud.training/certification-training/aws-certified-cloud-practitioner/architecting-for-the-cloud/

## 6. Question

Where can resources be launched when configuring AWS Auto Scaling?

1. Multiple VPCs
2. Multiple AZs and multiple regions
3. Multiple AZs within a region
4. A single subnet

Answer: 3

Explanation:

- AWS Auto Scaling is configured within the EC2 console and can launch instances within a VPC across multiple AZs. It cannot launch resources into another region

References:

https://digitalcloud.training/certification-training/aws-certified-cloud-practitioner/elastic-load-balancing-and-auto-scaling/

## 7. Question

When performing a total cost of ownership (TCO) analysis between on-premises and the AWS Cloud, which factors are only relevant to on-premises deployments? (choose 2)

1. Hardware procurement teams
2. Database administration
3. Application licensing
4. Operating system licensing
5. Facility operations costs

Answer: 1,5

**Explanation:**

- Facility operations and hardware procurement costs are something you no longer need to pay for in the AWS Cloud. These factors therefore must be included as an on-premise cost so you can understand the cost of staying in your own data centers.
- Database administration, operating system licensing and application licensing will still be required in the AWS Cloud.

**References:**

https://media.amazonwebservices.com/AWS_TCO_Web_Applications.pdf


## 8. Question

**What are two examples of the advantages of cloud computing? (choose 2)**

1. Trade operating costs for capital costs
2. Benefit from massive economies of scale
3. Increase speed and agility
4. Secure data centers
5. Trade variable expense for capital expense

**Answer: 2,3**

**Explanation:**

- The 6 advantages of cloud AWS discuss are:
    - Trade capital expense for variable expense
    - Benefit from massive economies of scale
    - Stop guessing about capacity
    - Increase speed and agility
    - Stop spending money running and maintaining data centers
    - Go global in minutes
- Secure data centers are not a reason to move to the cloud. Your on-premises data centers should also be secure

**References:**

https://digitalcloud.training/certification-training/aws-certified-cloud-practitioner/cloud-computing-concepts/


## 9. Question

**Which Amazon EC2 feature provides a static IPv4 public IP address that does not change when the instance is rebooted?**

1. Elastic IP
2. Dynamic IP
3. Elastic Network
4. Static IP

**Answer: 1**

**Explanation:**

- An Elastic IP address is a static IPv4 address designed for dynamic cloud computing. An Elastic IP address is associated with your AWS account. Elastic IP addresses do not change when the instance is rebooted and can be moved between instances as required
- All other answers are bogus

**References:**

https://docs.aws.amazon.com/AWSEC2/latest/UserGuide/elastic-ip-addresses-eip.html

## 10. Question

**Which of the following are architectural best practices for the AWS Cloud? (choose 2)**

1. Deploy into multiple Availability Zones
2. Design for fault tolerance
3. Create monolithic architectures
4. Deploy into a single availability zone
5. Close coupling

**Answer: 1,2**

**Explanation:**

- It is an architectural best practice to deploy your resources into multiple availability zones and design for fault tolerance. These both ensure that if resources or infrastructure fails, your application continues to run.
- You should not create monolithic architectures. With monolithic architectures you have a single instance running multiple components of the application, if any of these components fails, your application fails. It is better to design microservices architectures where components are spread across more instances.
- You should not deploy all of your resources into a single availability zone as any infrastructure failure will take down access to your resources.
- Close coupling is not an architectural best practice – loose coupling is. With loose coupling you reduce interdependencies between components of an application and often put a middle layer such as a message bus between components.

**References:**

https://digitalcloud.training/certification-training/aws-certified-cloud-practitioner/architecting-for-the-cloud/

https://aws.amazon.com/architecture/well-architected/

## 11. Question

**Which tool can be used to provide real time guidance on provisioning resources following AWS best practices?**

1. AWS Trusted Advisor
2. AWS Simple Monthly Calculator
3. AWS Personal Health Dashboard
4. AWS Inspector

**Answer: 1**

**Explanation:**

- Trusted Advisor is an online resource that helps to reduce cost, increase performance and improve security by optimizing your AWS environment. Trusted Advisor provides real time guidance to help you provision your resources following best practices
- Inspector is an automated security assessment service that helps improve the security and compliance of applications deployed on AWS
- AWS Personal Health Dashboard provides alerts and remediation guidance when AWS is experiencing events that may impact you
- The AWS Simple Monthly Calculator helps you to estimate the cost of using AWS services

**References:**

https://digitalcloud.training/certification-training/aws-certified-cloud-practitioner/cloud-security/

## 12. Question

**Which Amazon EC2 pricing option provides significant discounts for fixed term contracts?**

1. Reserved Instances
2. Dedicated Instances
3. Dedicated Hosts
4. Spot Instances

**Answer: 1**

**Explanation:**

- Reserved instances provide significant discounts, up to 75% compared to On-Demand pricing, by paying for capacity ahead of time
- Spot Instances allow you to purchase spare computing capacity with no upfront commitment at discounted hourly rates
- Dedicated hosts are EC2 servers dedicated to a single customer
- Dedicated Instances are Amazon EC2 instances that run in a VPC on hardware that's dedicated to a single customer

**References:**

https://digitalcloud.training/certification-training/aws-certified-cloud-practitioner/aws-billing-and-pricing/

## 13. Question

**What do Amazon S3 objects consist of? (choose 2)**

1. Key
2. Userdata
3. Value
4. ARN
5. AMI

Answer: 1,3

Explanation:

- Amazon S3 objects consist of:
  - Key (name of the object)
  - Value (data made up of a sequence of bytes)
  - Version ID (used for versioning)
  - Metadata (data about the data that is stored)

References:

https://digitalcloud.training/certification-training/aws-certified-cloud-practitioner/aws-storage/

## 14. Question

**Which of the following is an architectural best practice recommended by AWS?**

1. Design for success
2. Use manual operational processes
3. Think servers, not services
4. Design for failure

Answer: 4

Explanation:

- It is recommended that you design for failure. This means always considering what would happen if a component of an application fails and ensuring there is resilience in the architecture.
- Design for success sounds good, but this is not an architectural best practice. As much as we want our applications to be successful, we should always be cognizant of the potential failures that might occur and ensure we are prepared for them.
- AWS do not recommend that you "think servers, not services". What they do recommend is that you "think services, not servers". This means that you should consider using managed services and serverless services rather than just using Amazon EC2.
- You should not use manual operational processes; this is not an architectural best practice. You should automate as much as possible in the cloud.

References:

https://digitalcloud.training/certification-training/aws-certified-cloud-practitioner/architecting-for-the-cloud/

## 15. Question

**Which Amazon RDS deployment type is best used to enable fault tolerance in the event of the failure of an availability zone?**

1. Multiple Availability Zones
2. Write Replicas
3. Multiple Regions
4. Read Replicas

Answer: 1

**Explanation:**
- Multi AZ provides a mechanism to failover the RDS database to another synchronously replicated copy in the event of the failure of an AZ.
- There is no option for multiple region failover of Amazon RDS.
- Read replicas are used for offloading read traffic from a primary database but cannot be used for writing. You can failover the DB by promoting a read replica in a DR situation but this is not the best answer as the multi-AZ feature is preferred.
- There is no such thing as write replicas.

**References:**

https://digitalcloud.training/certification-training/aws-certified-cloud-practitioner/aws-databases/

## 16. Question

Which service can be used to manage configuration versions?

1. AWS Service Catalog
2. AWS Artifact
3. AWS Config
4. Amazon Inspector

**Answer: 3**

**Explanation:**
- AWS Config is a fully-managed service that provides you with an AWS resource inventory, configuration history, and configuration change notifications to enable security and regulatory compliance.
- AWS Service Catalog is used to create and manage catalogs of IT services that you have approved for use on AWS, including virtual machine images, servers, software, and databases to complete multi-tier application architectures.
- AWS Artifact is your go-to, central resource for compliance-related information that matters to you. This service can be used to get compliance information related to AWS' certifications/attestations.
- Inspector is an automated security assessment service that helps improve the security and compliance of applications deployed on AWS.

**References:**

https://digitalcloud.training/certification-training/aws-certified-cloud-practitioner/cloud-security/

## 17. Question

How does "elasticity" benefit an application design?

1. By selecting the correct storage tier for your workload
2. By reserving capacity to reduce cost
3. By reducing interdependencies between application components
4. By automatically scaling resources based on demand

**Answer: 4**

**Explanation:**

- Elasticity refers to the automatic scaling of resources based on demand. The benefit is that you provision only the necessary resources at a given time (optimizing cost) and don't have to worry about absorbing spikes in demand.
- Elasticity does not reduce interdependencies between systems – this is known as loose coupling.
- Reserving capacity to reduce cost refers to using reservations such as EC2 Reserved Instances.
- Selecting the correct storage tier would be an example of right-sizing not elasticity.

**References:**

https://digitalcloud.training/certification-training/aws-certified-cloud-practitioner/architecting-for-the-cloud/

https://wa.aws.amazon.com/wat.concept.elasticity.en.html

## 18. Question

**What are two components of Amazon S3? (choose 2)**

1. Buckets
2. Directories
3. Block devices
4. Objects
5. File systems

**Answer: 1,4**

**Explanation:**

- Amazon S3 is an object-based storage system that is accessed using a RESTful API over HTTP(S). It consists of buckets, which are root level folders, and objects, which are the files, images etc. that you upload
- The terms directory, file system and block device do not apply to S3

**References:**

https://digitalcloud.training/certification-training/aws-certified-cloud-practitioner/aws-storage/

## 19. Question

**What is the benefit of using fully managed services compared to deploying 3rd party software on EC2?**

1. You have greater control and flexibility
2. Reduced operational overhead
3. Improved security
4. You don't need to back-up your data

**Answer: 2**

**Explanation:**

- Fully managed services reduce your operational overhead as AWS manage not just the infrastructure layer but the service layers above it. Examples are Amazon Aurora and Amazon ElastiCache where the database is managed for you.

- You do not have greater control and flexibility with fully managed services. AWS take more responsibility for providing the service and you therefore have fewer options. For example you may not be able to configure the performance parameters of a database as you'd like to or use your own backup or operational software.
- Security is not necessarily improved by managing your own software stack. AWS are extremely good at securing their services and there is arguably less chance that they will expose vulnerabilities than a customer who deploys their own applications.
- You do still need to backup your data. For instance, with Amazon ElastiCache it's up to you to configure backups to S3.

**References:**

https://digitalcloud.training/certification-training/aws-certified-cloud-practitioner/architecting-for-the-cloud/

## 20. Question

Which of the advantages of cloud listed below is most closely addressed by the capabilities of AWS Auto Scaling?

1. Benefit from massive economies of scale
2. Go global in minutes
3. Stop guessing about capacity
4. Stop spending money running and maintaining data centers

**Answer: 3**

**Explanation:**

- AWS Auto Scaling helps you to adapt to the demand for your application and scale up and down as needed. This means you don't have to guess capacity upfront as you can provision what you need and allows Auto Scaling to manage the scaling

**References:**

https://digitalcloud.training/certification-training/aws-certified-cloud-practitioner/cloud-computing-concepts/

## 21. Question

Which AWS service allows you to automate the evaluation of recorded configurations against desired configuration?

1. AWS OpsWorks
2. AWS Service Catalog
3. AWS Config
4. AWS CloudFormation

**Answer: 3**

**Explanation:**

- AWS Config is a service that enables you to assess, audit, and evaluate the configurations of your AWS resources. Config continuously monitors and records your AWS resource configurations and allows you to automate the evaluation of recorded configurations against desired configurations
- AWS OpsWorks is a configuration management service that provides managed instances of Chef and Puppet
- AWS Service Catalog allows organizations to create and manage catalogs of IT services that are approved for use on AWS
- AWS CloudFormation provides a common language for you to describe and provision all the infrastructure resources in your cloud environment

**References:**

https://digitalcloud.training/certification-training/aws-certified-cloud-practitioner/additional-aws-services-tools/


## 22. Question

**Which of the below are components that can be configured in the VPC section of the AWS management console? (choose 2)**

1. Elastic Load Balancer
2. EBS volumes
3. Subnet
4. DNS records
5. Endpoints

**Answer: 3,5**

**Explanation:**

- You can have configured subnets and endpoints within the VPC section of AWS management console
- EBS volumes and ELB must be configured in the EC2 section of the AWS management console
- DNS records must be configured in Amazon Route 53

**References:**

https://digitalcloud.training/certification-training/aws-solutions-architect-associate/networking-and-content-delivery/amazon-vpc/


## 23. Question

**Which of the following is a benefit of moving to the AWS Cloud?**

1. Pay for what you use
2. Outsource all IT operations
3. Capital purchases
4. Long term commitments

**Answer: 1**

**Explanation:**

- With the AWS cloud you pay for what you use. This is a significant advantage compared to on-premises infrastructure where you need to purchase more equipment than you need to allow for peak capacity. You also need to pay for that equipment up-front.
- You do not outsource all IT operations when moving to the AWS Cloud. AWS provide some higher-level managed services which reduces your operations effort but does not eliminate it.
- Capital purchases are not a benefit of moving to the cloud. The AWS Cloud is mostly an operational expenditure which is favored by many CFOs.
- You do not need to enter into long term commitments with the AWS Cloud. There are options for 1- or 3-year commitments to lower prices with some services but this is not an advantage of the cloud.

**References:**

https://digitalcloud.training/certification-training/aws-certified-cloud-practitioner/aws-billing-and-pricing/

https://aws.amazon.com/pricing/

## 24. Question

**Which Amazon namespace is used to uniquely identify AWS resources?**

1. AMI
2. API
3. ARN
4. ACL

**Answer: 3**

**Explanation:**

- Amazon Resource Names (ARNs) uniquely identify AWS resources. We require an ARN when you need to specify a resource unambiguously across all of AWS, such as in IAM policies, Amazon Relational Database Service (Amazon RDS) tags, and API calls
- An application programming interface (API) is a set of subroutine definitions, communication protocols, and tools for building software
- An Amazon Machine Image (AMI) provides the information required to launch an instance, which is a virtual server in the cloud
- Amazon S3 access control lists (ACLs) enable you to manage access to buckets and objects

**References:**

https://docs.aws.amazon.com/general/latest/gr/aws-arns-and-namespaces.html

## 25. Question

**Which service can be used to assign a policy to a group?**

1. AWS Shield
2. Amazon STS
3. Amazon Cognito
4. AWS IAM

Answer: 4

Explanation:

- IAM is used to securely control individual and group access to AWS resources. Groups are collections of users and have policies attached to them. You can use IAM to attach a policy to a group
- Amazon Cognito is used for authentication using mobile apps
- The AWS Security Token Service (STS) is a web service that enables you to request temporary, limited-privilege credentials for IAM users or for users that you authenticate (federated users)
- AWS Shield is a managed Distributed Denial of Service (DDoS) protection service that safeguards applications running on AWS

References:

https://digitalcloud.training/certification-training/aws-certified-cloud-practitioner/identity-and-access-management/

## 26. Question

The AWS acceptable use policy for penetration testing allows?

1. Authorized security assessors to perform penetration tests against any AWS customer without authorization
2. AWS to perform penetration testing against customer resources without notification
3. Customers to carry out security assessments or penetration tests against their AWS infrastructure after obtaining authorization from AWS
4. Customers to carry out security assessments or penetration tests against their AWS infrastructure without prior approval for selected services

Answer: 4

Explanation:

- AWS updated their policy and now allow AWS customers carry out security assessments or penetration tests against their AWS infrastructure without prior approval for 8 services.

References:

https://digitalcloud.training/certification-training/aws-certified-cloud-practitioner/cloud-security/

https://aws.amazon.com/security/penetration-testing/

## 27. Question

Which type of connection should be used to connect an on-premises data center with the AWS cloud that is high speed, low latency and does not use the Internet?

1. VPC Endpoints
2. IPSec VPN
3. AWS Managed VPN
4. Direct Connect

Answer: 4

**Explanation:**

- AWS Direct Connect is a network service that provides an alternative to using the Internet to connect a customer's on-premise sites to AWS. Data is transmitted through a private network connection between AWS and a customer's datacenter or corporate network. Direct Connect is high bandwidth, and low latency
- The AWS Managed VPN (which is a type of IPSec VPN) is fast to setup but uses the public Internet and therefore latency is not as good and is unpredictable
- VPC endpoint enable private connectivity to services hosted in AWS, from within your VPC without using an Internet Gateway, VPN, Network Address Translation (NAT) devices, or firewall proxies

**References:**

https://digitalcloud.training/certification-training/aws-certified-cloud-practitioner/aws-networking/


## 28. Question

An organization has multiple AWS accounts and uses a mixture of on-demand and reserved instances. One account has a considerable amount of unused reserved instances. How can the organization reduce their costs? (choose 2)

1. Redeem their reserved instances
2. Switch to using placement groups
3. Create an AWS Organization configuration linking the accounts
4. Use Spot instances instead
5. Setup consolidated billing between the accounts

**Answer: 3,5**

**Explanation:**

- AWS organizations allow you to consolidate multiple AWS accounts into an organization that you create and centrally manage. Unused reserved instances (RIs) for EC2 are applied across the group so the organization can utilize their unused reserved instance instead of consuming on-demand instances which will lower their costs
- You cannot redeem your reserved instances. You can sell them on the AWS marketplace however
- Using placement groups will not lower their costs
- Spot instance pricing is variable so it is not guaranteed to lower the cost and it is not suitable for workloads that cannot be unexpectedly terminated by AWS

**References:**

https://digitalcloud.training/certification-training/aws-certified-cloud-practitioner/aws-billing-and-pricing/


## 29. Question

Which feature of AWS IAM enables you to identify unnecessary permissions that have been assigned to users?

1. Role Advisor
2. Group Advisor
3. Access Advisor
4. Permissions Advisor

Answer: 3

Explanation:

- The IAM console provides information about when IAM users and roles last attempted to access AWS services. This information is called service last accessed data. This data can help you identify unnecessary permissions so that you can refine your IAM policies to better adhere to the principle of "least privilege." That means granting the minimum permissions required to perform a specific task. You can find the data on the Access Advisor tab in the IAM console by examining the detail view for any IAM user, group, role, or managed policy

References:

https://docs.aws.amazon.com/IAM/latest/UserGuide/access_policies_access-advisor.html

## 30. Question

Which Amazon EC2 billing option gives you low cost, maximum flexibility, no upfront costs or commitment, and you only pay for what you use?

1. On-Demand Instances
2. Reserved Instances
3. Spot Instances
4. Dedicated Host

Answer: 1

Explanation:

- With On-Demand instances you pay for hours used with no commitment. There are no upfront costs so you have maximum flexibility
- Spot instances are used for getting a very low price which you bid on. You lose some flexibility as you are constrained by market prices and your workloads can be terminated if the market price exceeds your bid price
- Reserved instances are based on a commitment to 1 or 3 years in exchange for a large discount
- Dedicated hosts use physically dedicated EC2 servers to isolate your workloads and are expensive

References:

https://digitalcloud.training/certification-training/aws-certified-cloud-practitioner/aws-compute/

https://digitalcloud.training/certification-training/aws-solutions-architect-associate/compute/amazon-ec2/

## 31. Question

What is the scope of an Amazon Virtual Private Cloud (VPC)?

1. It spans multiple subnets
2. It spans a single CIDR block
3. It spans all Availability Zones within a region
4. It spans all Availability Zones in all regions

Answer: 3

Explanation:

- A virtual private cloud (VPC) is a virtual network dedicated to your AWS account. A VPC spans all the Availability Zones in the region
- You can have multiple CIDR blocks in a VPC
- A VPC spans AZs, subnets are created within AZs

References:

https://digitalcloud.training/certification-training/aws-certified-cloud-practitioner/aws-networking/

## 32. Question

You would like to collect custom metrics from a production application every 1 minute. What type of monitoring should you use?

1. CloudWatch with detailed monitoring
2. CloudWatch with basic monitoring
3. CloudTrail with basic monitoring
4. CloudTrail with detailed monitoring

Answer: 1

Explanation:

- Amazon CloudWatch is a monitoring service for AWS cloud resources and the applications you run on AWS. CloudWatch is for performance monitoring (CloudTrail is for auditing). Used to collect and track metrics, collect and monitor log files, and set alarms. Basic monitoring collects metrics every 5 minutes whereas detailed monitoring collects metrics every 1 minute
- AWS CloudTrail is a web service that records activity made on your account and delivers log files to an Amazon S3 bucket. CloudTrail is for auditing (CloudWatch is for performance monitoring). CloudTrail is about logging and saves a history of API calls for your AWS account

References:

https://digitalcloud.training/certification-training/aws-certified-cloud-practitioner/monitoring-and-logging-services/

## 33. Question

To reduce the price of your Amazon EC2 instances, which term lengths are available for reserved instances? (choose 2)

1. 1 year
2. 2 years
3. 3 years
4. 4 years
5. 5 years

Answer: 1,3

Explanation:

- Reserved instances provide significant discounts, up to 75% compared to On-Demand pricing, by paying for capacity ahead of time. Good for applications that have predictable usage, that need reserved capacity, and for customers who can commit to a 1 or 3-year term

References:

https://digitalcloud.training/certification-training/aws-certified-cloud-practitioner/aws-billing-and-pricing/

## 34. Question

Which Compute service should be used for running a Linux operating system upon which you will install custom software?

1. Amazon EC2
2. AWS Lambda
3. Amazon EKS
4. Amazon ECS

Answer: 1

Explanation:

- Amazon EC2 should be used when you need access to a full operating system instance
- Amazon Elastic Container Service (ECS) and Amazon Elastic Container Service for Kubernetes (EKS) are used for running software containers, not full operating system instances
- AWS Lambda runs code as functions in response to events

References:

https://digitalcloud.training/certification-training/aws-certified-cloud-practitioner/aws-compute/

## 35. Question

Which of the following security related activities are AWS customers responsible for? (choose 2)

1. Installing patches on network devices
2. Installing patches on Windows operating systems
3. Secure disposal of faulty disk drives
4. Implementing data center access controls
5. Implementing IAM password policies

Answer: 2,5

Explanation:

- Customers are responsible for configuring their own IAM password policies and installing operating system patches on Amazon EC2 instances
- AWS are responsible for installing patches on physical hardware devices, data center access controls and secure disposal of disk drives

References:

https://digitalcloud.training/certification-training/aws-certified-cloud-practitioner/aws-shared-responsibility-model/

## 36. Question

Your organization is looking to expand into the cloud for their web presence and development and test environments. Production systems will remain on-premises. What cloud computing deployment model will best suit the organization?

1. PaaS
2. Hybrid
3. Public
4. Private

Answer: 2

Explanation:

- A hybrid cloud computing model includes services deployed in private clouds and public clouds. This model suits the businesses requirements
- Platform as a Service (PaaS) is a type of service offering rather than a cloud computing deployment model

References:

https://digitalcloud.training/certification-training/aws-certified-cloud-practitioner/cloud-computing-concepts/


## 37. Question

What does an organization need to do to move to another AWS region?

1. Just start deploying resources in the additional region
2. Submit an application to extend their account to the additional region
3. Create a separate IAM account for that region
4. Apply for another AWS account in that region

Answer: 1

Explanation:

- You don't need to do anything except start deploying resources in the new region. With the AWS cloud you can use any region around the world at any time. There is no need for a separate account, and IAM is a global service.

References:

https://digitalcloud.training/certification-training/aws-certified-cloud-practitioner/identity-and-access-management/

https://digitalcloud.training/certification-training/aws-certified-cloud-practitioner/aws-global-infrastructure/


## 38. Question

Which of the following need to be included in a total cost of ownership (TCO) analysis? (choose 2)

1. Facility equipment installation

2. IT Manager salary
3. Application development
4. Company-wide marketing
5. Data center security costs

**Answer: 1,5**

**Explanation:**

- To perform a TCO you need to document all of the costs you're incurring today to run your IT operations. That includes facilities equipment installation and data center security costs. That way you get to compare the full cost of running your IT on-premises today, to running it in the cloud.
- Company-wide marketing campaigns are unaffected by moving to the cloud
- Application development still needs to continue as you will still have applications running in the cloud.
- The IT manager's salary should not be included, as it will still need to be paid when the organization moves to the cloud.

**References:**

https://digitalcloud.training/certification-training/aws-certified-cloud-practitioner/aws-billing-and-pricing/

https://aws.amazon.com/tco-calculator/

## 39. Question

**Which of the below are good use cases for a specific Amazon EC2 pricing model? (choose 2)**

1. Spot for consistent load over a long term
2. On-demand for ad-hoc requirements that cannot be interrupted
3. Reserved instances for applications with flexible start and end times
4. Reserved instances for steady state predictable usage
5. On-demand for regulatory requirements that do not allow multi-tenant virtualization

**Answer: 2,4**

**Explanation:**

Typical use cases for the pricing models listed are:
- On-demand: Good for users that want the low cost and flexibility of EC2 without any up-front payment or long-term commitment. Applications with short term, spiky, or unpredictable workloads that cannot be interrupted
- Reserved: Applications with steady state or predictable usage or that require reserved capacity
- Spot: Applications that have flexible start and end times and that are only feasible at very low compute prices. May be terminated
- Dedicated hosts: Useful for regulatory requirements that may not support multi-tenant virtualization. Great for licensing which does not support multi-tenancy or cloud deployments

**References:**

https://digitalcloud.training/certification-training/aws-certified-cloud-practitioner/aws-compute/

## 40. Question

**Which AWS service lets you add user sign up, sign-in and access control to web and mobile apps?**

1. AWS Directory Service
2. AWS Cognito
3. AWS Artifact
4. AWS CloudHSM

Answer: 2

Explanation:

- Amazon Cognito lets you add user sign-up, sign-in, and access control to your web and mobile apps quickly and easily. Amazon Cognito scales to millions of users and supports sign-in with social identity providers, such as Facebook, Google, and Amazon, and enterprise identity providers via SAML 2.0
- AWS Directory Service for Microsoft Active Directory, also known as AWS Managed Microsoft AD, enables your directory-aware workloads and AWS resources to use managed Active Directory in the AWS Cloud
- AWS Artifact is your go-to, central resource for compliance-related information that matters to you
- AWS CloudHSM is a cloud-based hardware security module (HSM) that enables you to easily generate and use your own encryption keys on the AWS Cloud

**References:**

https://digitalcloud.training/certification-training/aws-certified-cloud-practitioner/additional-aws-services-tools/

## 41. Question

**How are AWS Lambda functions triggered?**

1. Metrics
2. Schedules
3. Counters
4. Events

Answer: 4

Explanation:

- AWS Lambda lets you run code as functions without provisioning or managing server. Lambda-based applications (also referred to as serverless applications) are composed of functions triggered by events

**References:**

https://digitalcloud.training/certification-training/aws-certified-cloud-practitioner/aws-compute/

## 42. Question

**What types of monitoring can Amazon CloudWatch be used for? (choose 2)**

1. Infrastructure
2. Operational health
3. Application performance
4. API access
5. Data center

Answer: 2,3

Explanation:

- Amazon CloudWatch is a monitoring service for AWS cloud resources and the applications you run on AWS. CloudWatch performs performance monitoring and can monitor custom metrics generated by applications and the operational health of your AWS resources
- Amazon CloudTrail monitors API access
- Infrastructure and data center monitoring is not accessible to AWS customers

References:

https://digitalcloud.training/certification-training/aws-solutions-architect-associate/management-tools/amazon-cloudwatch/

## 43. Question

**What billing timeframes are available for Amazon EC2 on-demand instances? (choose 2)**

1. Per second
2. Per minute
3. Per hour
4. Per day
5. Per week

Answer: 1,3

Explanation:

- With EC2 you are billed either by the second, for some Linux instances, or by the hour for all other instance types

References:

https://aws.amazon.com/ec2/pricing/on-demand/

## 44. Question

**Which aspects of security on AWS are customer responsibilities? (choose 2)**

1. Availability of AWS regions
2. Physical access controls
3. Setting up account password policies
4. Patching of storage systems
5. Server-side encryption

Answer: 3,5

**Explanation:**

- AWS are responsible for the "security of the cloud". This includes protecting the infrastructure that runs all of the services offered in the AWS Cloud. This infrastructure is composed of the hardware, software, networking, and facilities that run AWS Cloud services.
- The customer is responsible for "security in the cloud". Customer responsibility depends on the service consumed but includes aspects such as Identity and Access Management (includes password policies), encryption of data, protection of network traffic, and operating system, network and firewall configuration.

**References:**

https://digitalcloud.training/certification-training/aws-certified-cloud-practitioner/aws-shared-responsibility-model/

https://aws.amazon.com/compliance/shared-responsibility-model/

## 45. Question

**Which service can be added to a database to provide improved performance for some requests?**

1. Amazon RedShift
2. Amazon EFS
3. Amazon ElastiCache
4. Amazon RDS

**Answer: 3**

**Explanation:**

- Amazon ElastiCache provides in-memory caching which improves performance for read requests when the data is cached in ElastiCache. ElastiCache can be placed in front of your database.
- Amazon RDS is a relational SQL type of database. It is not a service that you place in front of another database to improve performance. Instead you might use RDS as your back-end database and use ElastiCache in front of it to improve performance through its in-memory caching.
- Amazon EFS is an Elastic File System, not a caching service.
- Amazon RedShift is a data warehouse that is used for performing analytics on data.

**References:**

https://digitalcloud.training/certification-training/aws-certified-cloud-practitioner/aws-databases/

https://aws.amazon.com/elasticache/

## 46. Question

**Which AWS service uses a highly secure hardware storage device to store encryption keys?**

1. Amazon Cloud Directory
2. AWS WAF
3. AWS IAM
4. AWS CloudHSM

**Answer: 4**

**Explanation:**

- AWS CloudHSM is a cloud-based hardware security module (HSM) that allows you to easily add secure key storage and high-performance crypto operations to your AWS applications
- Amazon Cloud Directory enables you to build flexible cloud-native directories for organizing hierarchies of data along multiple dimensions
- AWS WAF is a web application firewall that helps protect your web applications from common web exploits
- AWS Identity and Access Management (IAM) is used for managing users, groups, and roles in AWS

**References:**

https://aws.amazon.com/cloudhsm/features/

## 47. Question

Which statement is correct in relation to the AWS Shared Responsibility Model?

1. Customers are responsible for security of the cloud
2. AWS are responsible for encrypting customer data
3. AWS are responsible for the security of regions and availability zones
4. Customers are responsible for patching storage systems

**Answer: 3**

**Explanation:**

- AWS are responsible for "Security of the Cloud". AWS is responsible for protecting the infrastructure that runs all of the services offered in the AWS Cloud. This infrastructure is composed of the hardware, software, networking, and facilities that run AWS Cloud services, and this includes regions, availability zones and edge locations
- Customers are responsible for "Security in the Cloud". This includes encrypting customer data, patching operating systems but not patching or maintaining the underlying infrastructure

**References:**

https://digitalcloud.training/certification-training/aws-certified-cloud-practitioner/aws-shared-responsibility-model/

## 48. Question

Which service can be used to improve performance for users around the world?

1. AWS LightSail
2. Amazon CloudFront
3. Amazon ElastiCache
4. Amazon Connect

**Answer: 2**

**Explanation:**

- Amazon CloudFront is a content delivery network (CDN) that caches content at Edge Locations around the world. This gets the content closer to users which improves performance.
- Amazon Connect Amazon Connect is a self-service, cloud-based contact center service that makes it easy for any business to deliver better customer service at lower cost.
- Amazon ElastiCache is a caching service for databases. Though it does improve read performance for database queries, it is not a global service that is designed to improve performance for users around the world.
- AWS LightSail is a compute service that offers a lower cost and easier to use alternative to Amazon EC2.

**References:**

https://digitalcloud.training/certification-training/aws-certified-cloud-practitioner/content-delivery-and-dns-services/

https://aws.amazon.com/cloudfront/faqs/

## 49. Question

**Which type of security control can be used to deny network access from a specific IP address?**

1. Security Group
2. AWS Shield
3. Network ACL
4. AWS WAF

**Answer: 3**

**Explanation:**

- A Network ACL supports allow and deny rules. You can create a deny rule specifying a specific IP address that you would like to block
- A Security Group only supports allow rules
- AWS WAF is a web application firewall
- AWS Shield is a managed Distributed Denial of Service (DDoS) protection service

**References:**

https://digitalcloud.training/certification-training/aws-certified-cloud-practitioner/aws-networking/

## 50. Question

**Which AWS service enables hybrid cloud storage between on-premises and the AWS Cloud?**

1. Amazon CloudFront
2. AWS Storage Gateway
3. Amazon S3 Cross Region Replication (CRR)
4. Amazon Elastic File System (EFS)

**Answer: 2**

**Explanation:**

- The AWS Storage Gateway service enables hybrid cloud storage between on-premises environments and the AWS Cloud. It seamlessly integrates on-premises enterprise applications and workflows with Amazon's block and object cloud storage services through industry standard storage protocols.
- Amazon S3 CRR is used for copying data from one S3 bucket to another S3 bucket in another region. That is not an examples of hybrid cloud.
- Amazon CloudFront is a content delivery network. It is used to get content closer to users, it is not a hybrid cloud storage solution.
- Amazon EFS is not a hybrid cloud storage solution. With EFS you can mount file systems from on-premises servers, however it does not offer a local cache or method of moving data into the cloud.

**References:**

https://aws.amazon.com/storagegateway/faqs/

https://digitalcloud.training/certification-training/aws-certified-cloud-practitioner/aws-storage/

## 51. Question

**Which team is available to support AWS customers on an Enterprise support plan with account issues?**

1. AWS Technical Account Manager
2. AWS Concierge
3. AWS Billing and Accounts
4. AWS Technical Support

Answer: 2

**Explanation:**

- Included as part of the Enterprise Support plan, the Support Concierge Team are AWS billing and account experts that specialize in working with enterprise accounts
- The Technical Account Manager provides expert monitor and optimized your environment and coordinate access to other programs and experts

**References:**

https://digitalcloud.training/certification-training/aws-certified-cloud-practitioner/aws-billing-and-pricing/

https://aws.amazon.com/premiumsupport/features/

## 52. Question

**Which type of AWS Storage Gateway can be used to backup data with popular backup software?**

1. File Gateway
2. Volume Gateway
3. Gateway Virtual Tape Library
4. Backup Gateway

Answer: 3

**Explanation:**

- The AWS Storage Gateway service enables hybrid storage between on-premises environments and the AWS Cloud. The Gateway Virtual Tape Library can be used with popular backup software such as NetBackup, Backup Exec and Veeam. Uses a virtual media changer and tape drives
- There is no such thing as a Backup Gateway in the AWS products
- File gateway provides a virtual on-premises file server, which enables you to store and retrieve files as objects in Amazon S3
- The volume gateway represents the family of gateways that support block-based volumes, previously referred to as gateway-cached and gateway-stored modes

**References:**

https://digitalcloud.training/certification-training/aws-certified-cloud-practitioner/additional-aws-services-tools/

https://digitalcloud.training/certification-training/aws-solutions-architect-associate/storage/aws-storage-gateway/


## 53. Question

**Which security service only requires a rule to be created in one direction as it automatically allows return traffic?**

1. Network ACL
2. VPC Router
3. Security Group
4. AWS Shield

**Answer: 3**

**Explanation:**

- Security groups are stateful so if you allow traffic to pass through, the return traffic is automatically allowed even if no rule matches the traffic
- Network ACLs are stateless so you must create rules in both directions to allow traffic through
- A VPC router is not a security service
- AWS Shield is a managed Distributed Denial of Service (DDoS) protection service that safeguards applications running on AWS

**References:**

https://digitalcloud.training/certification-training/aws-certified-cloud-practitioner/aws-networking/


## 54. Question

**What is the difference between an EBS volume and an Instance store?**

1. Instance store volumes can be used with all EC2 instance types whereas EBS cannot
2. EBS volumes are file-level storage devices whereas Instance store volumes are object-based
3. Instance store volumes are ephemeral whereas EBS volumes are persistent storage
4. EBS volumes are object storage devices whereas Instance store volume are block based

**Answer: 3**

**Explanation:**

- EBS-backed means the root volume is an EBS volume and storage is persistent. Instance store-backed means the root volume is an instance store volume and storage is not persistent
- Both EBS and Instance store volumes are block-based storage devices
- EBS volumes can be used with all EC2 instance types whereas Instance store volumes are more limited in compatibility

**References:**

https://digitalcloud.training/certification-training/aws-certified-cloud-practitioner/aws-storage/

## 55. Question

**Which of the options below are recommendations in the reliability pillar of the well-architected framework? (choose 2)**

1. Stop guessing about capacity
2. Scale vertically using big systems
3. Manually recover from failure
4. Test recovery procedures
5. Manage change in manual processes

**Answer: 1,4**

**Explanation:**

- The reliability pillar includes the ability of a system to recover from infrastructure or service disruptions, dynamically acquire computing resources to meet demand, and mitigate disruptions such as misconfigurations or transient network issues
- There are five design principles for reliability in the cloud:
    - Test recovery procedures
    - Automatically recover from failure
    - Scale horizontally to increase aggregate system availability
    - Stop guessing capacity
    - Manage change in automation

**References:**

https://aws.amazon.com/blogs/apn/the-5-pillars-of-the-aws-well-architected-framework/

https://digitalcloud.training/certification-training/aws-certified-cloud-practitioner/architecting-for-the-cloud/

## 56. Question

**In addition to DNS services, what other services does Amazon Route 53 provide? (choose 2)**

1. DHCP
2. Traffic flow
3. Caching
4. Domain registration
5. IP Routing

Answer: 2,4

Explanation:

- Route 53 features include domain registration, DNS, traffic flow, health checking, and failover.
- Route 53 does not support DHCP, IP routing or caching.
- The DNS features of Route 53 are called "routing policies", however this is not traditional IP routing which is performed by routers. It is intelligent DNS that responds with different results based on certain factors such as latency, weight, or failover configuration.

References:

https://digitalcloud.training/certification-training/aws-certified-cloud-practitioner/content-delivery-and-dns-services/


## 57. Question

What is the most cost-effective Amazon S3 storage tier for data that is not often accessed but requires high availability?

1. Amazon S3 Standard-IA
2. Amazon Glacier
3. Amazon S3 Standard
4. Amazon S3 One Zone-IA

Answer: 1

Explanation:

- S3 Standard-IA is for data that is accessed less frequently but requires rapid access when needed. S3 Standard-IA offers the high durability, high throughput, and low latency of S3 Standard with 99.9% availability
- S3 One Zone-IA is for data that is accessed less frequently but requires rapid access when needed. Unlike other S3 Storage Classes which store data in a minimum of three Availability Zones (AZs), S3 One Zone-IA stores data in a single AZ and offers lower availability
- Glacier is a data archiving solution so not suitable for a storage tier that requires infrequent access

References:

https://aws.amazon.com/s3/storage-classes/


## 58. Question

What does an organization need to do in Amazon IAM to enable user access to services being launched in new region?

1. Nothing, IAM is global
2. Enable global mode in IAM to provision the required access
3. Create new user accounts in the new region
4. Update the user accounts to allow access from another region

Answer: 1

Explanation:

- IAM is used to securely control individual and group access to AWS resources. IAM is universal (global) and does not apply to regions

**References:**

https://digitalcloud.training/certification-training/aws-certified-cloud-practitioner/identity-and-access-management/

## 59. Question

**Which types of root storage devices are available for Amazon EC2 instances? (choose 2)**

1. Instance Store
2. EBS volume
3. RAM
4. EFS file system
5. S3 Bucket

### Answer: 1,2

### Explanation:

- The only storage options for a root volume that can be booted from are EBS volumes and Instance Stores

**References:**

https://digitalcloud.training/certification-training/aws-certified-cloud-practitioner/aws-storage/

https://docs.aws.amazon.com/AWSEC2/latest/UserGuide/RootDeviceStorage.html

## 60. Question

**What are the fundamental charges for Elastic Block Store (EBS) volumes? (choose 2)**

1. Provisioned IOPS
2. The amount of data storage provisioned
3. Inbound data transfer
4. Number of snapshots
5. The amount of data storage consumed

### Answer: 1,2

### Explanation:

- With EBS volumes you are charged for the amount of data provisioned (not consumed) per month. This means you can have empty space within a volume and you still pay for it
- With provisioned IOPS volumes you are also charged for the amount you provision in IOPS
- You pay for the storage consumed by snapshots, not by the number of snapshots

**References:**

https://digitalcloud.training/certification-training/aws-certified-cloud-practitioner/aws-billing-and-pricing/

## 61. Question

**What can be assigned to an IAM user? (choose 2)**

1. A password for access to the management console
2. A password for logging into Linux
3. An access key ID and secret access key
4. A key pair
5. An SSL/TLS certificate

Answer: 1,3

Explanation:

- An IAM user is an entity that represents a person or service. Users can be assigned an access key ID and secret access key for programmatic access to the AWS API, CLI, SDK, and other development tools and a password for access to the management console
- Key pairs are used with Amazon EC2 as a method of using public key encryption to securely access EC2 instances
- You cannot assign an IAM user with a password for logging into a Linux instance
- You cannot assign an SSL/TLS certificate to a user

References:

https://digitalcloud.training/certification-training/aws-certified-cloud-practitioner/identity-and-access-management/

## 62. Question

**An organization has an on-premises cloud and accesses their AWS Cloud over the Internet. How can they create a private hybrid cloud connection?**

1. AWS VPC Endpoint
2. AWS Managed VPN
3. AWS VPN CloudHub
4. AWS Direct Connect

Answer: 4

Explanation:

- AWS Direct Connect is a low-latency, high-bandwidth, private connection to AWS. This can be used to create a private hybrid cloud connection between on-premises and the AWS Cloud.
- AWS Managed VPN and VPN CloudHub both use the Internet for network connections, so they are not creating a private connection. The connection is secured but uses the Internet.
- An AWS VPC Endpoint is a PrivateLink connection that connects an AWS public service to a VPC using a private connection. This does not connect on-premises environments to AWS.

References:

https://digitalcloud.training/certification-training/aws-certified-cloud-practitioner/aws-networking/

https://aws.amazon.com/directconnect/faqs/

### 63. Question

**Which AWS service provides a single location to track the progress of application migrations across multiple AWS and partner solutions?**

1. AWS Database Migration Service
2. AWS Batch
3. AWS Server Migration Service
4. AWS Migration Hub

Answer: 4

Explanation:

- AWS Migration Hub provides a single location to track the progress of application migrations across multiple AWS and partner solutions. Using Migration Hub allows you to choose the AWS and partner migration tools that best fit your needs, while providing visibility into the status of migrations across your portfolio of applications. This includes AWS Database Migration Service, AWS Server Migration Service, and partner migration tools
- AWS Database Migration Service helps you migrate databases to AWS quickly and securely
- AWS Server Migration Service (SMS) is an agentless service which makes it easier and faster for you to migrate thousands of on-premises workloads to AWS
- With AWS Batch, you simply package the code for your batch jobs, specify their dependencies, and submit your batch job using the AWS Management Console, CLIs, or SDK

References:

https://digitalcloud.training/certification-training/aws-certified-cloud-practitioner/additional-aws-services-tools/


### 64. Question

**Which read/write capacity modes are available for DynamoDB? (choose 2)**

1. Reserved capacity mode
2. On-demand capacity mode
3. Dedicated capacity mode
4. Spot capacity mode
5. Provisioned capacity mode

Answer: 2,5

Explanation:

- On-demand capacity mode: DynamoDB charges you for the data reads and writes your application performs on your tables. You do not need to specify how much read and write throughput you expect your application to perform because DynamoDB instantly accommodates your workloads as they ramp up or down.
- Provisioned capacity mode: you specify the number of reads and writes per second that you expect your application to require. You can use auto scaling to automatically adjust your table's capacity based on the specified utilization rate to ensure application performance while reducing cost
- Reserved pricing is available for provisioned mode but is not actually a "read/write mode". There is no Spot pricing option for DynamoDB.

**References:**

https://digitalcloud.training/certification-training/aws-solutions-architect-associate/database/amazon-dynamodb/

https://docs.aws.amazon.com/amazondynamodb/latest/developerguide/HowItWorks.ReadWriteCapacityMode.html

## 65. Question

**Which storage type can be mounted using the NFS protocol to many EC2 instances simultaneously?**

1. Amazon S3
2. Amazon EFS
3. Amazon EBS
4. Amazon Instance Store

**Answer: 2**

**Explanation:**

- EFS is a fully-managed service that makes it easy to set up and scale file storage in the Amazon Cloud. EFS uses the NFSv4.1 protocol. Can concurrently connect 1 to 1000s of EC2 instances, from multiple AZs
- EBS volumes can only be attached to a single EC2 instance at a time and are block devices (not NFS)
- Amazon S3 is an object store and is connected to using a RESTful protocol over HTTP
- Amazon Instance Store is a type of ephemeral block-based volume that can be attached to a single EC2 instance at a time

**References:**

https://digitalcloud.training/certification-training/aws-certified-cloud-practitioner/aws-storage/

https://digitalcloud.training/certification-training/aws-solutions-architect-associate/storage/amazon-efs/

# SET 5: PRACTICE QUESTIONS ONLY

### 1. Question

Which AWS support plan provides email only support by Cloud Support Associates?

1. Enterprise
2. Business
3. Developer
4. Basic

### 2. Question

Which AWS program can help an organization to design, build, and manage their workloads on AWS?

1. APN Consulting Partners
2. APN Technology Consultants
3. AWS Business Development Manager
4. AWS Technical Account Manager

### 3. Question

How do AWS charge for the use of NAT Gateways? (choose 2)

1. Price per port
2. Price per instance session
3. Price per protocol
4. Price per GB processed
5. Price per gateway hour

### 4. Question

What is the name of the online, self-service portal that AWS provides to enable customers to view reports and, such as PCI reports, and accept agreements?

1. AWS Compliance Portal
2. AWS Documentation Portal
3. AWS Artifact
4. AWS DocuFact

### 5. Question

Which combination of AWS services could be used to deploy a stateless web application that can automatically and elastically scale?

1. EC2, EBS and Auto Scaling
2. EC2, Auto Scaling and Elastic Load Balancing
3. EC2, CloudFront and RDS
4. EC2, DynamoDB and ElastiCache

## 6. Question

**Which AWS service enables developers and data scientists to build, train, and deploy machine learning models?**

1. Amazon Rekognition
2. Amazon Comprehend
3. Amazon SageMaker
4. Amazon MQ


## 7. Question

**Which tools can you use to manage identities in IAM? (choose 2)**

1. Amazon CloudWatch API
2. Amazon Workspaces
3. EC2 Management Console
4. AWS Management Console
5. AWS Command Line Tools


## 8. Question

**How can a company protect their Amazon S3 data from a regional disaster?**

1. Use lifecycle actions to move to another S3 storage class
2. Use Cross-Region Replication (CRR) to copy to another region
3. Archive to Amazon Glacier
4. Enable Multi-Factor Authentication (MFA) delete


## 9. Question

**What are two correct statements about AWS Organizations with consolidated billing? (choose 2)**

1. Volume pricing discounts applied across multiple accounts
2. Linked accounts lose their management independence
3. CloudTrail can be configured per organization
4. One bill provided for multiple accounts
5. Multiple bills are provided per organization


## 10. Question

**Which AWS components aid in the construction of fault-tolerant applications? (choose 2)**

1. AMIs
2. Elastic IP addresses
3. Tags
4. Block device mappings
5. ARNs

## 11. Question

Which cloud model should a company use for an application that has a requirement for a bespoke, specialized hardware configuration?

1. SaaS
2. Private
3. Public
4. Hybrid

## 12. Question

What are the primary benefits of using AWS Elastic Load Balancing? (choose 2)

1. Caching
2. High availability
3. Regional resilience
4. Elasticity
5. Automation

## 13. Question

Which AWS services form the app-facing services of the AWS serverless infrastructure? (choose 2)

1. Amazon DynamoDB
2. Amazon API Gateway
3. AWS Lambda
4. AWS Step Functions
5. Amazon EFS

## 14. Question

Which AWS service is part of the suite of "serverless" services and runs code as functions?

1. AWS Lambda
2. Amazon EKS
3. Amazon ECS
4. AWS CodeCommit

## 15. Question

Which service is used introduce fault tolerance into an application architecture?

1. Amazon CloudFront
2. Amazon ElastiCache
3. Amazon Elastic Load Balancing
4. Amazon DynamoDB

## 16. Question

Which of the below is an example of optimizing for cost?

1. Choosing the fastest EC2 instance to ensure performance

2. Deploy resources with AWS CloudFormation
3. Provision extra capacity to allow for growth
4. Replace an EC2 compute instance with AWS Lambda

## 17. Question

Which type of Amazon RDS automated backup allows you to restore the database with a granularity of as little as 5 minutes?

1. Snapshot backup
2. Full backup
3. Point-in-time recovery
4. Incremental backup

## 18. Question

Which of the following would be good reasons to move from on-premises to the AWS Cloud? (choose 2)

1. Gain access to free technical support services
2. Gain end-to-end operational management of the entire infrastructure stack
3. Outsource all security responsibility
4. Improve agility and elasticity
5. Reduce costs through easier right-sizing of workloads

## 19. Question

How can a company connect from their on-premises network to VPCs in multiple regions using private connections?

1. AWS Direct Connect Gateway
2. AWS Managed VPN
3. Inter-Region VPC Peering
4. Amazon CloudFront

## 20. Question

Under the AWS Shared Responsibility Model, which of the following is the customer NOT responsible for?

1. Installing firmware updates on host servers
2. Applying encryption to data stored on an EBS volume
3. Applying bucket policies to share Amazon S3 data
4. Adding firewall rules to security groups and network ACLs

## 21. Question

Which of the following configuration items are important to enabling an EC2 web server to serve web pages on the Internet? (choose 2)

1. Security groups rules configured to allow SSH
2. An established VPN connection

3. A private IP address assigned to the instance
4. Security group rules configured to allow HTTP/HTTPS
5. A public IP address assigned to the instance

## 22. Question

**What are two benefits of using AWS Lambda? (choose 2)**

1. No servers to manage
2. Integrated snapshots
3. Flexible operating system choices
4. Open source software
5. Continuous scaling (scale out)

## 23. Question

**Why would a company choose a NAT Gateway over a NAT instance? (choose 2)**

1. They are managed by AWS, not by you
2. Can be used for port forwarding
3. You can use security groups to assign firewall rules to them
4. They are elastically scalable
5. They can be additionally used as bastion hosts

## 24. Question

**What is the relationship between subnets and availability zones?**

1. You can create one subnet per availability zone
2. Subnets span across multiple availability zones
3. You can create one or more subnets within each availability zone
4. Subnets contain one or more availability zones

## 25. Question

**Which services allow you to store files on AWS? (choose 2)**

1. AWS Lambda
2. Amazon SQS
3. Amazon LightSail
4. Amazon EFS
5. Amazon EBS

## 26. Question

**What feature of Amazon S3 enables you to set rules to automatically transfer objects between different storage classes at defined time intervals?**

1. Object Lifecycle Management
2. S3 Archiving
3. Elastic Data Management
4. Auto Lifecycle Scaling

## 27. Question
Which AWS service can be used to prepare and load data for analytics using an extract, transform and load (ETL) process?

1. Amazon EMR
2. AWS Glue
3. AWS Lambda
4. Amazon Athena

## 28. Question
What are the benefits of using IAM roles for applications that run on EC2 instances? (choose 2)

1. It is easier to manage IAM roles
2. Can apply multiple roles to a single instance
3. More secure than storing access keys within applications
4. Easier to configure than using storing access keys within the EC2 instance
5. Role credentials are permanent

## 29. Question
Which type of data storage system is typically considered to hold "structured" data?

1. Non-relational database
2. Relational database
3. File system
4. Email system

## 30. Question
Which DynamoDB feature provides in-memory acceleration to tables that result in significant performance improvements?

1. Amazon ElastiCache
2. Amazon EFS
3. Amazon DynamoDB Accelerator (DAX)
4. Amazon CloudFront

## 31. Question
An Elastic IP Address can be remapped between EC2 instances across which boundaries?

1. DB Subnets
2. Regions
3. Edge Locations
4. Availability Zones

## 32. Question
Which type of EBS volumes can be encrypted?

1. Only root volumes can have encryption applied at launch time

2. Only non-root volumes created from snapshots
3. Both non-root and root volumes
4. Non-root volumes only

## 33. Question

**Which AWS IAM best practice recommends applying the minimum permissions necessary to perform a task when creating IAM policies?**

1. Enable MFA for privileged users
2. Use roles to delegate permissions
3. Create individual IAM users
4. Grant least privilege

## 34. Question

**What information must be entered into the AWS TCO Calculator?**

1. The number of end users in your company
2. The number of applications in your company
3. The number of storage systems in your company
4. The number of servers in your company

## 35. Question

**Which service runs your application code only when needed without needing to run servers?**

1. AWS LightSail
2. AWS Lambda
3. Amazon ECS
4. Amazon EC2

## 36. Question

**A company wants to utilize a pay as you go cloud model for all of their applications without CAPEX costs and which is highly elastic. Which cloud delivery model will suit them best?**

1. Public
2. Hybrid
3. On-premise
4. Private

## 37. Question

**Which of the following descriptions is incorrect in relation to the design of Availability Zones?**

1. Each subnet in a VPC is mapped to all AZs in the region
2. AZs are physically separated within a typical metropolitan region and are located in lower risk flood plains
3. Each AZ is designed as an independent failure zone
4. AZ's have direct, low-latency, high throughput and redundant network connections between each other

## 38. Question

Which AWS services have a global (rather than regional) scope? (choose 2)

1. Amazon EFS
2. AWS CloudFront
3. Amazon S3
4. AWS WAF
5. AWS Lambda

## 39. Question

Which AWS service can be used to send automated notifications to HTTP endpoints?

1. Amazon SWF
2. Amazon SQS
3. Amazon SES
4. Amazon SNS

## 40. Question

Which of the following constitute the five pillars for the AWS Well-Architected Framework? (choose 2)

1. Operational excellence, security, and reliability
2. Data consistency, and cost optimization
3. Operational excellence, elasticity and scalability
4. Cost prioritization, and cost optimization
5. Performance efficiency, and cost optimization

## 41. Question

Which of the following are advantages of using the AWS cloud computing over legacy IT? (choose 2)

1. You don't need to worry about over provisioning as you can elastically scale
2. You are able to pass responsibility for the availability of your application to AWS
3. You don't need to patch your operating systems
4. You can bring new applications to market faster
5. You can bring services closer to your end users

## 42. Question

Which AWS service can assist with providing recommended actions on cost optimization?

1. AWS Artifact
2. Amazon CloudWatch Events
3. AWS Trusted Advisor
4. AWS Inspector

## 43. Question

What offerings are included in the Amazon Lightsail product set? (choose 2)

1. Object storage

2. Serverless functions
3. Managed MySQL database
4. NoSQL database
5. Virtual Private Server

## 44. Question

**What is the name of the AWS managed Docker registry service used by the Amazon Elastic Container Service (ECS)?**

1. Elastic Container Registry
2. ECS Container Registry
3. Docker Container Registry
4. Docker Image Repository

## 45. Question

**How do AWS charge for Amazon CloudFront? (choose 2)**

1. Data transfer in
2. Number of users
3. Number of requests
4. Data transfer out
5. Uptime

## 46. Question

**When designing a VPC, what is the purpose of an Internet Gateway?**

1. Provides Internet access for EC2 instances in private subnets
2. It's a bastion host for inbound management connections
3. It's used for making VPN connections to a VPC
4. Enables Internet communications for instances in public subnets

## 47. Question

**Which service provides alerts and remediation guidance when AWS is experiencing events that may impact you?**

1. AWS Trusted Advisor
2. AWS Personal Health Dashboard
3. AWS Inspector
4. AWS Shield

## 48. Question

**Which AWS service lets connected devices easily and securely interact with cloud applications and other devices?**

1. Amazon Workspaces
2. AWS Directory Service
3. AWS IoT Core

4. AWS SMS

## 49. Question
Which AWS security service provides a firewall at the subnet level within a VPC?

1. Security Group
2. IAM Policy
3. Network Access Control List
4. Bucket Policy

## 50. Question
With which service can a developer upload code from a Git repository and have the service handle the end-to-end deployment of the resources?

1. AWS CodeDeploy
2. AWS CodeCommit
3. AWS Elastic Beanstalk
4. Amazon ECS

## 51. Question
A developer needs a way to automatically provision a collection of AWS resources. Which AWS service is primarily used for deploying infrastructure as code?

1. AWS Elastic Beanstalk
2. Jenkins
3. Amazon CloudFormation
4. AWS CodeDeploy

## 52. Question
To reward customers for using their services, what are two ways AWS reduce prices? (choose 2)

1. Reduced cost for reserved capacity
2. Reduction in inbound data transfer charges
3. Removal of termination fees for customers who spend more
4. Discounts for using a wider variety of services
5. Volume based discounts when you use more services

## 53. Question
What is an Edge location?

1. A virtual private gateway for VPN
2. A content delivery network (CDN) endpoint for CloudFront
3. A VPC peering connection endpoint
4. A public endpoint for Amazon S3

### 54. Question

Which service allows an organization to bring their own licensing on host hardware that is physically isolated from other AWS accounts?

1. EC2 Reserved Instances
2. EC2 Dedicated Instances
3. EC2 Dedicated Hosts
4. EC2 Spot Instances

### 55. Question

Which of the following is NOT an AWS service used for transferring large amounts of data into Amazon S3?

1. AWS Snowball
2. AWS DMS
3. AWS Snowmobile
4. S3 Transfer Acceleration

### 56. Question

What charges are applicable to Amazon S3 Standard storage class? (choose 2)

1. Data egress
2. Data ingress
3. Per GB/month storage fee
4. Retrieval fee
5. Minimum capacity charge per object

### 57. Question

Which support plan is the lowest cost option that allows unlimited cases to be open?

1. Developer
2. Enterprise
3. Basic
4. Business

### 58. Question

Assuming you have configured them correctly, which AWS services can scale automatically without intervention? (choose 2)

1. Amazon EBS
2. Amazon DynamoDB
3. Amazon S3
4. Amazon EC2
5. Amazon RDS

## 59. Question

**How can an online education company ensure their video courses play with minimal latency for their users around the world?**

1. Use Amazon Aurora Global Database
2. Use Amazon S3 Transfer Acceleration to speed up downloads
3. Use Amazon CloudFront to get the content closer to users
4. Use Amazon EBS Cross Region Replication to get the content close to the users

## 60. Question

**Which service can you use to monitor, store and access log files generated by EC2 instances and on-premises servers?**

1. Amazon Kinesis
2. Amazon CloudWatch Logs
3. AWS OpsWorks
4. Amazon CloudTrail

## 61. Question

**Which AWS feature of Amazon EC2 allows an administrator to create a standardized image that can be used for launching new instances?**

1. Amazon Golden Image
2. Amazon Block Template
3. Amazon Machine Image
4. Amazon EBS Mount Point

## 62. Question

**How can you configure Amazon Route 53 to monitor the health and performance of your application?**

1. Using DNS lookups
2. Using CloudWatch
3. Using Route 53 health checks
4. Using the Route 53 API

## 63. Question

**What is the availability model of Amazon DynamoDB?**

1. Data is asynchronously replicated across all regions
2. Data is synchronously replicated across all regions
3. Data is asynchronously replicated across 3 facilities in a region
4. Data is synchronously replicated across 3 facilities in a region

## 64. Question

**Which type of storage stores objects comprised of key, value pairs?**

1. Amazon DynamoDB

2. Amazon EBS
3. Amazon S3
4. Amazon EFS

## 65. Question
**Which service is used for caching data?**

1. Amazon Elastic File System (EFS)
2. Amazon Simple Queue Service (SQS)
3. Amazon DynamoDB DAX
4. Amazon Key Management Service (KMS)

# SET 5: PRACTICE QUESTIONS, ANSWERS & EXPLANATIONS

## 1. Question

Which AWS support plan provides email only support by Cloud Support Associates?

1. Enterprise
2. Business
3. Developer
4. Basic

Answer: 3

Explanation:

- Developer provides email support by the Cloud Support Associates team whereas Business and Enterprise provide email, 24×7 phone and chat access to Cloud Support Engineers
- Basic does not provide email support at all

References:

https://digitalcloud.training/certification-training/aws-certified-cloud-practitioner/aws-billing-and-pricing/

## 2. Question

Which AWS program can help an organization to design, build, and manage their workloads on AWS?

1. APN Consulting Partners
2. APN Technology Consultants
3. AWS Business Development Manager
4. AWS Technical Account Manager

Answer: 1

Explanation:

- APN Consulting Partners are professional services firms that help customers of all sizes design, architect, build, migrate, and manage their workloads and applications on AWS. Consulting Partners include System Integrators (SIs), Strategic Consultancies, Agencies, Managed Service Providers (MSPs), and Value-Added Resellers (VARs).
- None of the other options are AWS Programs that can assist a customer with the design, build and management of their workloads.

References:

https://aws.amazon.com/partners/consulting/

## 3. Question

How do AWS charge for the use of NAT Gateways? (choose 2)

1. Price per port

2. Price per instance session
3. Price per protocol
4. Price per GB processed
5. Price per gateway hour

**Answer: 4,5**

**Explanation:**

- If you choose to create a NAT gateway in your VPC, you are charged for each "NAT Gateway-hour" that your NAT gateway is provisioned and available. Data processing charges apply for each Gigabyte processed through the NAT gateway regardless of the traffic's source or destination

**References:**

https://aws.amazon.com/vpc/pricing/


## 4. Question

What is the name of the online, self-service portal that AWS provides to enable customers to view reports and, such as PCI reports, and accept agreements?

1. AWS Compliance Portal
2. AWS Documentation Portal
3. AWS Artifact
4. AWS DocuFact

**Answer: 3**

**Explanation:**

- AWS Artifact is your go-to, central resource for compliance-related information that matters to you. It provides on-demand access to AWS' security and compliance reports and select online agreements. Reports available in AWS Artifact include our Service Organization Control (SOC) reports, Payment Card Industry (PCI) reports, and certifications from accreditation bodies across geographies and compliance verticals that validate the implementation and operating effectiveness of AWS security controls.
- Agreements available in AWS Artifact include the Business Associate Addendum (BAA) and the Nondisclosure Agreement (NDA)
- All other options are fabricated and do not exist on AWS

**References:**

https://digitalcloud.training/certification-training/aws-certified-cloud-practitioner/additional-aws-services-tools/

https://aws.amazon.com/artifact/


## 5. Question

Which combination of AWS services could be used to deploy a stateless web application that can automatically and elastically scale?

1. EC2, EBS and Auto Scaling

2. EC2, Auto Scaling and Elastic Load Balancing
3. EC2, CloudFront and RDS
4. EC2, DynamoDB and ElastiCache

Answer: 2

Explanation:

- Whenever EC2 is included you need to use Auto Scaling to automatically scale the number of instances which only leaves 2 potential answers. EBS volumes can only be mounted to a single instance and so data cannot be shared therefore that rules out the other potential answer. Therefore, EC2 with Auto Scaling and an ELB sitting in front is the correct solution
- DynamoDB can be used for storing session state for stateless web applications but is not necessary for the answer

References:

https://digitalcloud.training/certification-training/aws-certified-cloud-practitioner/aws-compute/

https://digitalcloud.training/certification-training/aws-certified-cloud-practitioner/elastic-load-balancing-and-auto-scaling/

## 6. Question

Which AWS service enables developers and data scientists to build, train, and deploy machine learning models?

1. Amazon Rekognition
2. Amazon Comprehend
3. Amazon SageMaker
4. Amazon MQ

Answer: 3

Explanation:

- Amazon SageMaker is a fully-managed platform that enables developers and data scientists to quickly and easily build, train, and deploy machine learning models at any scale. Amazon SageMaker removes all the barriers that typically slow down developers who want to use machine learning
- Amazon Comprehend is a natural language processing (NLP) service that uses machine learning to find insights and relationships in text
- Amazon Rekognition makes it easy to add image and video analysis to your applications
- Amazon MQ is a managed message broker service for Apache ActiveMQ that makes it easy to set up and operate message brokers in the cloud

References:

https://digitalcloud.training/certification-training/aws-certified-cloud-practitioner/additional-aws-services-tools/

## 7. Question

Which tools can you use to manage identities in IAM? (choose 2)

1. Amazon CloudWatch API
2. Amazon Workspaces
3. EC2 Management Console
4. AWS Management Console
5. AWS Command Line Tools

**Answer: 4,5**

**Explanation:**

- You can manage AWS Identity and Access Management identities through the AWS Management Console, AWS Command Line Tools, AWS SDKs, and IAM HTTPS API
- CloudWatch is not used for managing identities in IAM. It is a service used for monitoring the state of your AWS resources
- The EC2 management console cannot be used for managing identities in IAM.
- Amazon WorkSpaces is a managed desktop computing service running on the AWS cloud

**References:**

https://digitalcloud.training/certification-training/aws-certified-cloud-practitioner/identity-and-access-management/

## 8. Question

**How can a company protect their Amazon S3 data from a regional disaster?**

1. Use lifecycle actions to move to another S3 storage class
2. Use Cross-Region Replication (CRR) to copy to another region
3. Archive to Amazon Glacier
4. Enable Multi-Factor Authentication (MFA) delete

**Answer: 2**

**Explanation:**

- The only option here that will help is to use CRR to copy the data to another region. This will provide disaster recovery
- Moving to Glacier or another S3 storage class does not copy the data out of the region
- Enabling MFA delete will not protect the data from a regional disaster

**References:**

https://digitalcloud.training/certification-training/aws-certified-cloud-practitioner/aws-storage/

https://aws.amazon.com/s3/features/

## 9. Question

**What are two correct statements about AWS Organizations with consolidated billing? (choose 2)**

1. Volume pricing discounts applied across multiple accounts
2. Linked accounts lose their management independence
3. CloudTrail can be configured per organization
4. One bill provided for multiple accounts

5. Multiple bills are provided per organization

**Answer: 1,4**

**Explanation:**

- With AWS organizations you create a paying account and linked accounts. One bill is provided for multiple accounts within an organization. Volume pricing discounts can be applied across resources in multiple accounts
- Linked accounts can still be managed independently
- CloudTrail is on a per account basis and per region basis but can be aggregated into a single bucket in the paying account

**References:**

https://digitalcloud.training/certification-training/aws-certified-cloud-practitioner/aws-billing-and-pricing/

## 10. Question

Which AWS components aid in the construction of fault-tolerant applications? (choose 2)

1. AMIs
2. Elastic IP addresses
3. Tags
4. Block device mappings
5. ARNs

**Answer: 1,2**

**Explanation:**

- Elastic IP addresses can be easily remapped between EC2 instances in the event of a failure. Amazon Machine Images (AMIs) can be used to quickly launch replacement instances when there is a failure
- Amazon Resource Names (ARNs), tags and block device mappings don't really help with fault tolerance

**References:**

https://d36cz9buwru1tt.cloudfront.net/AWS_Building_Fault_Tolerant_Applications.pdf

## 11. Question

Which cloud model should a company use for an application that has a requirement for a bespoke, specialized hardware configuration?

1. SaaS
2. Private
3. Public
4. Hybrid

**Answer: 2**

**Explanation:**

- You cannot choose the hardware stack in the public cloud so if you have an application that requires access to bespoke, specialized hardware you need to build it on-premise in a private cloud
- Hybrid could be an option if other components of the application, such as a web front-end, can run in a public cloud
- Software as a Service (SaaS) is a type of cloud service that delivers a managed application

**References:**

https://digitalcloud.training/certification-training/aws-certified-cloud-practitioner/cloud-computing-concepts/

## 12. Question

**What are the primary benefits of using AWS Elastic Load Balancing? (choose 2)**

1. Caching
2. High availability
3. Regional resilience
4. Elasticity
5. Automation

**Answer: 2,4**

**Explanation:**

- High availability – ELB automatically distributes traffic across multiple EC2 instances in different AZs within a region
- Elasticity – ELB is capable of handling rapid changes in network traffic patterns
- An ELB can distribute incoming traffic across your Amazon EC2 instances in a single Availability Zone or multiple Availability Zones, but not across regions (for regional resilience)
- Automation is not a primary benefit of ELB
- Caching is not a benefit of ELB

**References:**

https://digitalcloud.training/2018/10/19/cloud-computing-basics-compute/

## 13. Question

**Which AWS services form the app-facing services of the AWS serverless infrastructure? (choose 2)**

1. Amazon DynamoDB
2. Amazon API Gateway
3. AWS Lambda
4. AWS Step Functions
5. Amazon EFS

**Answer: 2,3**

**Explanation:**

- AWS Lambda and Amazon API Gateway are both app-facing components of the AWS Serverless infrastructure
- Amazon DynamoDB and EFS are database and storage services of the serverless infrastructure
- AWS Step Functions is an orchestration service

**References:**

https://aws.amazon.com/serverless/

## 14. Question

Which AWS service is part of the suite of "serverless" services and runs code as functions?

1. AWS Lambda
2. Amazon EKS
3. Amazon ECS
4. AWS CodeCommit

Answer: 1

**Explanation:**

- AWS Lambda is a serverless compute service that runs your code in response to events and automatically manages the underlying compute resources for you. The code you run on AWS Lambda is called a "Lambda function"
- Amazon ECS and EKS are both used for running software containers such as Docker containers
- AWS CodeCommit is a fully-managed source control service that hosts secure Git-based repositories

**References:**

https://digitalcloud.training/certification-training/aws-certified-cloud-practitioner/aws-compute/

https://aws.amazon.com/lambda/features/

## 15. Question

**Which service is used introduce fault tolerance into an application architecture?**

1. Amazon CloudFront
2. Amazon ElastiCache
3. Amazon Elastic Load Balancing
4. Amazon DynamoDB

Answer: 3

**Explanation:**

- Amazon Elastic Load Balancing is used to spread load and introduce fault tolerance by distributing connections across multiple identically configured back-end EC2 instances
- Amazon DynamoDB is fault tolerant; however, it is not something you add to an architecture to introduce fault tolerance to the application stack
- Amazon CloudFront is a content delivery network that is used for caching content and serving it to web-based users quickly

- Amazon ElastiCache is an in-memory database cache and is used to introduce improved performance rather than fault tolerance

**References:**

https://digitalcloud.training/certification-training/aws-certified-cloud-practitioner/aws-databases/

## 16. Question

**Which of the below is an example of optimizing for cost?**

1. Choosing the fastest EC2 instance to ensure performance
2. Deploy resources with AWS CloudFormation
3. Provision extra capacity to allow for growth
4. Replace an EC2 compute instance with AWS Lambda

**Answer: 4**

**Explanation:**

- Where possible, you should replace EC2 workloads with AWS managed services that don't require you to take any capacity decisions. AWS Lambda is a serverless services and you only pay for actual processing time. Other examples of services that you don't need to make capacity decisions with include: ELB, CloudFront, SQS, Kinesis Firehose, SES, and CloudSearch
- You should not choose the fastest EC2 instance if you're trying to optimize for cost as this will be expensive, you should right-size your EC2 instances, so you use the cheapest EC2 instance to suit your workload's requirements
- Provisioning extra capacity for growth is not an example of cost optimization. With cloud computing you no longer need to do this as you can configure applications, databases and storage systems to grow on demand
- Deploying resources with CloudFormation is great for consistently deploying application configurations from a template. However, this is not an example of cost optimization, it is more an example of operational optimization

**References:**

https://digitalcloud.training/certification-training/aws-certified-cloud-practitioner/architecting-for-the-cloud/

## 17. Question

**Which type of Amazon RDS automated backup allows you to restore the database with a granularity of as little as 5 minutes?**

1. Snapshot backup
2. Full backup
3. Point-in-time recovery
4. Incremental backup

**Answer: 3**

**Explanation:**

- You can restore a DB instance to a specific point in time with a granularity of 5 minutes. RDS uses transaction logs which it uploads to Amazon S3 to do this

**References:**

https://docs.aws.amazon.com/AmazonRDS/latest/UserGuide/USER_PIT.html

## 18. Question

**Which of the following would be good reasons to move from on-premises to the AWS Cloud? (choose 2)**

1. Gain access to free technical support services
2. Gain end-to-end operational management of the entire infrastructure stack
3. Outsource all security responsibility
4. Improve agility and elasticity
5. Reduce costs through easier right-sizing of workloads

**Answer: 4,5**

**Explanation:**

- There are many benefits to moving to the AWS Cloud and these include reducing costs through right-sizing workloads. This is easier with elastic computing and the ability to easily adjust workloads, monitor utilization and programmatically make changes. You can improve agility and elasticity through services such as Auto Scaling, Elastic Load Balancing and highly scalable services such as S3 and Lambda.
- You do not get free technical support services with AWS.
- You do not gain end-to-end operational management of your entire infrastructure stack. AWS manage the infrastructure and, for some services, the application too.
- You do not outsource all security responsibility with AWS – you are still responsible for ensuring the security of your applications, users, and data.

**References:**

https://digitalcloud.training/certification-training/aws-certified-cloud-practitioner/cloud-computing-concepts/

https://docs.aws.amazon.com/whitepapers/latest/aws-overview/six-advantages-of-cloud-computing.html

## 19. Question

**How can a company connect from their on-premises network to VPCs in multiple regions using private connections?**

1. AWS Direct Connect Gateway
2. AWS Managed VPN
3. Inter-Region VPC Peering
4. Amazon CloudFront

**Answer: 1**

**Explanation:**

- You can use an AWS Direct Connect gateway to connect your AWS Direct Connect connection over a private virtual interface to one or more VPCs in your account that are located in the same or different Regions
- AWS Managed VPN uses the public Internet and is therefore not a private connection
- Amazon CloudFront is a content delivery network used for caching data
- Inter-Region VPC peering does not help you to connect from an on-premise network

**References:**

https://docs.aws.amazon.com/directconnect/latest/UserGuide/direct-connect-gateways.html

## 20. Question

**Under the AWS Shared Responsibility Model, which of the following is the customer NOT responsible for?**

1. Installing firmware updates on host servers
2. Applying encryption to data stored on an EBS volume
3. Applying bucket policies to share Amazon S3 data
4. Adding firewall rules to security groups and network ACLs

**Answer: 1**

**Explanation:**

- AWS customers are not responsible for installing firmware updates on the underlying infrastructure
- AWS customers must protect their AWS services through policies, encryption, and firewall rules

**References:**

https://digitalcloud.training/certification-training/aws-certified-cloud-practitioner/aws-shared-responsibility-model/

## 21. Question

**Which of the following configuration items are important to enabling an EC2 web server to serve web pages on the Internet? (choose 2)**

1. Security groups rules configured to allow SSH
2. An established VPN connection
3. A private IP address assigned to the instance
4. Security group rules configured to allow HTTP/HTTPS
5. A public IP address assigned to the instance

**Answer: 4,5**

**Explanation:**

- To connect to a web page on a web server you use the HTTP/HTTPS protocol. You therefore need to ensure the instance's security group allows these protocols in an inbound rule

- A public IP address assigned to an instance in a public subnet is required in order to be able to directly access the instance from the Internet. There also needs to be an Internet Gateway attached to the VPC and an entry in the route table for the subnet that points to it
- A private IP address will always be assigned to instances in EC2, but these do not enable access from the Internet
- An established VPN connection is not required, connections will come through an Internet Gateway to a public subnet

**References:**

https://digitalcloud.training/2018/10/19/cloud-computing-basics-compute/

## 22. Question

**What are two benefits of using AWS Lambda? (choose 2)**

1. No servers to manage
2. Integrated snapshots
3. Flexible operating system choices
4. Open source software
5. Continuous scaling (scale out)

**Answer: 1,5**

**Explanation:**

- With AWS Lambda you don't have any servers to manage (serverless). Lambda functions scale out rather than up by creating additional functions
- You do not have integrated snapshots (or any persistent storage) with Lambda
- You do not manage the operating system on which the functions run so have no choice of software
- Lambda is AWS proprietary not open source

**References:**

https://digitalcloud.training/certification-training/aws-certified-cloud-practitioner/aws-compute/

## 23. Question

**Why would a company choose a NAT Gateway over a NAT instance? (choose 2)**

1. They are managed by AWS, not by you
2. Can be used for port forwarding
3. You can use security groups to assign firewall rules to them
4. They are elastically scalable
5. They can be additionally used as bastion hosts

**Answer: 1,4**

**Explanation:**

- NAT Gateways are elastically scalable, managed by AWS, and provide automatic HA.
- You cannot assign a NAT Gateway to a security group, use them as bastion hosts, or configure port forwarding

**References:**

https://digitalcloud.training/certification-training/aws-certified-cloud-practitioner/aws-networking/

## 24. Question

**What is the relationship between subnets and availability zones?**

1. You can create one subnet per availability zone
2. Subnets span across multiple availability zones
3. You can create one or more subnets within each availability zone
4. Subnets contain one or more availability zones

**Answer: 3**

**Explanation:**

- You can create one or more subnets within each availability zone but subnets cannot span across availability zones

**References:**

https://digitalcloud.training/certification-training/aws-certified-cloud-practitioner/aws-networking/

## 25. Question

**Which services allow you to store files on AWS? (choose 2)**

1. AWS Lambda
2. Amazon SQS
3. Amazon LightSail
4. Amazon EFS
5. Amazon EBS

**Answer: 4,5**

**Explanation:**

- You can store files on the Elastic Block Store (EBS), and Elastic File System (EFS). EBS volumes are mounted as block devices to EC2 instances and EFS volumes are mounted to the instance using NFS v2 protocol.
- AWS Lambda is a compute service for running code as functions.
- Amazon LightSail is a compute service for running instances.
- Amazon Simple Queue Service (SQS) is a message bus for temporarily storing data that is being passed between application components.

**References:**

https://digitalcloud.training/certification-training/aws-certified-cloud-practitioner/aws-storage/

https://aws.amazon.com/ebs/

https://aws.amazon.com/efs/

## 26. Question

**What feature of Amazon S3 enables you to set rules to automatically transfer objects between different storage classes at defined time intervals?**

1. Object Lifecycle Management
2. S3 Archiving
3. Elastic Data Management
4. Auto Lifecycle Scaling

Answer: 1

Explanation:

- Object lifecycle management can be used with objects so that they are stored cost effectively throughout their lifecycle. Objects can be transitioned to another storage class or expired
- All other options are bogus and do not exist

References:

https://digitalcloud.training/certification-training/aws-certified-cloud-practitioner/aws-storage/

https://docs.aws.amazon.com/AmazonS3/latest/dev/object-lifecycle-mgmt.html

## 27. Question

**Which AWS service can be used to prepare and load data for analytics using an extract, transform and load (ETL) process?**

1. Amazon EMR
2. AWS Glue
3. AWS Lambda
4. Amazon Athena

Answer: 2

Explanation:

- AWS Glue is a fully managed extract, transform, and load (ETL) service that makes it easy for customers to prepare and load their data for analytics
- Amazon Elastic Map Reduce (EMR) provides a managed Hadoop framework that makes it easy, fast, and cost-effective to process vast amounts of data across dynamically scalable Amazon EC2 instances
- Amazon Athena is an interactive query service that makes it easy to analyze data in Amazon S3 using standard SQL
- AWS Lambda is a serverless application that runs code as functions in response to events

References:

https://digitalcloud.training/certification-training/aws-certified-cloud-practitioner/additional-aws-services-tools/

## 28. Question

**What are the benefits of using IAM roles for applications that run on EC2 instances? (choose 2)**

1. It is easier to manage IAM roles
2. Can apply multiple roles to a single instance
3. More secure than storing access keys within applications
4. Easier to configure than using storing access keys within the EC2 instance
5. Role credentials are permanent

Answer: 1,3

Explanation:

- Using IAM roles instead of storing credentials within EC2 instances is more secure It is also easier to manage roles
- It is not easier to configure as there are extra steps that need to be completed
- You cannot apply multiple roles to a single instance
- Role credentials are temporary, not permanent, and are rotated automatically

References:

https://docs.aws.amazon.com/IAM/latest/UserGuide/id_roles_use_switch-role-ec2.html

## 29. Question

**Which type of data storage system is typically considered to hold "structured" data?**

1. Non-relational database
2. Relational database
3. File system
4. Email system

Answer: 2

Explanation:

- Relation databases such as Structured Query Language (SQL) databases hold data in a structured format. Examples are Amazon RDS and Microsoft SQL Server
- File systems, email systems and non-relational databases hold data in an "unstructured" format. This means that though there is some structure to it, the data cannot be easily searched using standard data processing algorithms or structured queries. Unstructured data is more human-friendly than machine-friendly

References:

https://www.webopedia.com/TERM/S/structured_data.html

## 30. Question

**Which DynamoDB feature provides in-memory acceleration to tables that result in significant performance improvements?**

1. Amazon ElastiCache
2. Amazon EFS
3. Amazon DynamoDB Accelerator (DAX)
4. Amazon CloudFront

Answer: 3

Explanation:
- Amazon DynamoDB Accelerator (DAX) is a fully managed, highly available, in-memory cache for DynamoDB that delivers up to a 10x performance improvement – from milliseconds to microseconds – even at millions of requests per second
- DAX does all the heavy lifting required to add in-memory acceleration to your DynamoDB tables, without requiring developers to manage cache invalidation, data population, or cluster management

References:

https://aws.amazon.com/dynamodb/dax/

## 31. Question

**An Elastic IP Address can be remapped between EC2 instances across which boundaries?**

1. DB Subnets
2. Regions
3. Edge Locations
4. Availability Zones

Answer: 4

Explanation:
- Elastic IP addresses are for use in a specific region only and can therefore only be remapped between instances within that region. You can use Elastic IP addresses to mask the failure of an instance in one Availability Zone by rapidly remapping the address to an instance in another Availability Zone
- Edge Locations are used by CloudFront and are not places where you can run EC2 instances
- DB subnets (groups) are used by the RDS relational database service and are not used for running EC2 instances

References:

https://docs.aws.amazon.com/AWSEC2/latest/UserGuide/elastic-ip-addresses-eip.html

https://digitalcloud.training/certification-training/aws-certified-cloud-practitioner/aws-global-infrastructure/

## 32. Question

**Which type of EBS volumes can be encrypted?**

1. Only root volumes can have encryption applied at launch time
2. Only non-root volumes created from snapshots
3. Both non-root and root volumes
4. Non-root volumes only

Answer: 3

**Explanation:**

- All volumes can now be encrypted at launch time and it's possible to set this as the default setting.

**References:**

https://aws.amazon.com/blogs/aws/new-encrypted-ebs-boot-volumes/

https://aws.amazon.com/blogs/aws/new-opt-in-to-default-encryption-for-new-ebs-volumes/

## 33. Question

**Which AWS IAM best practice recommends applying the minimum permissions necessary to perform a task when creating IAM policies?**

1. Enable MFA for privileged users
2. Use roles to delegate permissions
3. Create individual IAM users
4. Grant least privilege

**Answer: 4**

**Explanation:**

- When you create IAM policies, follow the standard security advice of granting least privilege—that is, granting only the permissions required to perform a task. Determine what users need to do and then craft policies for them that let the users perform only those tasks

**References:**

https://docs.aws.amazon.com/IAM/latest/UserGuide/best-practices.html#grant-least-privilege

## 34. Question

**What information must be entered into the AWS TCO Calculator?**

1. The number of end users in your company
2. The number of applications in your company
3. The number of storage systems in your company
4. The number of servers in your company

**Answer: 4**

**Explanation:**

- The TCO calculator asks for the number of servers (Physical or VMs) you are running on-premises. You also need to supply the resource information (CPU, RAM) and specify whether the server is a DB or non-DB.
- You don't need to specify the number of storage systems; you just need to specify the raw capacity.
- You do not need to supply the number of end users or applications.

**References:**

https://aws.amazon.com/tco-calculator/

https://awstcocalculator.com/

## 35. Question

Which service runs your application code only when needed without needing to run servers?

1. AWS LightSail
2. AWS Lambda
3. Amazon ECS
4. Amazon EC2

Answer: 2

Explanation:

- AWS Lambda is a server-less service that runs code as "functions". That means that your code is run when needed but there are no servers running (at least not servers that you see or manage). This reduces cost and operational overhead.
- Amazon EC2 is used for running server instances so this is an incorrect answer.
- Amazon ECS is used for running Docker containers which do need to run waiting for requests.
- AWS LightSail is a service that is used for running virtual instances and databases using a simplified user interface for users who are less experienced with AWS (also at a much lower cost than EC2).

References:

https://digitalcloud.training/certification-training/aws-certified-cloud-practitioner/aws-compute/

https://aws.amazon.com/lambda/

## 36. Question

A company wants to utilize a pay as you go cloud model for all of their applications without CAPEX costs and which is highly elastic. Which cloud delivery model will suit them best?

1. Public
2. Hybrid
3. On-premise
4. Private

Answer: 1

Explanation:

- The public cloud is offered under a purely pay as you go model (unless you choose to reserve) and allows companies to completely avoid CAPEX costs. The public cloud is also highly elastic so companies can grow and shrink the applications as demand changes
- Private and on-premise clouds are essentially the same, though both could be managed by a third party and even could be delivered under an OPEX model by some vendors. However, they are typically more CAPEX heavy and the elasticity is limited
- A hybrid model combines public and private and this company wants to go all in on a single model

References:

https://digitalcloud.training/certification-training/aws-certified-cloud-practitioner/cloud-computing-concepts/

## 37. Question

**Which of the following descriptions is incorrect in relation to the design of Availability Zones?**

1. Each subnet in a VPC is mapped to all AZs in the region
2. AZs are physically separated within a typical metropolitan region and are located in lower risk flood plains
3. Each AZ is designed as an independent failure zone
4. AZ's have direct, low-latency, high throughput and redundant network connections between each other

**Answer: 1**

**Explanation:**

- Subnets are created within a single AZ and do not get mapped to multiple AZs

**References:**

https://digitalcloud.training/certification-training/aws-certified-cloud-practitioner/aws-global-infrastructure/

https://digitalcloud.training/certification-training/aws-certified-cloud-practitioner/aws-networking/

## 38. Question

**Which AWS services have a global (rather than regional) scope? (choose 2)**

1. Amazon EFS
2. AWS CloudFront
3. Amazon S3
4. AWS WAF
5. AWS Lambda

**Answer: 2,4**

**Explanation:**

- AWS WAF and AWS CloudFront are both services that are global in scope. When you configure these services in the AWS management console you will see that the scope is set to "Global"
- All other services listed are regional in scope. When you configure these through the AWS management console you will need to select a region and will see the name of the region listed instead of "Global"
- NOTE: S3 uses a global namespace, meaning that bucket names must be unique globally. However, you still create buckets within a region

**References:**

https://digitalcloud.training/certification-training/aws-certified-cloud-practitioner/aws-global-infrastructure/

## 39. Question

Which AWS service can be used to send automated notifications to HTTP endpoints?

1. Amazon SWF
2. Amazon SQS
3. Amazon SES
4. Amazon SNS

Answer: 4

Explanation:

- Amazon Simple Notification Service (Amazon SNS) is a web service that makes it easy to set up, operate, and send notifications from the cloud. SNS can be used to send automated or manual notifications to email, mobile (SMS), SQS, and HTTP endpoints
- Amazon Simple Queue Service (SQS) is a fully managed message queuing service that enables you to decouple and scale microservices, distributed systems, and serverless applications
- Amazon SWF helps developers build, run, and scale background jobs that have parallel or sequential step
- Amazon Simple Email Service (Amazon SES) is a cloud-based email sending service designed to help digital marketers and application developers send marketing, notification, and transactional emails

References:

https://digitalcloud.training/certification-training/aws-certified-cloud-practitioner/notification-services/

## 40. Question

Which of the following constitute the five pillars for the AWS Well-Architected Framework? (choose 2)

1. Operational excellence, security, and reliability
2. Data consistency, and cost optimization
3. Operational excellence, elasticity and scalability
4. Cost prioritization, and cost optimization
5. Performance efficiency, and cost optimization

Answer: 1,5

Explanation:

- The five pillars of the AWS Well-Architected Framework are operational excellence, security, reliability, performance efficiency, and cost optimization

References:

https://aws.amazon.com/blogs/apn/the-5-pillars-of-the-aws-well-architected-framework/

## 41. Question

Which of the following are advantages of using the AWS cloud computing over legacy IT? (choose 2)

1. You don't need to worry about over provisioning as you can elastically scale
2. You are able to pass responsibility for the availability of your application to AWS

3. You don't need to patch your operating systems
4. You can bring new applications to market faster
5. You can bring services closer to your end users

**Answer: 1,4**

**Explanation:**

- With cloud computing you no longer need to guess about capacity as you can elastically scale. This means you don't end up overprovisioning but instead react to the load on your servers. You can also be faster and more agile with development and release of applications
- You do not pass responsibility for your application to AWS. AWS runs the infrastructure but you still manage the application
- You still need to patch your own operating systems
- The cloud is centralized so you won't necessarily bring services closer to your end users

**References:**

https://digitalcloud.training/certification-training/aws-certified-cloud-practitioner/cloud-computing-concepts/

## 42. Question

**Which AWS service can assist with providing recommended actions on cost optimization?**

1. AWS Artifact
2. Amazon CloudWatch Events
3. AWS Trusted Advisor
4. AWS Inspector

**Answer: 3**

**Explanation:**

- Trusted Advisor is an online resource that helps to reduce cost, increase performance and improve security by optimizing your AWS environment.
- Inspector is an automated security assessment service that helps improve the security and compliance of applications deployed on AWS.
- AWS Artifact is a resource for obtaining compliance-related information.
- Amazon CloudWatch Events delivers a near real-time stream of system events that describe changes in Amazon Web Services (AWS) resources.

**References:**

https://digitalcloud.training/certification-training/aws-certified-cloud-practitioner/cloud-security/

https://aws.amazon.com/premiumsupport/technology/trusted-advisor/

## 43. Question

**What offerings are included in the Amazon Lightsail product set? (choose 2)**

1. Object storage
2. Serverless functions

3. Managed MySQL database
4. NoSQL database
5. Virtual Private Server

Answer: 3,5

Explanation:

- Amazon Lightsail provides an easy, low cost way to consume cloud services without needing the skill set for using VPC resources. The product set includes virtual private servers (instances), managed MySQL databases, HA storage, and load balancing
- You can connect to other AWS services such as S3, DynamoDB, and CloudFront, however these are not part of the Lightsail product range

References:

https://digitalcloud.training/certification-training/aws-certified-cloud-practitioner/aws-compute/

https://aws.amazon.com/lightsail/features/

## 44. Question

What is the name of the AWS managed Docker registry service used by the Amazon Elastic Container Service (ECS)?

1. Elastic Container Registry
2. ECS Container Registry
3. Docker Container Registry
4. Docker Image Repository

Answer: 1

Explanation:

- The Elastic container registry (ECR) is a managed AWS Docker registry service for storing, managing and deploying Docker images

References:

https://digitalcloud.training/certification-training/aws-certified-cloud-practitioner/aws-compute/

## 45. Question

How do AWS charge for Amazon CloudFront? (choose 2)

1. Data transfer in
2. Number of users
3. Number of requests
4. Data transfer out
5. Uptime

Answer: 3,4

Explanation:

- With Amazon CloudFront the basic elements you are charged for include the amount of data transfer out and the number of requests. There are additional chargeable items such as invalidation requests, field-level encryption requests, and custom SSL certificates

**References:**

https://digitalcloud.training/certification-training/aws-certified-cloud-practitioner/aws-billing-and-pricing/

## 46. Question

When designing a VPC, what is the purpose of an Internet Gateway?

1. Provides Internet access for EC2 instances in private subnets
2. It's a bastion host for inbound management connections
3. It's used for making VPN connections to a VPC
4. Enables Internet communications for instances in public subnets

**Answer: 4**

**Explanation:**

- An internet gateway is a horizontally scaled, redundant, and highly available VPC component that allows communication between instances in your VPC and the internet. It therefore imposes no availability risks or bandwidth constraints on your network traffic
- An internet gateway serves two purposes: to provide a target in your VPC route tables for internet-routable traffic, and to perform network address translation (NAT) for instances that have been assigned public IPv4 addresses
- You cannot use an Internet Gateway as a bastion host, deploy an EC2 instance in a public subnet for this purpose
- You cannot connect instances in a private subnet to the Internet using an Internet Gateway, you need a NAT Gateway or NAT Instance for this purpose
- You cannot use the Internet Gateway for making VPN connections to a VPC, you need a Virtual Private Gateway for this purpose

**References:**

https://digitalcloud.training/certification-training/aws-certified-cloud-practitioner/aws-networking/

https://docs.aws.amazon.com/vpc/latest/userguide/VPC_Internet_Gateway.html

## 47. Question

Which service provides alerts and remediation guidance when AWS is experiencing events that may impact you?

1. AWS Trusted Advisor
2. AWS Personal Health Dashboard
3. AWS Inspector
4. AWS Shield

**Answer: 2**

**Explanation:**

- AWS Personal Health Dashboard provides alerts and remediation guidance when AWS is experiencing events that may impact you
- Trusted Advisor is an online resource that helps to reduce cost, increase performance and improve security by optimizing your AWS environment
- Inspector is an automated security assessment service that helps improve the security and compliance of applications deployed on AWS
- AWS Shield is a managed Distributed Denial of Service (DDoS) protection service

**References:**

https://digitalcloud.training/certification-training/aws-certified-cloud-practitioner/cloud-security/

## 48. Question

**Which AWS service lets connected devices easily and securely interact with cloud applications and other devices?**

1. Amazon Workspaces
2. AWS Directory Service
3. AWS IoT Core
4. AWS SMS

**Answer: 3**

**Explanation:**

- AWS IoT Core is a managed cloud service that lets connected devices easily and securely interact with cloud applications and other devices. AWS IoT Core can support billions of devices and trillions of messages, and can process and route those messages to AWS endpoints and to other devices reliably and securely
- AWS Directory Service for Microsoft Active Directory, also known as AWS Managed Microsoft AD, enables your directory-aware workloads and AWS resources to use managed Active Directory in the AWS Cloud
- Amazon WorkSpaces is a managed, secure cloud desktop service
- AWS Server Migration Service (SMS) is an agentless service which makes it easier and faster for you to migrate thousands of on-premises workloads to AWS

**References:**

https://digitalcloud.training/certification-training/aws-certified-cloud-practitioner/additional-aws-services-tools/

## 49. Question

**Which AWS security service provides a firewall at the subnet level within a VPC?**

1. Security Group
2. IAM Policy
3. Network Access Control List
4. Bucket Policy

**Answer: 3**

**Explanation:**

- A Network ACL is a firewall that is associated with a subnet within your VPC. It is used to filter the network traffic that enters and exits the subnet.
- An IAM Policy is used to assign permissions to users and roles.
- A Bucket Policy is used with Amazon S3 buckets to control access.
- A Security Group is a firewall that is associated with an EC2 instances (not the subnet). Security Groups control the traffic the inbound and outbound network traffic from/to the instance.

**References:**

https://digitalcloud.training/certification-training/aws-certified-cloud-practitioner/aws-networking/

https://docs.aws.amazon.com/vpc/latest/userguide/vpc-network-acls.html

## 50. Question

With which service can a developer upload code from a Git repository and have the service handle the end-to-end deployment of the resources?

1. AWS CodeDeploy
2. AWS CodeCommit
3. AWS Elastic Beanstalk
4. Amazon ECS

**Answer: 3**

**Explanation:**

- AWS Elastic Beanstalk can be used to quickly deploy and manage applications in the AWS Cloud. Developers upload applications and Elastic Beanstalk handles the deployment details of capacity provisioning, load balancing, auto-scaling, and application health monitoring
- AWS CodeCommit is a fully-managed source control service that hosts secure Git-based repositories
- AWS CodeDeploy is a fully managed deployment service that automates software deployments to a variety of compute services such as Amazon EC2, AWS Lambda, and your on-premises servers
- Amazon Elastic Container Service is a managed service for running Docker containers

**References:**

https://digitalcloud.training/certification-training/aws-solutions-architect-associate/compute/aws-elastic-beanstalk/

## 51. Question

A developer needs a way to automatically provision a collection of AWS resources. Which AWS service is primarily used for deploying infrastructure as code?

1. AWS Elastic Beanstalk
2. Jenkins
3. Amazon CloudFormation
4. AWS CodeDeploy

**Answer: 3**

**Explanation:**

- AWS CloudFormation is a service that gives developers and businesses an easy way to create a collection of related AWS resources and provision them in an orderly and predictable fashion. AWS CloudFormation provides a common language for you to describe and provision all the infrastructure resources in your cloud environment. Think of CloudFormation as deploying infrastructure as code
- Elastic Beanstalk is more focused on deploying applications on EC2 (PaaS)
- AWS CodeDeploy is a fully managed deployment service that automates software deployments to a variety of compute services such as Amazon EC2, AWS Lambda, and your on-premises servers
- Jenkins deploys infrastructure as code but is not an AWS service

**References:**

https://digitalcloud.training/certification-training/aws-certified-cloud-practitioner/additional-aws-services-tools/

## 52. Question

**To reward customers for using their services, what are two ways AWS reduce prices? (choose 2)**

1. Reduced cost for reserved capacity
2. Reduction in inbound data transfer charges
3. Removal of termination fees for customers who spend more
4. Discounts for using a wider variety of services
5. Volume based discounts when you use more services

**Answer: 1,5**

**Explanation:**

- AWS provide volume-based discount so that when you use more services you reduce the cost per service. You can also reserve capacity by locking in to fixed 1- or 3-year contracts to get significant discounts
- You never pay for inbound data transfer
- You don't get discounts for using a variety of services, only when you use more services
- There are never termination fees with AWS

**References:**

https://digitalcloud.training/certification-training/aws-certified-cloud-practitioner/aws-billing-and-pricing/

https://aws.amazon.com/pricing/

## 53. Question

**What is an Edge location?**

1. A virtual private gateway for VPN
2. A content delivery network (CDN) endpoint for CloudFront
3. A VPC peering connection endpoint
4. A public endpoint for Amazon S3

**Answer: 2**

**Explanation:**

- Edge locations are Content Delivery Network (CDN) endpoints for CloudFront. There are many more edge locations than regions

**References:**

https://digitalcloud.training/certification-training/aws-certified-cloud-practitioner/aws-global-infrastructure/

## 54. Question

Which service allows an organization to bring their own licensing on host hardware that is physically isolated from other AWS accounts?

1. EC2 Reserved Instances
2. EC2 Dedicated Instances
3. EC2 Dedicated Hosts
4. EC2 Spot Instances

**Answer: 3**

**Explanation:**

- An Amazon EC2 Dedicated Host is a physical server with EC2 instance capacity fully dedicated to your use. Dedicated Hosts allow you to use your existing per-socket, per-core, or per-VM software licenses, including Windows Server, Microsoft SQL Server, SUSE, Linux Enterprise Server, and so on
- Dedicated Instances are Amazon EC2 instances that run in a VPC on hardware that's dedicated to a single customer. Bring your own licensing (BYOL) is not supported for dedicated instances
- Spot instances allow you to bid in the marketplace for EC2 instances to reduce cost, they do not allow BYOL
- Reserved instances allow you to reduce on-demand price by up to 70% by committing to a 1- or 3-year term

**References:**

https://docs.aws.amazon.com/AWSEC2/latest/UserGuide/dedicated-hosts-overview.html

https://digitalcloud.training/certification-training/aws-certified-cloud-practitioner/aws-compute/

## 55. Question

Which of the following is NOT an AWS service used for transferring large amounts of data into Amazon S3?

1. AWS Snowball
2. AWS DMS
3. AWS Snowmobile
4. S3 Transfer Acceleration

Answer: 2

Explanation:

- AWS DMS is used for migrating databases into or within AWS
- All other options are valid services that are used for transferring large amounts of data into Amazon S3

References:

https://aws.amazon.com/s3/features/


## 56. Question

**What charges are applicable to Amazon S3 Standard storage class? (choose 2)**

1. Data egress
2. Data ingress
3. Per GB/month storage fee
4. Retrieval fee
5. Minimum capacity charge per object

Answer: 1,3

Explanation:

- With the standard storage class, you pay a per GB/month storage fee, and data transfer out of S3
- Standard-IA and One Zone-IA have a minimum capacity charge per object
- Standard-IA, One Zone-IA, and Glacier also have a retrieval fee
- You don't pay for data into S3 under any storage class

References:

https://digitalcloud.training/certification-training/aws-certified-cloud-practitioner/aws-storage/

https://digitalcloud.training/certification-training/aws-solutions-architect-associate/storage/amazon-s3/


## 57. Question

**Which support plan is the lowest cost option that allows unlimited cases to be open?**

1. Developer
2. Enterprise
3. Basic
4. Business

Answer: 1

Explanation:

- With the Developer plan you can open unlimited cases
- You can also open unlimited cases with the Business and Enterprise plans but these are more expensive
- You cannot open any support cases with the basic support plan

References:

https://digitalcloud.training/certification-training/aws-certified-cloud-practitioner/aws-billing-and-pricing/

## 58. Question

**Assuming you have configured them correctly, which AWS services can scale automatically without intervention? (choose 2)**

1. Amazon EBS
2. Amazon DynamoDB
3. Amazon S3
4. Amazon EC2
5. Amazon RDS

**Answer: 2,3**

**Explanation:**

- Both S3 and DynamoDB automatically scale as demand dictates. In the case of DynamoDB you can either configure the on-demand or provisioned capacity mode. With on-demand capacity mode DynamoDB automatically adjusts the read and write throughput for you
- EC2 cannot scale automatically. You need to use Auto Scaling to scale the number of EC2 instances deployed
- EBS and RDS do not scale automatically. You must intervene to adjust volume sizes and database instance types to scale these resources

**References:**

https://digitalcloud.training/certification-training/aws-solutions-architect-associate/database/amazon-dynamodb/

https://digitalcloud.training/certification-training/aws-solutions-architect-associate/storage/amazon-s3/

## 59. Question

**How can an online education company ensure their video courses play with minimal latency for their users around the world?**

1. Use Amazon Aurora Global Database
2. Use Amazon S3 Transfer Acceleration to speed up downloads
3. Use Amazon CloudFront to get the content closer to users
4. Use Amazon EBS Cross Region Replication to get the content close to the users

**Answer: 3**

**Explanation:**

- Amazon CloudFront is a content delivery network (CDN) that enables you to cache content in Edge Locations that are located around the world. This brings your media closer to your end users which reduces latency and improves the user experience.
- Amazon EBS Cross Region Replication does not exist (S3 Cross Region Replication does). You can copy EBS volumes across regions manually (or programmatically), however EBS is not a good way

- to get your content closer to your users as you would need to mount the volume to an EC2 instance (additional cost) and would also need to find a way to keep your files in sync.
- Amazon S3 Transfer Acceleration is a feature that is used for accelerating uploads to Amazon S3, not for downloads.
- Amazon Aurora Global Database is designed for globally distributed applications, allowing a single Amazon Aurora database to span multiple AWS regions. This is a way to have an SQL database across regions, which is not a good use case for hosting media files.

**References:**

https://digitalcloud.training/certification-training/aws-certified-cloud-practitioner/content-delivery-and-dns-services/

https://aws.amazon.com/cloudfront/

## 60. Question

**Which service can you use to monitor, store and access log files generated by EC2 instances and on-premises servers?**

1. Amazon Kinesis
2. Amazon CloudWatch Logs
3. AWS OpsWorks
4. Amazon CloudTrail

**Answer: 2**

**Explanation:**

- You can use Amazon CloudWatch Logs to monitor, store, and access your log files from Amazon Elastic Compute Cloud (Amazon EC2) instances, AWS CloudTrail, Route 53, and other sources
- You can then retrieve the associated log data from CloudWatch Logs
- Amazon CloudTrail is used for recording a history of API actions taken on your account.
- Amazon Kinesis is a set of services used for collecting, processing and analyzing streaming data

**References:**

https://docs.aws.amazon.com/AmazonCloudWatch/latest/logs/WhatIsCloudWatchLogs.html

## 61. Question

**Which AWS feature of Amazon EC2 allows an administrator to create a standardized image that can be used for launching new instances?**

1. Amazon Golden Image
2. Amazon Block Template
3. Amazon Machine Image
4. Amazon EBS Mount Point

**Answer: 3**

**Explanation:**

- An Amazon Machine Image (AMI) provides the information required to launch an instance. You can use an AMI to launch identical instances from a standard template. This is also known as a Golden Image (though no such feature exists in AWS with this name). An AMI is created from an EBS snapshot and also includes launch permissions and a block device mapping.
- Amazon Block Templates and Amazon Machine Images do not exist.
- An Amazon EBS Mount Point is not an AWS feature. You do mount EBS volumes however this is within the operating system. Block device mappings are used in AMIs to specify how to mount the EBS volume.

**References:**

https://digitalcloud.training/certification-training/aws-certified-cloud-practitioner/aws-compute/

https://docs.aws.amazon.com/AWSEC2/latest/UserGuide/AMIs.html

## 62. Question

**How can you configure Amazon Route 53 to monitor the health and performance of your application?**

1. Using DNS lookups
2. Using CloudWatch
3. Using Route 53 health checks
4. Using the Route 53 API

**Answer: 3**

**Explanation:**

- Amazon Route 53 health checks monitor the health and performance of your web applications, web servers, and other resources
- None of the other options provide a solution that can check the health and performance of an application

**References:**

https://docs.aws.amazon.com/Route53/latest/DeveloperGuide/dns-failover.html

## 63. Question

**What is the availability model of Amazon DynamoDB?**

1. Data is asynchronously replicated across all regions
2. Data is synchronously replicated across all regions
3. Data is asynchronously replicated across 3 facilities in a region
4. Data is synchronously replicated across 3 facilities in a region

**Answer: 4**

**Explanation:**

- Amazon DynamoDB stores three geographically distributed replicas of each table to enable high availability and data durability. Data is synchronously replicated across 3 facilities (AZs) in a region

**References:**

https://digitalcloud.training/certification-training/aws-solutions-architect-associate/database/amazon-dynamodb/

## 64. Question

**Which type of storage stores objects comprised of key, value pairs?**

1. Amazon DynamoDB
2. Amazon EBS
3. Amazon S3
4. Amazon EFS

Answer: 3

Explanation:

- Amazon S3 is an object-based storage system that stores objects that are comprised of key, value pairs
- Amazon DynamoDB stores items, not objects, based on key, value pairs
- Amazon EBS is a block-based storage system
- Amazon EFS is a file-based storage system

References:

https://digitalcloud.training/certification-training/aws-certified-cloud-practitioner/aws-storage/

## 65. Question

**Which service is used for caching data?**

1. Amazon Elastic File System (EFS)
2. Amazon Simple Queue Service (SQS)
3. Amazon DynamoDB DAX
4. Amazon Key Management Service (KMS)

Answer: 3

Explanation:

- Amazon DynamoDB Accelerator (DAX) is a fully managed, highly available, in-memory cache for DynamoDB that delivers up to a 10x performance improvement – from milliseconds to microseconds – even at millions of requests per second
- Amazon Simple Queue Service (SQS) is a fully managed message queuing service that enables you to decouple and scale microservices, distributed systems, and serverless applications
- AWS Key Management Service (KMS) makes it easy for you to create and manage keys and control the use of encryption across a wide range of AWS services and in your applications
- Amazon Elastic File System (Amazon EFS) provides a simple, scalable, elastic file system for Linux-based workloads for use with AWS Cloud services and on-premises resources

References:

https://digitalcloud.training/certification-training/aws-certified-cloud-practitioner/aws-databases/

# SET 6: PRACTICE QUESTIONS ONLY

### 1. Question

What are the advantages of running a database service such as Amazon RDS in the cloud versus deploying on-premise? (choose 2)

1. You have full control of the operating system and can install your own operational tools
2. Scalability is improved as it is quicker to implement and there is an abundance of capacity
3. You can use any database software you like, allowing greater flexibility
4. High availability is easier to implement due to built-in functionality for deploying read replicas and multi-AZ
5. There are no costs for replicating data between DBs in different data centers or regions

### 2. Question

Where do Amazon Identity and Access Management (IAM) accounts need to be created for a global organization?

1. In each geographical area where the users are located
2. In each region where the users are located
3. Create them globally, and then replicate them regionally
4. Just create them once, as IAM is a global service

### 3. Question

Which AWS service makes it easy to coordinate the components of distributed applications as a series of steps in a visual workflow?

1. Amazon SWF
2. AWS Step Functions
3. Amazon SNS
4. Amazon SES

### 4. Question

A Solutions Architect needs to design a cloud-native application architecture using AWS services. What is a typical use case for Amazon Simple Queue Service (SQS)?

1. Providing fault tolerance for EC2 instances
2. Co-ordination of work items between different human and non-human workers
3. Running serverless processes as functions
4. Decoupling application components to ensure that there is no dependency on the availability of a single component

### 5. Question

With which AWS Storage Gateway Volume Gateway configuration is data stored on-premise and asynchronously backed up to Amazon S3?

1. Cached volume mode

2. Stored volume mode
3. File gateway mode
4. VTL mode

## 6. Question

Which AWS technology can be referred to as a "virtual hard disk in the cloud"?

1. Amazon S3 Bucket
2. Amazon ENI
3. Amazon EFS Filesystem
4. Amazon EBS volume

## 7. Question

Which of the following are examples of horizontal scaling? (choose 2)

1. Add more instances as demand increases
2. Add more CPU/RAM to existing instances as demand increases
3. Scalability is limited by maximum instance size
4. Requires a restart to scale up or down
5. Automatic using services such as AWS Auto Scaling

## 8. Question

Which HTTP code indicates a successful upload of an object to Amazon S3?

1. 500
2. 400
3. 300
4. 200

## 9. Question

Which AWS database service is a SQL database that supports complex queries and joins?

1. Amazon DynamoDB
2. Amazon ElastiCache
3. Amazon RDS
4. Amazon SimpleDB

## 10. Question

You need to connect your company's on-premise network into AWS and would like to establish an AWS managed VPN service. Which of the following configuration items needs to be setup on the Amazon VPC side of the connection?

1. A Customer Gateway
2. A Virtual Private Gateway
3. A Firewall
4. A Network Address Translation device

## 11. Question

Which AWS service is designed to be used for operational analytics?

1. Amazon EMR
2. Amazon Athena
3. Amazon QuickSight
4. Amazon Elasticsearch Service


## 12. Question

Which of the following are NOT features of AWS IAM? (choose 2)

1. Charged for what you use
2. Shared access to your AWS account
3. Logon using local user accounts
4. Identity federation
5. PCI DSS compliance


## 13. Question

Which AWS storage service is accessed using the Network File System (NFS) protocol?

1. Amazon EBS
2. Amazon Instance Store
3. Amazon S3
4. Amazon EFS


## 14. Question

You are evaluating AWS services that can assist with creating scalable application environments. Which of the statements below best describes the Elastic Load Balancer service?

1. A network service that provides an alternative to using the Internet to connect customers' on-premise sites to AWS
2. Helps you ensure that you have the correct number of Amazon EC2 instances available to handle the load for your application
3. A highly available and scalable Domain Name System (DNS) service
4. Automatically distributes incoming application traffic across multiple targets, such as Amazon EC2 instances, containers, and IP addresses


## 15. Question

What are two of the core concepts related to Amazon SNS? (choose 2)

1. Tables
2. Conversations
3. Topics
4. Subscriptions
5. Templates

## 16. Question

**To which destinations can Amazon S3 NOT send event notifications? (choose 2)**

1. SQS Queue
2. CloudWatch
3. SNS Topics
4. Lambda functions
5. DynamoDB Table


## 17. Question

**What methods are available for scaling an Amazon RDS database? (choose 2)**

1. You can scale up by moving to a larger instance size
2. You can scale up automatically using AWS Auto Scaling
3. You can scale out automatically with EC2 Auto Scaling
4. You can scale up by increasing storage capacity
5. You can scale out by implementing Elastic Load Balancing


## 18. Question

**Which type of scaling does AWS Auto Scaling provide?**

1. Incremental
2. Horizontal
3. Linear
4. Vertical


## 19. Question

**You need to provision a single EBS volume that is 500 GiB in size and needs to support 20,000 IOPS. Which EBS volume type will you select?**

1. Throughput Optimized HDD
2. Provisioned IOPS SSD
3. Cold HDD
4. General Purpose SSD


## 20. Question

**Which service allows you to monitor and troubleshoot systems using system and application log files generated by those systems?**

1. CloudWatch Logs
2. CloudWatch Metrics
3. CloudTrail Logs
4. CloudTrail Metrics


## 21. Question

**Under the AWS Shared Responsibility Model, who is responsible for what? (choose 2)**

1. AWS are responsible for network and firewall configuration
2. AWS are responsible for networking infrastructure
3. Customers are responsible for compute infrastructure
4. Customers are responsible for networking traffic protection
5. Customers are responsible for edge locations

## 22. Question

A Solutions Architect is creating the business process workflows associated with an order fulfilment system. Which AWS service can assist with coordinating tasks across distributed application components?

1. Amazon SNS
2. Amazon SQS
3. Amazon STS
4. Amazon SWF

## 23. Question

When using Identity and Access Management (IAM) what is the process of gaining access to a resource?

1. With IAM you do not need to authenticate or be authorized
2. First you authenticate, then you are authorized, and then you gain access
3. First you are authorized, then you authenticate, and then you gain access
4. First you authenticate, then you gain access, and then you are authorized

## 24. Question

How can a company configure automatic, asynchronous copying of objects in Amazon S3 buckets across regions?

1. Using lifecycle actions
2. Using cross-region replication
3. By configuring multi-master replication
4. This is done by default by AWS

## 25. Question

Which of the authentication options below can be used to authenticate using AWS APIs? (choose 2)

1. Access keys
2. Key pairs
3. Security groups
4. Server certificates
5. Server passwords

## 26. Question

Your company has recently migrated to AWS. How can your CTO monitor the organization's costs?

1. AWS Consolidated Billing

2. AWS CloudTrail
3. AWS Cost Explorer
4. AWS Simple Monthly calculator

## 27. Question

**What type of cloud computing service type do AWS Elastic Beanstalk and Amazon RDS correspond to?**

1. Hybrid
2. IaaS
3. PaaS
4. SaaS

## 28. Question

**What is an example of scaling vertically?**

1. Increasing the instance size with Amazon RDS
2. AWS Lambda adding concurrently executing functions
3. AWS Auto Scaling adding more EC2 instances
4. Adding read replicas to an Amazon RDS database

## 29. Question

**Up to what layer of the OSI model does AWS Web Application Firewall operate?**

1. Layer 7
2. Layer 3
3. Layer 4
4. Layer 5

## 30. Question

**Which AWS technology enables you to group resources that share one or more tags?**

1. Tag groups
2. Organization groups
3. Resource groups
4. Consolidation groups

## 31. Question

**Which of the following is not a best practice for protecting the root user of an AWS account?**

1. Enable MFA
2. Lock away the AWS root user access keys
3. Don't share the root user credentials
4. Remove administrative permissions

## 32. Question

What do you need to create to specify how your AWS Auto Scaling Group scales and shrinks?

1. IAM Policy
2. Launch Configuration
3. Scaling Plan
4. Scaling Policy


## 33. Question

Which AWS database service is schema-less and can be scaled dynamically without incurring downtime?

1. Amazon RedShift
2. Amazon Aurora
3. Amazon DynamoDB
4. Amazon RDS


## 34. Question

What is the easiest way to store a backup of an EBS volume on Amazon S3?

1. Write a custom script to copy the data into a bucket
2. Use S3 lifecycle actions to backup the volume
3. Use Amazon Kinesis to process the data and store the results in S3
4. Create a snapshot of the volume


## 35. Question

What is the name for the top-level container used to hold objects within Amazon S3?

1. Folder
2. Directory
3. Bucket
4. Instance Store


## 36. Question

Which types of scaling policies are available when using AWS Auto Scaling? (choose 2)

1. Simple scaling
2. Deferred scaling
3. Warm scaling
4. Agile scaling
5. Step scaling


## 37. Question

Your manager has asked you to explain the benefits of using IAM groups. Which of the below statements are valid benefits? (choose 2)

1. You can restrict access to the subnets in your VPC

2. Groups let you specify permissions for multiple users, which can make it easier to manage the permissions for those users
  3. Provide the ability to nest groups to create an organizational hierarchy
  4. Enables you to attach IAM permission policies to more than one user at a time
  5. Provide the ability to create custom permission policies

## 38. Question

Which AWS Glacier data access option retrieves data from an archive in 1-5 minutes?

  1. Expedited
  2. Standard
  3. Express
  4. Accelerated

## 39. Question

Which of the following are pillars from the five pillars of the AWS Well-Architected Framework? (Choose 2)

  1. Resilience
  2. Operational excellence
  3. Confidentiality
  4. Economics
  5. Performance efficiency

## 40. Question

Which resource should you use to access AWS security and compliance reports?

  1. AWS Business Associate Addendum (BAA)
  2. AWS Organizations
  3. AWS IAM
  4. AWS Artifact

## 41. Question

How many snapshots are required in order to restore an Amazon EBS volume?

  1. All snapshots
  2. The first snapshot only
  3. The most recent snapshot only
  4. The first and most recent snapshot

## 42. Question

Which type of Elastic Load Balancer only distributes traffic using the HTTP, and HTTPS protocol information?

  1. No load balancers operate at the TCP level
  2. Application Load Balancer (ALB)
  3. Network Load Balancer (NLB

4. Classic Load Balancer (CLB)

## 43. Question

**Which feature of Amazon S3 enables you to create rules to control the transfer of objects between different storage classes?**

1. Versioning
2. Object sharing
3. Lifecycle management
4. Bucket policies

## 44. Question

**What advantages does the AWS cloud provide in relation to cost? (choose 2)**

1. Enterprise licensing discounts
2. Fine-grained billing
3. Itemized power costs
4. Ability to turn off resources and not pay for them
5. One-off payments for on-demand resources

## 45. Question

**What do you need to log into the AWS console?**

1. Access key and secret ID
2. Key pair
3. User name and password
4. Certificate

## 46. Question

**How can a systems administrator specify a script to be run on an EC2 instance during launch?**

1. User Data
2. Metadata
3. Run Command
4. AWS Config

## 47. Question

**Which type of consistency model does Amazon S3 provide for PUTS of new objects?**

1. Read-after-write consistency
2. Asynchronous consistency
3. Write-after-PUT consistency
4. Eventual consistency

## 48. Question

Your organization has offices around the world and some employees travel between offices. How should their accounts be setup?

1. IAM is a global service, just create the users in one place
2. Set the user account as a "global" account when created
3. Enable MFA for the accounts
4. Create a separate account in IAM within each region in which they will travel

## 49. Question

Which type of Elastic Load Balancer only distributes traffic using layer 4 protocol information?

1. No load balancers operate at the TCP level
2. Classic Load Balancer (CLB)
3. Network Load Balancer (NLB)
4. Application Load Balancer (ALB)

## 50. Question

Your manager has asked you to explain some of the security features available in the AWS cloud. How can you describe the function of Amazon CloudHSM?

1. It can be used to generate, use and manage encryption keys in the cloud
2. It provides server-side encryption for S3 objects
3. it is a firewall for use with web applications
4. It is a Public Key Infrastructure (PKI)

## 51. Question

When using Amazon RDS with Read Replicas, which of the deployment options below are valid? (choose 2)

1. Within an Availability Zone
2. Cross-edge location
3. Cross-subnet
4. Cross-data center
5. Cross-Availability Zone

## 52. Question

What types of rules can be defined in a security group? (choose 2)

1. Outbound
2. Tags
3. Deny
4. Inbound
5. Stateful

## 53. Question

Which AWS security tool uses an agent installed in EC2 instances and assesses applications for vulnerabilities and deviations from best practices?

1. AWS Trusted Advisor
2. AWS Personal Health Dashboard
3. AWS TCO Calculator
4. AWS Inspector

## 54. Question

Which type of AWS database is ideally suited to analytics using SQL queries?

1. Amazon RDS
2. Amazon RedShift
3. Amazon DynamoDB
4. Amazon S3

## 55. Question

According to the AWS Shared Responsibility Model, which of the following is a shared control?

1. Operating system patching
2. Client-side data encryption
3. Protection of infrastructure
4. Awareness and training

## 56. Question

How can you deploy your EC2 instances so that if a single data center fails you still have instances available?

1. Across Availability Zones
2. Across regions
3. Across subnets
4. Across VPCs

## 57. Question

How can a database administrator reduce operational overhead for a MySQL database?

1. Use AWS CloudFormation to manage operations
2. Migrate the database onto an Amazon RDS instance
3. Migrate the database onto an EC2 instance
4. Migrate the database onto AWS Lambda

## 58. Question

Which of the statements below do not characterize cloud computing?

1. Cloud computing allows you to swap variable expense for capital expense
2. With cloud computing you can increase your speed and agility

3. With cloud computing you get to benefit from massive economies of scale
4. Cloud computing is the on-demand delivery of compute power

## 59. Question

Which AWS support plans provide 24×7 access to customer service?

1. Basic
2. Business
3. Developer
4. All plans

## 60. Question

Which types of servers can be migrated using the AWS Server Migration Service? (choose 2)

1. Hyper-V VMs
2. VMware vSphere VMs
3. OpenStack VMs
4. Azure Instances
5. Oracle VMs

## 61. Question

How can a Solutions Architect reduce the latency between end-users and applications or content? (choose 2)

1. Deploy applications in regions closest to the end-users
2. Use Amazon CloudFront to cache content closer to end-users
3. Use S3 Transfer Acceleration to improve application performance
4. Deploy applications in multiple AZs
5. Use larger EC2 instance types for the applications

## 62. Question

In which ways does AWS' pricing model benefit organizations?

1. Eliminates licensing costs
2. Focus spend on capital expenditure, rather than operational expenditure
3. Reduce the cost of maintaining idle resources
4. Reduces the people cost of application development

## 63. Question

Where are Amazon EBS snapshots stored?

1. On Amazon S3
2. On an Amazon EFS filesystem
3. On an Amazon EBS instance store
4. Within the EBS block store

## 64. Question

**To reduce cost, which of the following services support reservations? (choose 2)**

1. Amazon S3
2. AWS Elastic Beanstalk
3. Amazon RedShift
4. Amazon CloudFormation
5. Amazon ElastiCache

## 65. Question

**How can a company facilitate the sharing of data over private connections between two accounts they own within a region?**

1. Create a subnet peering connection
2. Create an internal ELB
3. Create a VPC peering connection
4. Configure matching CIDR address ranges

# SET 6: PRACTICE QUESTIONS, ANSWERS & EXPLANATIONS

## 1. Question

What are the advantages of running a database service such as Amazon RDS in the cloud versus deploying on-premise? (choose 2)

1. You have full control of the operating system and can install your own operational tools
2. Scalability is improved as it is quicker to implement and there is an abundance of capacity
3. You can use any database software you like, allowing greater flexibility
4. High availability is easier to implement due to built-in functionality for deploying read replicas and multi-AZ
5. There are no costs for replicating data between DBs in different data centers or regions

Answer: 2,4

Explanation:

- The advantages of using Amazon RDS include being able to easily scale by increasing your instance type without having to go through a long procurement cycle for getting new hardware or worrying about whether capacity exists on your existing private cloud infrastructure. You can also implement fault tolerance and scalability features through multi-AZ and read replicas easily
- With Amazon RDS you do not have control of the operating system and you cannot use any database software you like as you are restricted to a list of several engines. There are costs for replicating data between AZs and regions so this must be taken into account in any cost analysis

References:

https://digitalcloud.training/certification-training/aws-certified-cloud-practitioner/architecting-for-the-cloud/

## 2. Question

Where do Amazon Identity and Access Management (IAM) accounts need to be created for a global organization?

1. In each geographical area where the users are located
2. In each region where the users are located
3. Create them globally, and then replicate them regionally
4. Just create them once, as IAM is a global service

Answer: 4

Explanation:

- IAM is a global service so you only need to create your users once and can then use those user accounts anywhere globally
- The other options are all incorrect as you do not create IAM accounts regionally, replicate them regionally, or create them within geographical areas

References:

https://digitalcloud.training/certification-training/aws-certified-cloud-practitioner/identity-and-access-management/

## 3. Question

Which AWS service makes it easy to coordinate the components of distributed applications as a series of steps in a visual workflow?

1. Amazon SWF
2. AWS Step Functions
3. Amazon SNS
4. Amazon SES

Answer: 2

Explanation:

1. AWS Step Functions lets you coordinate multiple AWS services into serverless workflows so you can build and update apps quickly. AWS Step Functions lets you build visual workflows that enable fast translation of business requirements into technical requirements
2. Amazon SWF helps developers build, run, and scale background jobs that have parallel or sequential steps. SWF is not a visual workflow tool
3. Amazon Simple Notification Service (SNS) is a highly available, durable, secure, fully managed pub/sub messaging service
4. Amazon Simple Email Service (Amazon SES) is a cloud-based email sending service designed to help digital marketers and application developers send marketing, notification, and transactional emails

References:

https://aws.amazon.com/step-functions/

## 4. Question

A Solutions Architect needs to design a cloud-native application architecture using AWS services. What is a typical use case for Amazon Simple Queue Service (SQS)?

1. Providing fault tolerance for EC2 instances
2. Co-ordination of work items between different human and non-human workers
3. Running serverless processes as functions
4. Decoupling application components to ensure that there is no dependency on the availability of a single component

Answer: 4

Explanation:

- Amazon Simple Queue Service (SQS) is a fully managed message queuing service that enables you to decouple and scale microservices, distributed systems, and serverless applications

References:

https://digitalcloud.training/certification-training/aws-certified-cloud-practitioner/additional-aws-services-tools/

https://digitalcloud.training/certification-training/aws-solutions-architect-associate/application-integration/amazon-sqs/

## 5. Question

**With which AWS Storage Gateway Volume Gateway configuration is data stored on-premise and asynchronously backed up to Amazon S3?**

1. Cached volume mode
2. Stored volume mode
3. File gateway mode
4. VTL mode

**Answer: 2**

**Explanation:**

- The volume gateway represents the family of gateways that support block-based volumes, previously referred to as gateway-cached and gateway-stored modes
- Stored Volume mode – the entire dataset is stored on-site and is asynchronously backed up to S3 (EBS point-in-time snapshots). Snapshots are incremental and compressed
- Cached Volume mode – the entire dataset is stored on S3 and a cache of the most frequently accessed data is cached on-site
- A file gateway is not a mode but a different type of AWS Storage Gateway that provides a virtual on-premises file server, which enables you to store and retrieve files as objects in Amazon S3
- Virtual Tape Library is not a mode but a gateway that is preconfigured with a media changer and tape drives

**References:**

https://digitalcloud.training/certification-training/aws-solutions-architect-associate/storage/aws-storage-gateway/


## 6. Question

**Which AWS technology can be referred to as a "virtual hard disk in the cloud"?**

1. Amazon S3 Bucket
2. Amazon ENI
3. Amazon EFS Filesystem
4. Amazon EBS volume

**Answer: 4**

**Explanation:**

- An Amazon Elastic Block Store (EBS) volume is often described as a "virtual hard disk in the cloud". EBS volumes are block-level storage volumes that are attached to EC2 instances much as you would attach a virtual hard disk to a virtual machine in a virtual infrastructure
- An Amazon EFS filesystem is a file-level storage system that is accessed using the NFS protocol. Filesystems are mounted at the file, rather than the block level and are therefore not similar to a virtual hard disk

- Amazon S3 is an object-level storage service and is not mounted or attached. You use a REST API over HTTPS to access objects in an object store
- An Amazon Elastic Network Interface is a networking construct, not a storage construct

**References:**

https://digitalcloud.training/certification-training/aws-certified-cloud-practitioner/aws-compute/

## 7. Question

**Which of the following are examples of horizontal scaling? (choose 2)**

1. Add more instances as demand increases
2. Add more CPU/RAM to existing instances as demand increases
3. Scalability is limited by maximum instance size
4. Requires a restart to scale up or down
5. Automatic using services such as AWS Auto Scaling

**Answer: 1,5**

**Explanation:**

- With horizontal scaling you add more instances to a fleet of instances to service demand as it increases. This can be achieved automatically by using AWS Auto Scaling to add instances in response to CloudWatch performance metrics
- With vertical scaling you are adding CPU, RAM or storage to an existing instance. This may involve modifying the instance type which typically requires a restart. With vertical scaling on AWS scalability is limited by the maximum instance size

**References:**

https://digitalcloud.training/certification-training/aws-certified-cloud-practitioner/architecting-for-the-cloud/

## 8. Question

**Which HTTP code indicates a successful upload of an object to Amazon S3?**

1. 500
2. 400
3. 300
4. 200

**Answer: 4**

**Explanation:**

- A HTTP 200 codes indicates a successful upload
- A HTTP 300 code indicates a redirection
- A HTTP 400 code indicates a client error
- A HTTP 500 code indicates a server error

**References:**

https://digitalcloud.training/certification-training/aws-certified-cloud-practitioner/aws-storage/

https://en.wikipedia.org/wiki/List_of_HTTP_status_codes

## 9. Question

Which AWS database service is a SQL database that supports complex queries and joins?

1. Amazon DynamoDB
2. Amazon ElastiCache
3. Amazon RDS
4. Amazon SimpleDB

Answer: 3

Explanation:

- Amazon RDS is a relational database of the SQL type and can be used for complex queries and joins
- All other options listed are NoSQL types of database which are not suitable for complex queries and joins

References:

https://digitalcloud.training/certification-training/aws-certified-cloud-practitioner/aws-databases/

## 10. Question

You need to connect your company's on-premise network into AWS and would like to establish an AWS managed VPN service. Which of the following configuration items needs to be setup on the Amazon VPC side of the connection?

1. A Customer Gateway
2. A Virtual Private Gateway
3. A Firewall
4. A Network Address Translation device

Answer: 2

Explanation:

- A virtual private gateway is the VPN concentrator on the Amazon side of the VPN connection. You create a virtual private gateway and attach it to the VPC from which you want to create the VPN connection
- A customer gateway is a physical device or software application on your side of the VPN connection
- NAT devices and firewalls are not required for an AWS managed VPN

References:

https://digitalcloud.training/certification-training/aws-certified-cloud-practitioner/aws-networking/

https://docs.aws.amazon.com/vpc/latest/userguide/VPC_VPN.html#VPN

## 11. Question

Which AWS service is designed to be used for operational analytics?

1. Amazon EMR
2. Amazon Athena
3. Amazon QuickSight
4. Amazon Elasticsearch Service

**Answer: 4**

**Explanation:**

- For operational analytics such as application monitoring, log analytics and clickstream analytics, Amazon Elasticsearch Service allows you to search, explore, filter, aggregate, and visualize your data in near real-time
- For big data processing using the Spark and Hadoop frameworks, Amazon EMR provides a managed service that makes it easy, fast, and cost-effective to process vast amounts data
- For interactive analysis, Amazon Athena makes it easy to analyze data directly in S3 and Glacier using standard SQL queries
- For dashboards and visualizations, Amazon QuickSight provides you a fast, cloud-powered business analytics service, that that makes it easy to build stunning visualizations and rich dashboards that can be accessed from any browser or mobile device

**References:**

https://aws.amazon.com/big-data/datalakes-and-analytics/

## 12. Question

**Which of the following are NOT features of AWS IAM? (choose 2)**

1. Charged for what you use
2. Shared access to your AWS account
3. Logon using local user accounts
4. Identity federation
5. PCI DSS compliance

**Answer: 1,3**

**Explanation:**

- You cannot use IAM to create local user accounts on any system. You are also not charged for what you use, IAM is free to use
- The other options are all features of AWS IAM

**References:**

https://digitalcloud.training/certification-training/aws-certified-cloud-practitioner/identity-and-access-management/

## 13. Question

**Which AWS storage service is accessed using the Network File System (NFS) protocol?**

1. Amazon EBS
2. Amazon Instance Store
3. Amazon S3

4. Amazon EFS

## Answer: 4

### Explanation:

- The Amazon Elastic File System (EFS) storage service can be accessed using the NFSv4 protocol
- Amazon EBS and Instance store are both block-based storage systems (not file-based like EFS)
- Amazon S3 is an object-based storage system and is accessed by HTTP/HTTPS

### References:

https://digitalcloud.training/certification-training/aws-certified-cloud-practitioner/aws-storage/

## 14. Question

You are evaluating AWS services that can assist with creating scalable application environments. Which of the statements below best describes the Elastic Load Balancer service?

1. A network service that provides an alternative to using the Internet to connect customers' on-premise sites to AWS
2. Helps you ensure that you have the correct number of Amazon EC2 instances available to handle the load for your application
3. A highly available and scalable Domain Name System (DNS) service
4. Automatically distributes incoming application traffic across multiple targets, such as Amazon EC2 instances, containers, and IP addresses

## Answer: 4

### Explanation:

- Elastic Load Balancing automatically distributes incoming application traffic across multiple targets, such as Amazon EC2 instances, containers, and IP addresses
- Elastic Load Balancing provides fault tolerance for applications by automatically balancing traffic across targets – Amazon EC2 instances, containers and IP addresses – and Availability Zones while ensuring only healthy targets receive traffic

### References:

https://digitalcloud.training/certification-training/aws-certified-cloud-practitioner/elastic-load-balancing-and-auto-scaling/

## 15. Question

What are two of the core concepts related to Amazon SNS? (choose 2)

1. Tables
2. Conversations
3. Topics
4. Subscriptions
5. Templates

## Answer: 3,4

**Explanation:**

- The core concepts of SNS are:
  - Topics – how you label and group different endpoints that you send messages to
  - Subscriptions – the endpoints that a topic sends messages to
  - Publishers – the person/alarm/event that gives SNS the message that needs to be sent

**References:**

https://digitalcloud.training/certification-training/aws-certified-cloud-practitioner/notification-services/

## 16. Question

**To which destinations can Amazon S3 NOT send event notifications? (choose 2)**

1. SQS Queue
2. CloudWatch
3. SNS Topics
4. Lambda functions
5. DynamoDB Table

**Answer: 2,5**

**Explanation:**

- The Amazon S3 notification feature enables you to receive notifications when certain events happen in your bucket
- Notifications can be sent to: SNS Topics, SWS Queues, and Lambda functions

**References:**

https://digitalcloud.training/certification-training/aws-solutions-architect-associate/storage/amazon-s3/

https://docs.aws.amazon.com/AmazonS3/latest/dev/NotificationHowTo.html#notification-how-to-event-types-and-destinations

## 17. Question

**What methods are available for scaling an Amazon RDS database? (choose 2)**

1. You can scale up by moving to a larger instance size
2. You can scale up automatically using AWS Auto Scaling
3. You can scale out automatically with EC2 Auto Scaling
4. You can scale up by increasing storage capacity
5. You can scale out by implementing Elastic Load Balancing

**Answer: 1,4**

**Explanation:**

- There are only two ways you can scale an Amazon RDS database. You can modify the instance size and you can also independently modify the storage type and capacity
- You cannot use EC2 Auto Scaling or AWS (Application) Auto Scaling to automatically scale your RDS database. EC2 Auto Scaling is involved with launching additional instances (scale out) and this is not a method of scaling an RDS database and application auto scaling is involved with

automatically adjusting the assignment of resources to the database which is not supported with RDS (you can do it with DynamoDB)
- You cannot use Elastic Load Balancing with RDS because there is only ever one master database serving writes. If you want to scale reads you can implement Read Replicas

**References:**

https://digitalcloud.training/certification-training/aws-certified-cloud-practitioner/aws-databases/

https://aws.amazon.com/blogs/database/scaling-your-amazon-rds-instance-vertically-and-horizontally/

## 18. Question

**Which type of scaling does AWS Auto Scaling provide?**

1. Incremental
2. Horizontal
3. Linear
4. Vertical

**Answer: 2**

**Explanation:**

- AWS Auto Scaling scales horizontally by adding additional compute instances

**References:**

https://digitalcloud.training/certification-training/aws-certified-cloud-practitioner/architecting-for-the-cloud/

## 19. Question

**You need to provision a single EBS volume that is 500 GiB in size and needs to support 20,000 IOPS. Which EBS volume type will you select?**

1. Throughput Optimized HDD
2. Provisioned IOPS SSD
3. Cold HDD
4. General Purpose SSD

**Answer: 2**

**Explanation:**

- Provisioned IOPS SSD supports up to 50 IOPS per GiB with up to 32,000 IOPS per volume
- General purpose SSD supports 3 IOPS per GiB and can burst up to 3000 IOPS (volumes > 334GB), and a maximum of 16,000 per volume
- The HDD options provide much lower IOPS per volume (500, 250)

**References:**

https://digitalcloud.training/certification-training/aws-certified-cloud-practitioner/aws-storage/

## 20. Question

**Which service allows you to monitor and troubleshoot systems using system and application log files generated by those systems?**

1. CloudWatch Logs
2. CloudWatch Metrics
3. CloudTrail Logs
4. CloudTrail Metrics

### Answer: 1

### Explanation:

- Amazon CloudWatch Logs lets you monitor and troubleshoot your systems and applications using your existing system, application and custom log files. CloudWatch Logs can be used for real time application and system monitoring as well as long term log retention
- CloudWatch metrics are the standard method by which CloudWatch collects data
- CloudTrail is used for logging who does what in AWS by recording API calls. It is used for auditing, not performance or system operational monitoring

### References:

https://digitalcloud.training/certification-training/aws-certified-cloud-practitioner/monitoring-and-logging-services/

## 21. Question

**Under the AWS Shared Responsibility Model, who is responsible for what? (choose 2)**

1. AWS are responsible for network and firewall configuration
2. AWS are responsible for networking infrastructure
3. Customers are responsible for compute infrastructure
4. Customers are responsible for networking traffic protection
5. Customers are responsible for edge locations

### Answer: 2,4

### Explanation:

- Customers are responsible for networking traffic protection
- AWS are responsible for networking infrastructure
- AWS are responsible for compute infrastructure
- Customers are responsible for network and firewall configuration
- AWS are responsible for edge locations

### References:

https://digitalcloud.training/certification-training/aws-certified-cloud-practitioner/aws-shared-responsibility-model/

## 22. Question

A Solutions Architect is creating the business process workflows associated with an order fulfilment system. Which AWS service can assist with coordinating tasks across distributed application components?

1. Amazon SNS
2. Amazon SQS
3. Amazon STS
4. Amazon SWF

Answer: 4

Explanation:

- Amazon Simple Workflow Service (SWF) is a web service that makes it easy to coordinate work across distributed application components. SWF enables applications for a range of use cases, including media processing, web application back-ends, business process workflows, and analytics pipelines, to be designed as a coordination of tasks
- Amazon Security Token Service (STS) is used for requesting temporary credentials
- Amazon Simple Queue Service (SQS) is a message queue used for decoupling application components
- Amazon Simple Notification Service (SNS) is a web service that makes it easy to set up, operate, and send notifications from the cloud
- SNS supports notifications over multiple transports including HTTP/HTTPS, Email/Email-JSON, SQS and SMS

References:

https://digitalcloud.training/certification-training/aws-certified-cloud-practitioner/additional-aws-services-tools/

https://aws.amazon.com/swf/

## 23. Question

When using Identity and Access Management (IAM) what is the process of gaining access to a resource?

1. With IAM you do not need to authenticate or be authorized
2. First you authenticate, then you are authorized, and then you gain access
3. First you are authorized, then you authenticate, and then you gain access
4. First you authenticate, then you gain access, and then you are authorized

Answer: 2

Explanation:

- The process is that you are first authenticated (the system checks you are who you say you are), then you are authorized (the system determined the resources you are allowed to access), and then you are able to access the resources

References:

https://digitalcloud.training/certification-training/aws-certified-cloud-practitioner/identity-and-access-management/

## 24. Question

How can a company configure automatic, asynchronous copying of objects in Amazon S3 buckets across regions?

1. Using lifecycle actions
2. Using cross-region replication
3. By configuring multi-master replication
4. This is done by default by AWS

Answer: 2

Explanation:

- Cross-region replication (CRR) enables automatic, asynchronous copying of objects across buckets in different AWS Regions. Buckets configured for cross-region replication can be owned by the same AWS account or by different account
- Multi-master replication is not something you can do with Amazon S3 (Amazon Aurora has this feature)
- Lifecycle actions cannot be configured to move to another storage class in a different region

References:

https://digitalcloud.training/certification-training/aws-certified-cloud-practitioner/aws-storage/

https://docs.aws.amazon.com/AmazonS3/latest/dev/crr.html

## 25. Question

Which of the authentication options below can be used to authenticate using AWS APIs? (choose 2)

1. Access keys
2. Key pairs
3. Security groups
4. Server certificates
5. Server passwords

Answer: 1,4

Explanation:

1. Key pairs are used for encrypting logon information when accessing EC2 instances
2. Access keys are a combination of an access key ID and a secret access key
3. A server password cannot be used to authenticate with an API
4. Server certificates are SSL/TLS certificates that you can use to authenticate with some AWS services
5. Security groups are an instance-level firewall used for controlling access to AWS resources

References:

https://digitalcloud.training/certification-training/aws-certified-cloud-practitioner/identity-and-access-management/

## 26. Question

Your company has recently migrated to AWS. How can your CTO monitor the organization's costs?

1. AWS Consolidated Billing
2. AWS CloudTrail
3. AWS Cost Explorer
4. AWS Simple Monthly calculator

Answer: 3

Explanation:

- AWS Cost Explorer – enables you to visualize your usage patterns over time and to identify your underlying cost drivers.
- AWS Simple Monthly calculator – shows you how much you would pay in AWS if you move your resources.
- AWS CloudTrail provides a record of API activity in your account. I.e. who did what to which resource.
- AWS Consolidated Billing is a feature of AWS Organizations that allows you to consolidate billing across multiple linked accounts and benefit from volume pricing discounts.

References:

https://digitalcloud.training/certification-training/aws-certified-cloud-practitioner/aws-billing-and-pricing/

https://aws.amazon.com/aws-cost-management/aws-cost-explorer/

## 27. Question

What type of cloud computing service type do AWS Elastic Beanstalk and Amazon RDS correspond to?

1. Hybrid
2. IaaS
3. PaaS
4. SaaS

Answer: 3

Explanation:

- Both Elastic Beanstalk and RDS are services that are managed at the platform level meaning you don't need to manage the infrastructure level yourself. Therefore, tasks like OS management and patching are performed for you
- IaaS is a model where the underlying hardware platform and hypervisor are managed for you and you are delivered tools and interfaces for working with operating system instances
- SaaS is a model where the whole stack is managed for you right up to the application and you are delivered working software that you can customize and populate with data

- Hybrid is a type of cloud delivery model in which you consume both public and private cloud and connect the two together

**References:**

https://digitalcloud.training/certification-training/aws-certified-cloud-practitioner/cloud-computing-concepts/

## 28. Question

**What is an example of scaling vertically?**

1. Increasing the instance size with Amazon RDS
2. AWS Lambda adding concurrently executing functions
3. AWS Auto Scaling adding more EC2 instances
4. Adding read replicas to an Amazon RDS database

**Answer: 1**

**Explanation:**

- A good example of vertical scaling is changing the instance size of an EC2 instance or RDS database to one with more CPU and RAM
- All of the other options are examples of scaling horizontally

**References:**

https://digitalcloud.training/certification-training/aws-certified-cloud-practitioner/architecting-for-the-cloud/

## 29. Question

**Up to what layer of the OSI model does AWS Web Application Firewall operate?**

1. Layer 7
2. Layer 3
3. Layer 4
4. Layer 5

**Answer: 1**

**Explanation:**

- The AWS Web Application Firewall operates up to the application layer (layer 7). You can use AWS WAF to create custom rules that block common attack patterns, such as SQL injection or cross-site scripting, and rules that are designed for your specific application

**References:**

https://aws.amazon.com/waf/

## 30. Question

**Which AWS technology enables you to group resources that share one or more tags?**

1. Tag groups
2. Organization groups
3. Resource groups
4. Consolidation groups

Answer: 3

Explanation:

- Resource groups make it easy to group resources using the tags that are assigned to them. You can group resources that share one or more tags
- The other options are bogus and do not exist

References:

https://digitalcloud.training/certification-training/aws-certified-cloud-practitioner/aws-billing-and-pricing/

## 31. Question

Which of the following is not a best practice for protecting the root user of an AWS account?

1. Enable MFA
2. Lock away the AWS root user access keys
3. Don't share the root user credentials
4. Remove administrative permissions

Answer: 4

Explanation:

- You cannot remove administrative permissions from the root user of an AWS account. Therefore, you must protect the account through creating a complex password, enabling MFA, locking away access keys (assuming they're even required), and not sharing the account details

References:

https://digitalcloud.training/certification-training/aws-certified-cloud-practitioner/identity-and-access-management/

## 32. Question

What do you need to create to specify how your AWS Auto Scaling Group scales and shrinks?

1. IAM Policy
2. Launch Configuration
3. Scaling Plan
4. Scaling Policy

Answer: 4

Explanation:

- Scaling policies determine when, if, and how the ASG scales and shrinks (on-demand/dynamic scaling, cyclic/scheduled scaling)
- Scaling Plans define the triggers and when instances should be provisioned/de-provisioned
- A launch configuration is the template used to create new EC2 instances and includes parameters such as instance family, instance type, AMI, key pair and security groups
- An IAM policy is not used to control Auto Scaling

**References:**

https://digitalcloud.training/certification-training/aws-certified-cloud-practitioner/elastic-load-balancing-and-auto-scaling/

## 33. Question

Which AWS database service is schema-less and can be scaled dynamically without incurring downtime?

1. Amazon RedShift
2. Amazon Aurora
3. Amazon DynamoDB
4. Amazon RDS

**Answer: 3**

**Explanation:**

- Amazon DynamoDB is a fully managed NoSQL database service that provides fast and predictable performance with seamless scalability. Push button scaling means that you can scale the DB at any time without incurring downtime. DynamoDB is schema-less
- All other options are SQL type of databases and therefore have a schema. They also rely on EC2 instances so cannot be scaled dynamically without incurring downtime (you have to change instance types)

**References:**

https://digitalcloud.training/certification-training/aws-certified-cloud-practitioner/aws-databases/

## 34. Question

What is the easiest way to store a backup of an EBS volume on Amazon S3?

1. Write a custom script to copy the data into a bucket
2. Use S3 lifecycle actions to backup the volume
3. Use Amazon Kinesis to process the data and store the results in S3
4. Create a snapshot of the volume

**Answer: 4**

**Explanation:**

- All you need to do is create a snapshot as EBS snapshots are stored on S3
- Writing a custom script could work but would not be the easiest method
- You cannot apply S3 lifecycle actions to EBS volumes

- Amazon Kinesis is used for processing streaming data, not data in EBS volumes

**References:**

https://digitalcloud.training/certification-training/aws-certified-cloud-practitioner/aws-storage/

## 35. Question

**What is the name for the top-level container used to hold objects within Amazon S3?**

1. Folder
2. Directory
3. Bucket
4. Instance Store

**Answer: 3**

**Explanation:**

- Amazon S3 is an object-based storage system. You upload your objects into buckets
- Though S3 is a flat structure (not hierarchical), folders can be used for grouping objects
- Directories are usually associated with filesystems rather than object-based storage systems
- An Instance Store is a type of ephemeral block-based storage service available to EC2 instances

**References:**

https://docs.aws.amazon.com/AmazonS3/latest/dev/UsingBucket.html#create-bucket-intro

https://docs.aws.amazon.com/AmazonS3/latest/user-guide/using-folders.html

https://digitalcloud.training/certification-training/aws-certified-cloud-practitioner/aws-storage/

## 36. Question

**Which types of scaling policies are available when using AWS Auto Scaling? (choose 2)**

1. Simple scaling
2. Deferred scaling
3. Warm scaling
4. Agile scaling
5. Step scaling

**Answer: 1,5**

**Explanation:**

With AWS Auto Scaling the types of scaling policy are Scheduled Scaling and Dynamic Scaling.

Dynamic Scaling includes the following policy types:

- Target tracking scaling
- Step scaling
- Simple scaling

The other options are bogus and do not exist.

**References:**

https://digitalcloud.training/certification-training/aws-certified-cloud-practitioner/elastic-load-balancing-and-auto-scaling/

https://digitalcloud.training/certification-training/aws-solutions-architect-associate/compute/aws-auto-scaling/

### 37. Question

**Your manager has asked you to explain the benefits of using IAM groups. Which of the below statements are valid benefits? (choose 2)**

1. You can restrict access to the subnets in your VPC
2. Groups let you specify permissions for multiple users, which can make it easier to manage the permissions for those users
3. Provide the ability to nest groups to create an organizational hierarchy
4. Enables you to attach IAM permission policies to more than one user at a time
5. Provide the ability to create custom permission policies

**Answer: 2,4**

**Explanation:**

- Groups are collections of users and have policies attached to them
- A group is not an identity and cannot be identified as a principal in an IAM policy
- Use groups to assign permissions to users
- Use the principal of least privilege when assigning permissions
- You cannot nest groups (groups within groups)

**References:**

https://digitalcloud.training/certification-training/aws-certified-cloud-practitioner/identity-and-access-management/

### 38. Question

**Which AWS Glacier data access option retrieves data from an archive in 1-5 minutes?**

1. Expedited
2. Standard
3. Express
4. Accelerated

**Answer: 1**

**Explanation:**

- You can use the expedited access to retrieve data within 1-5 minutes
- Standard takes 3-5 hours
- The other options are bogus and do not exist

**References:**

https://digitalcloud.training/certification-training/aws-certified-cloud-practitioner/aws-billing-and-pricing/

## 39. Question

Which of the following are pillars from the five pillars of the AWS Well-Architected Framework? (Choose 2)

1. Resilience
2. Operational excellence
3. Confidentiality
4. Economics
5. Performance efficiency

Answer: 2,5

Explanation:
- The five pillars of the AWS Well-Architected Framework are operation excellence, security, reliability, performance efficiency, and cost optimization

References:

https://aws.amazon.com/blogs/apn/the-5-pillars-of-the-aws-well-architected-framework/

## 40. Question

Which resource should you use to access AWS security and compliance reports?

1. AWS Business Associate Addendum (BAA)
2. AWS Organizations
3. AWS IAM
4. AWS Artifact

Answer: 4

Explanation:
- AWS Artifact, available in the console, is a self-service audit artifact retrieval portal that provides our customers with on-demand access to AWS' compliance documentation and AWS agreements
- The Business Associate Addendum (BAA) is an agreement you can choose to accept within AWS Artifact Agreements
- AWS Identity and Access Management (IAM) is the service used for creating and managing users, groups, roles and policies
- AWS Organizations helps you centrally govern your environment as you grow and scale your workloads on AWS. Using AWS Organizations, you can automate account creation, create groups of accounts to reflect your business needs, and apply policies for these groups for governance

References:

https://digitalcloud.training/certification-training/aws-certified-cloud-practitioner/cloud-security/

## 41. Question

How many snapshots are required in order to restore an Amazon EBS volume?

1. All snapshots
2. The first snapshot only

3. The most recent snapshot only
4. The first and most recent snapshot

**Answer: 3**

**Explanation:**

- If you make periodic snapshots of a volume, the snapshots are incremental, which means that only the blocks on the device that have changed after your last snapshot are saved in the new snapshot
- Even though snapshots are saved incrementally, the snapshot deletion process is designed so that you need to retain only the most recent snapshot in order to restore the volume

**References:**

https://digitalcloud.training/certification-training/aws-certified-cloud-practitioner/aws-storage/

## 42. Question

Which type of Elastic Load Balancer only distributes traffic using the HTTP, and HTTPS protocol information?

1. No load balancers operate at the TCP level
2. Application Load Balancer (ALB)
3. Network Load Balancer (NLB
4. Classic Load Balancer (CLB)

**Answer: 2**

**Explanation:**

- ALBs process traffic at the HTTP, HTTPS level (layer 7)
- NLBs process traffic at the TCP level (layer 4)
- CLBs process traffic at the TCP, SSL, HTTP and HTTPS levels (layer 4 & 7)

**References:**

https://digitalcloud.training/certification-training/aws-certified-cloud-practitioner/elastic-load-balancing-and-auto-scaling/

https://digitalcloud.training/certification-training/aws-solutions-architect-associate/compute/elastic-load-balancing/

## 43. Question

Which feature of Amazon S3 enables you to create rules to control the transfer of objects between different storage classes?

1. Versioning
2. Object sharing
3. Lifecycle management
4. Bucket policies

**Answer: 3**

**Explanation:**

- With lifecycle management you can set rules to transfer objects between storage classes at defined time intervals
- Object sharing refers to the ability to make any object publicly available via a URL
- Versioning enabled you to automatically keep multiple versions of an object (when enabled)
- Bucket policies are used for controlling access to buckets, they can't be used to move data between storage classes

**References:**

https://digitalcloud.training/certification-training/aws-certified-cloud-practitioner/aws-storage/

## 44. Question

**What advantages does the AWS cloud provide in relation to cost? (choose 2)**

1. Enterprise licensing discounts
2. Fine-grained billing
3. Itemized power costs
4. Ability to turn off resources and not pay for them
5. One-off payments for on-demand resources

**Answer: 2,4**

**Explanation:**

- With the AWS cloud you get fine-grained billing and can turn off resources you are not using easily and not have to pay for them (pay for what you use model)
- You do not get the option for one-off payments for on-demand resources. You can for reserved instances which can be paid all upfront
- You do not get enterprise licensing discounts from AWS and you do not pay anything for power as the cost is built in

**References:**

https://digitalcloud.training/certification-training/aws-certified-cloud-practitioner/architecting-for-the-cloud/

## 45. Question

**What do you need to log into the AWS console?**

1. Access key and secret ID
2. Key pair
3. User name and password
4. Certificate

**Answer: 3**

**Explanation:**

- You can log into the AWS console using a user name and password
- You cannot log in to the AWS console using a key pair, access key & secret ID or certificate

**References:**

https://aws.amazon.com/console/

## 46. Question

How can a systems administrator specify a script to be run on an EC2 instance during launch?

1. User Data
2. Metadata
3. Run Command
4. AWS Config

**Answer: 1**

**Explanation:**

- When you launch an instance in Amazon EC2, you have the option of passing user data to the instance that can be used to perform common automated configuration tasks and even run scripts after the instance starts
- You can pass two types of user data to Amazon EC2: shell scripts and cloud-init directives
- User data is data that is supplied by the user at instance launch in the form of a script
- User data is limited to 16KB
- User data and meta data are not encrypted

**References:**

https://digitalcloud.training/certification-training/aws-certified-cloud-practitioner/aws-compute/

## 47. Question

Which type of consistency model does Amazon S3 provide for PUTS of new objects?

1. Read-after-write consistency
2. Asynchronous consistency
3. Write-after-PUT consistency
4. Eventual consistency

**Answer: 1**

**Explanation:**

- Amazon S3 provides read-after-write consistency for PUTs of new objects and eventual consistency for overwrite PUTs and DELETES
- Write-after-PUT consistency is incorrect and asynchronous consistency is not a concept related to Amazon S3

**References:**

https://digitalcloud.training/certification-training/aws-certified-cloud-practitioner/aws-storage/

## 48. Question

Your organization has offices around the world and some employees travel between offices. How should their accounts be setup?

1. IAM is a global service, just create the users in one place
2. Set the user account as a "global" account when created
3. Enable MFA for the accounts
4. Create a separate account in IAM within each region in which they will travel

Answer: 1

Explanation:

- IAM is a global service and all users that are created are able to login to the AWS Management Console from any location.
- You do not create separate IAM accounts in different regions as IAM is a global service.
- There is no such thing as setting the account as "global".
- Enabling multi-factor authentication is a good security practice but not necessary to enable users to travel to different locations.

References:

https://digitalcloud.training/certification-training/aws-certified-cloud-practitioner/identity-and-access-management/

https://docs.aws.amazon.com/IAM/latest/UserGuide/introduction_identity-management.html

## 49. Question

Which type of Elastic Load Balancer only distributes traffic using layer 4 protocol information?

1. No load balancers operate at the TCP level
2. Classic Load Balancer (CLB)
3. Network Load Balancer (NLB)
4. Application Load Balancer (ALB)

Answer: 3

Explanation:

- NLBs process traffic at the TCP level (layer 4)
- ALBs process traffic at the HTTP, HTTPS level (layer 7)
- CLBs process traffic at the TCP, SSL, HTTP and HTTPS levels (layer 4 & 7)

References:

https://digitalcloud.training/certification-training/aws-certified-cloud-practitioner/elastic-load-balancing-and-auto-scaling/

https://digitalcloud.training/certification-training/aws-solutions-architect-associate/compute/elastic-load-balancing/

## 50. Question

Your manager has asked you to explain some of the security features available in the AWS cloud. How can you describe the function of Amazon CloudHSM?

1. It can be used to generate, use and manage encryption keys in the cloud
2. It provides server-side encryption for S3 objects
3. it is a firewall for use with web applications
4. It is a Public Key Infrastructure (PKI)

Answer: 1

Explanation:

- AWS CloudHSM is a cloud-based hardware security module (HSM) that allows you to easily add secure key storage and high-performance crypto operations to your AWS applications
- CloudHSM has no upfront costs and provides the ability to start and stop HSMs on-demand, allowing you to provision capacity when and where it is needed quickly and cost-effectively
- CloudHSM is a managed service that automates time-consuming administrative tasks, such as hardware provisioning, software patching, high availability, and backups

References:

https://aws.amazon.com/cloudhsm/details/

## 51. Question

When using Amazon RDS with Read Replicas, which of the deployment options below are valid? (choose 2)

1. Within an Availability Zone
2. Cross-edge location
3. Cross-subnet
4. Cross-data center
5. Cross-Availability Zone

Answer: 1,5

Explanation:

- Read replicas are used for offloading read traffic from the primary RDS database. You can configure read replicas to be within an AZ, across AZs, and across regions
- You cannot specify the subnet or data center to deploy a read replica in

References:

https://digitalcloud.training/certification-training/aws-solutions-architect-associate/database/amazon-rds/

## 52. Question

What types of rules can be defined in a security group? (choose 2)

1. Outbound
2. Tags

3. Deny
4. Inbound
5. Stateful

**Answer: 1,4**

**Explanation:**

- You can create inbound and outbound rules in a security group
- You can tag a security group but this is not a type of rule
- You cannot create deny rules with a security group, all rules entries allow traffic
- A security group is stateful but this is not a rule type

**References:**

https://digitalcloud.training/certification-training/aws-certified-cloud-practitioner/aws-networking/

## 53. Question

**Which AWS security tool uses an agent installed in EC2 instances and assesses applications for vulnerabilities and deviations from best practices?**

1. AWS Trusted Advisor
2. AWS Personal Health Dashboard
3. AWS TCO Calculator
4. AWS Inspector

**Answer: 4**

**Explanation:**

- Inspector is an automated security assessment service that helps improve the security and compliance of applications deployed on AWS. Inspector automatically assesses applications for vulnerabilities or deviations from best practices. Uses an agent installed on EC2 instances
- Trusted Advisor is an online resource that helps to reduce cost, increase performance and improve security by optimizing your AWS environment
- AWS Personal Health Dashboard provides alerts and remediation guidance when AWS is experiencing events that may impact you
- The AWS TCO calculator can be used to compare the cost of running your applications in an on-premises or colocation environment to AWS

**References:**

https://digitalcloud.training/certification-training/aws-certified-cloud-practitioner/cloud-security/

## 54. Question

**Which type of AWS database is ideally suited to analytics using SQL queries?**

1. Amazon RDS
2. Amazon RedShift
3. Amazon DynamoDB
4. Amazon S3

**Answer: 2**

**Explanation:**

- Amazon Redshift is a fast, fully managed data warehouse that makes it simple and cost-effective to analyze all your data using standard SQL and existing Business Intelligence (BI) tools. RedShift is a SQL based data warehouse used for analytics applications
- Amazon DynamoDB is a NoSQL type of database and is not suited to analytics using SQL queries
- Amazon RDS is a transactional DB, not an analytics DB
- Amazon S3 is an object storage solution not a database

**References:**

https://digitalcloud.training/certification-training/aws-certified-cloud-practitioner/aws-databases/

## 55. Question

According to the AWS Shared Responsibility Model, which of the following is a shared control?

1. Operating system patching
2. Client-side data encryption
3. Protection of infrastructure
4. Awareness and training

**Answer: 4**

**Explanation:**

- Shared Controls are controls which apply to both the infrastructure layer and customer layers, but in completely separate contexts or perspectives. In a shared control, AWS provides the requirements for the infrastructure and the customer must provide their own control implementation within their use of AWS services. Examples include patch management, configuration management, and awareness and training
- Though patch management is a shared control, operating system patching specifically is a customer responsibility
- Protection of infrastructure is solely an AWS responsibility
- Client and server-side data encryption are both customer responsibilities

**References:**

https://digitalcloud.training/certification-training/aws-certified-cloud-practitioner/aws-shared-responsibility-model/

## 56. Question

How can you deploy your EC2 instances so that if a single data center fails you still have instances available?

1. Across Availability Zones
2. Across regions
3. Across subnets
4. Across VPCs

Answer: 1

Explanation:

- An AZ spans one or more data centers and each AZ is physically isolated from other AZs and connected by high speed networking. If you want to deploy a highly available application you should spread your instances across AZs and they will be resilient to the failure of a single DC
- Subnets are created within AZs. Therefore, if you deploy resources into multiple subnets within an AZ and a data center fails, you may lose all of your instances
- You could deploy your instances across separate regions but this is not necessary to create a highly available application and introduces complexity and cost. For example, you may need multiple ELBs (one per region), complex name resolution and potential data transfer charges

References:

https://digitalcloud.training/certification-training/aws-certified-cloud-practitioner/aws-global-infrastructure/

https://docs.aws.amazon.com/AWSEC2/latest/UserGuide/using-regions-availability-zones.html


## 57. Question

**How can a database administrator reduce operational overhead for a MySQL database?**

1. Use AWS CloudFormation to manage operations
2. Migrate the database onto an Amazon RDS instance
3. Migrate the database onto an EC2 instance
4. Migrate the database onto AWS Lambda

Answer: 2

Explanation:

- Amazon RDS is a managed database service that supports MySQL. The DBA can reduce operational overhead by moving to RDS and having less work to do to manage the database
- AWS Lambda provides functions as a service. It therefore a compute service, not a database service and cannot be used to run a MySQL database
- AWS CloudFormation is used for automating the deployment of infrastructure on AWS, not for automating operations
- Migrating onto an EC2 instance will not reduce operational overhead as the DBA will still need to manage both the operating system and the database

References:

https://digitalcloud.training/certification-training/aws-certified-cloud-practitioner/aws-databases/


## 58. Question

**Which of the statements below do not characterize cloud computing?**

1. Cloud computing allows you to swap variable expense for capital expense
2. With cloud computing you can increase your speed and agility
3. With cloud computing you get to benefit from massive economies of scale
4. Cloud computing is the on-demand delivery of compute power

Answer: 1

Explanation:

- Cloud computing is not a one-off capital expense, it is an ongoing operating expense. The caveat to this is that if you purchase reserved capacity you have an option to partially or fully pay upfront. however, it is still an operating cost as you do not own and depreciate the assets

References:

https://digitalcloud.training/certification-training/aws-certified-cloud-practitioner/cloud-computing-concepts/

## 59. Question

Which AWS support plans provide 24×7 access to customer service?

1. Basic
2. Business
3. Developer
4. All plans

Answer: 4

Explanation:

- All support plans provide 24×7 access to customer service, documentation, whitepapers, and support forums

References:

https://digitalcloud.training/certification-training/aws-certified-cloud-practitioner/aws-billing-and-pricing/

## 60. Question

Which types of servers can be migrated using the AWS Server Migration Service? (choose 2)

1. Hyper-V VMs
2. VMware vSphere VMs
3. OpenStack VMs
4. Azure Instances
5. Oracle VMs

Answer: 1,2

Explanation:

- AWS Server Migration Service (SMS) is an agentless service which makes it easier and faster for you to migrate thousands of on-premises workloads to AWS
- AWS SMS allows you to automate, schedule, and track incremental replications of live server volumes, making it easier for you to coordinate large-scale server migrations

- Currently, you can migrate virtual machines from VMware vSphere and Windows Hyper-V to AWS using AWS Server Migration Service

**References:**

https://aws.amazon.com/server-migration-service/

https://aws.amazon.com/server-migration-service/faqs/

## 61. Question

**How can a Solutions Architect reduce the latency between end-users and applications or content? (choose 2)**

1. Deploy applications in regions closest to the end-users
2. Use Amazon CloudFront to cache content closer to end-users
3. Use S3 Transfer Acceleration to improve application performance
4. Deploy applications in multiple AZs
5. Use larger EC2 instance types for the applications

Answer: 1,2

Explanation:

- To reduce latency, which corresponds with the distance over which network communications travel, you should aim to host your applications closer to your end-users. This means deploying them in the closest regions
- Amazon CloudFront, which is a content delivery network (CDN) can be used to cache content closer to end users
- Deploying in multiple AZs may create resiliency but won't change latency much as AZs are geographically close to each other
- S3 Transfer Acceleration is used to improve upload speeds for S3 objects and does not affect application performance
- Using a larger instance type for your application may improve application performance but will not reduce latency

**References:**

https://digitalcloud.training/certification-training/aws-certified-cloud-practitioner/architecting-for-the-cloud/

## 62. Question

**In which ways does AWS' pricing model benefit organizations?**

1. Eliminates licensing costs
2. Focus spend on capital expenditure, rather than operational expenditure
3. Reduce the cost of maintaining idle resources
4. Reduces the people cost of application development

Answer: 3

Explanation:

- Using AWS, you can provision only what you need and adjust resources automatically and elastically. This reduces the amount of resources that are sitting idle which reduces cost
- AWS does not eliminate licensing costs or application development costs as you still need to license and develop your application
- AWS allows you to focus your spend on operational costs, not capital costs

**References:**

https://digitalcloud.training/certification-training/aws-certified-cloud-practitioner/cloud-computing-concepts/

## 63. Question

**Where are Amazon EBS snapshots stored?**

1. On Amazon S3
2. On an Amazon EFS filesystem
3. On an Amazon EBS instance store
4. Within the EBS block store

**Answer: 1**

**Explanation:**

- Snapshots capture a point-in-time state of an instance. Snapshots are stored on S3

**References:**

https://digitalcloud.training/certification-training/aws-certified-cloud-practitioner/aws-storage/

## 64. Question

**To reduce cost, which of the following services support reservations? (choose 2)**

1. Amazon S3
2. AWS Elastic Beanstalk
3. Amazon RedShift
4. Amazon CloudFormation
5. Amazon ElastiCache

**Answer: 3,5**

**Explanation:**

- Amazon ElastiCache and Redshift both support reserved nodes
- The use of CloudFormation and Elastic Beanstalk is not chargeable so you can't reserve anything
- Amazon S3 is a pure pay per use service, you cannot reserve capacity

**References:**

https://digitalcloud.training/certification-training/aws-certified-cloud-practitioner/aws-billing-and-pricing/

https://d1.awsstatic.com/whitepapers/aws_pricing_overview.pdf

## 65. Question

**How can a company facilitate the sharing of data over private connections between two accounts they own within a region?**

1. Create a subnet peering connection
2. Create an internal ELB
3. Create a VPC peering connection
4. Configure matching CIDR address ranges

**Answer: 3**

**Explanation:**

- A VPC peering connection helps you to facilitate the transfer of data. For example, if you have more than one AWS account, you can peer the VPCs across those accounts to create a file sharing network. You can also use a VPC peering connection to allow other VPCs to access resources you have in one of your VPCs
- An internal ELB will not help you to transfer data between accounts
- You cannot peer subnets
- Configuring matching CIDR address ranges will not mean you can route between accounts. Also, you cannot peer with an account with a matching (or overlapping) address range

**References:**

https://digitalcloud.training/certification-training/aws-solutions-architect-associate/networking-and-content-delivery/amazon-vpc/

# CONCLUSION

Congratulations on completing these exam-difficulty practice tests! We truly hope that these high-quality questions along with the supporting explanations and reference links helped to fully prepare you for the AWS Certified Cloud Practitioner exam.

The CLF-C01 exam covers a broad set of technologies and it's vital to ensure you are armed with the knowledge to answer whatever questions come up in your certification exam, so it's best to review these practice questions until you're confident in all areas. We recommend re-taking these practice tests until you consistently score 80% or higher - that's when you're ready to sit the exam and achieve a great score!

## Reach out with any question

If anything is not 100% to your liking, please email us at feedback@digitalcloud.training. We promise to address all questions and concerns. For technical support, contact us at:

support@digitalcloud.training.

Also, remember to join our private Facebook group to ask questions and share knowledge and exam tips with the AWS community:

https://www.facebook.com/groups/awscertificationqa

## Limited Time Bonus Offer

As a special bonus, we are now offering **FREE Access to the Exam Simulator** on the Digital Cloud Training website. The exam simulator randomly selects 65 questions from our pool of over 500 unique questions - mimicking the real AWS exam environment. The practice exam has the same format, style, time limit, and passing score as the real AWS exam.

To gain FREE access to these 500 Practice Questions, simply send us a **screenshot of your review on Amazon** to info@digitalcloud.training with "CCP500" in the subject line. You will then get FREE access to our Online Exam Simulator within 48 hours.

Your review helps us improve our courses and help your fellow AWS students make the right choices. We celebrate every honest review and truly appreciate it. You can leave a review at any time by visiting amazon.com/ryp or your local amazon store (e.g. amazon.co.uk/ryp).

**Best wishes for your AWS certification journey!**

# OTHER BOOKS & COURSES BY NEAL DAVIS

## AWS Certified Cloud Practitioner Video Course

AVAILABLE ON DIGITALCLOUD.TRAINING

We have fully aligned this instructor-led video training with the AWS Certified Cloud Practitioner exam blueprint (CLF-C01) and structured the course so that you can study at a pace that suits you best. We start with some basic background to get everyone up to speed on what cloud computing is, before progressing through each knowledge domain.

**Here's why this ultimate exam prep is your best chance to ace your AWS certification exam:**

**HIGHLY FLEXIBLE COURSE STRUCTURE**: We understand that not everyone has the time to go through lengthy lectures. That's why we give you options to maximize your time efficiency and accommodate different learning styles

**6 HOURS OF THEORY LECTURES**: You can move quickly through the course, focusing on the theory lectures that are 100% conform with the CLF-C01 exam blueprint - everything you need to know to pass your exam first attempt

**4 HOURS OF GUIDED HANDS-ON EXERCISES**: To gain more practical experience with AWS services, you have the option to explore the guided hands-on exercises

**1 HOUR OF EXAM-CRAM LECTURES**: Get through the key exam facts in the shortest time possible with the exam-cram lectures that you'll find at the end of each section

**HIGH-QUALITY VISUALS**: We've spared no effort to create a highly visual training course with lots of table and graphs to illustrate the concepts. All practical exercises are backed by logical diagrams so you can visualize what we're building.

To learn more, visit: https://digitalcloud.training/aws-certified-cloud-practitioner-training-course/

# AWS Certified Cloud Practitioner (online) Practice Tests

AVAILABLE ON DIGITALCLOUD.TRAINING

Get access to the online Exam Simulator from Digital Cloud Training with over **500 Practice questions plus 6 sets of practice exams** with 65 Questions each. All questions are unique and conform to the latest AWS CLF-C01 exam blueprint.

Our AWS Practice Tests are delivered in 3 different modes:

**Simulation mode**: the number of questions, time limit and pass mark are the same as the real AWS exam. You need to complete the exam before you get to check your score and review answers and explanations.

**Training mode**: You are shown the answer and explanation for every question after clicking "check". Upon completion of the exam, the score report shows your overall score and performance in each knowledge area.

**Knowledge reviews**: Collections of practice questions for a specific knowledge area. When you complete a practice exam you can use the score report to identify your strengths and weaknesses and then use the knowledge reviews to focus your efforts where they are needed most.

Learn more on how to fast-track your AWS Certified Cloud Practitioner Exam Success:

https://digitalcloud.training/aws-certified-cloud-practitioner-practice-tests-2019

# AWS Certified Cloud Practitioner Training Notes

AVAILABLE ON AMAZON AND DIGITALCLOUD.TRAINING

Save valuable time by getting straight to the facts you need to know to be successful and ensure you pass your AWS Certified Cloud Practitioner exam first time!

This book is based on the CLF-C01 exam blueprint and provides a deep dive into the subject matter in a concise and easy-to-read format so you can fast-track your time to success.

The Cloud Practitioner certification is a great first step into the world of Cloud Computing and requires a foundational knowledge of the AWS Cloud, its architectural principles, value proposition, billing and pricing, key services and more.

AWS Solutions Architect and successful instructor, Neal Davis, has consolidated the information you need to be successful from numerous training sources and AWS FAQ pages to save you time.

In addition to the book, you are provided with access to a 65-question practice exam on an interactive exam simulator to evaluate your progress and ensure you're prepared for the style and difficulty of the real AWS exam.

**Deep dive into the CLF-C01 exam objectives with over 200 pages of detailed facts, tables, and diagrams – everything you need to know!**

To learn more, visit:

https://digitalcloud.training/product/aws-certified-cloud-practitioner-offline-training-notes/

# AWS Certified Solutions Architect Associate Video Course

AVAILABLE ON DIGITALCLOUD.TRAINING

This popular AWS Certified Solutions Architect Associate (SAA-C02) video course is delivered through practical AWS Hands-On Labs.

You will be looking over my shoulder and building applications on Amazon Web Services. By the end of the course, you will have a strong experience-based skillset thanks to the guided AWS Practice Labs.

We will use a process of repetition and incremental learning to ensure that you retain the knowledge as repeated practice is the best way to learn and build your cloud skills. We take you from opening your first AWS Free Tier account through to creating complex multi-tier architectures, always sticking to the **SAA-C02 exam blueprint** to ensure you're learning practical skills and also preparing for your exam.

We back the +20 hours of AWS Hands-On Labs with high-quality logical diagrams so you can visualize what you're building and check your progress.

Our AWS Hands-On Labs teach you how to design and build multi-tier web architectures with services such as EC2 Auto Scaling, Elastic Load Balancing, Route 53, ECS, Lambda, API Gateway and Elastic File System.

To learn more, visit: https://digitalcloud.training/aws-training-courses/

# AWS Certified Solutions Architect Associate (online) Practice Tests

AVAILABLE ON DIGITALCLOUD.TRAINING

Get access to the **online Exam Simulator** from Digital Cloud Training with over 500 Questions **plus 6 sets of practice exams** with 65 Questions each. All questions are unique, 100% scenario-based and conform to the latest AWS SAA-C02 exam blueprint.

Our AWS Practice Tests are delivered in 3 different modes:

**Simulation mode:** the number of questions, time limit, and pass mark are the same as the real AWS exam. You must complete the exam before you are able to check your score and review answers and explanations.

**Training mode:** You are shown the answer and explanation for every question after clicking "check". Upon completion of the exam the score report shows your overall score and performance in each knowledge area.

**Knowledge reviews:** Collections of practice questions for a specific knowledge area. When you complete a practice exam you can use the score report to identify your strengths and weaknesses and then use the knowledge reviews to focus your efforts where they're needed most.

Each exam includes questions from the four domains of the SAA-C02 AWS exam blueprint. All questions are also available in the knowledge reviews where they are split into more than 15 categories for focused training.

Learn more on how to fast-track your AWS Certified Solutions Architect Associate Exam Success:

https://digitalcloud.training/aws-certified-solutions-architect-associate-practice-tests-2019/

# AWS Certified Solutions Architect Associate (offline) Practice Tests

AVAILABLE ON AMAZON ONLY

The AWS Solutions Architect Associate certification is extremely valuable in the Cloud Computing industry today and preparing to answer the difficult scenario-based questions requires a significant commitment in time and effort.

The latest **SAA-C02 exam** is composed entirely of scenario-based questions that test your knowledge and experience working with Amazon Web Services. Our practice tests are patterned to reflect the difficulty of the AWS exam and are the closest to the real AWS exam experience available anywhere.

There are **6 practice exams with 65 questions** each covering the five domains of the AWS exam blueprint. Each set of questions is repeated once without answers and explanations, and once with answers and explanations, so you get to choose from two methods of preparation:

- **To simulate the exam experience and assess your exam readiness**, use the "PRACTICE QUESTIONS ONLY" sets.

- **To use the practice questions as a learning tool**, use the "PRACTICE QUESTIONS, ANSWERS & EXPLANATIONS" sets to view the answers and read the in-depth explanations as you move through the questions.

These Practice Questions will prepare you for your AWS exam in the following ways:

- **Master the new 2020 exam pattern**: All 390 practice questions are based on the SAA-C02 exam blueprint and use the question format of the real AWS exam

- **6 sets of exam-difficulty practice questions**: Presented with and without answers so you can study or simulate an exam

- **Ideal exam prep tool that will shortcut your study time**: Assess your exam readiness to maximize your chance of passing the AWS exam first time

The exam covers a broad set of technologies and it's vital to ensure you are armed with the knowledge to answer whatever questions come up in your certification exam. We recommend reviewing these practice questions until you're confident in all areas and ready to ace your AWS exam.

To learn more, visit: https://www.amazon.com/gp/product/1079185720.

# AWS Certified Solutions Architect Associate Training Notes

AVAILABLE ON AMAZON AND DIGITAL CLOUD TRAINING

Save valuable time by getting straight to the facts you need to know to pass your AWS Certified Solutions Architect Associate exam first time!

This book is based on the 2020 SAA-C02 exam blueprint and provides a deep dive into the subject matter in a concise and easy-to-read format so you can fast-track your time to success.

AWS Solutions Architect and successful instructor, Neal Davis, has consolidated the information you need to be successful from numerous training sources and AWS FAQ pages to save you time.

In addition to the book, you are provided with access to a 65-question practice exam on an interactive exam simulator to evaluate your progress and ensure you're prepared for the style and difficulty of the real AWS exam.

This book will help you prepare for your AWS Certified Solutions Architect – Associate exam in the following ways:

• Deep dive into the SAA-C02 exam objectives with over 300 pages of detailed facts, tables and diagrams.

• Familiarize yourself with the exam question format with the practice questions included in each section.

• Use our online exam simulator to evaluate progress and ensure you're ready for the real thing.

To learn more, visit: https://digitalcloud.training/product/aws-certified-solutions-architect-associate-offline-training-notes/

# ABOUT THE AUTHOR

**Neal Davis** is the founder of Digital Cloud Training, AWS Cloud Solutions Architect and successful IT instructor. With more than 20 years of experience in the tech industry, Neal is a true expert in virtualization and cloud computing. His passion is to help others achieve career success by offering in-depth AWS certification training resources.

Neal started **Digital Cloud Training** to provide a variety of training resources for Amazon Web Services (AWS) certifications that represent a higher standard of quality than is otherwise available in the market. Digital Cloud Training provides **AWS Certification exam preparation resources** including instructor-led Video Courses, guided Hands-on Labs, in-depth Training Notes, Exam-Cram lessons for quick revision, Quizzes to test your knowledge and exam-difficulty Practice Exams to assess your exam readiness.

With Digital Cloud Training, you get access to highly experienced staff who support you on your AWS Certification journey and help you elevate your career through achieving highly valuable certifications. Join the AWS Community of over 40,000 happy students that are currently enrolled in Digital Cloud Training courses

**Connect with Neal / Digital Cloud Training on social media**:

digitalcloud.training

facebook.com/digitalcloudtraining/

linkedin.com/company/digitalcloudtraining

Twitter @DigitalCloudT

Instagram @digitalcloudtraining

Made in the USA
Middletown, DE
16 July 2020